Lecture Notes in Computer Science 11459

More information about this series at http://www.springer.com/series/7409

Chen Zheng · Jianfeng Zhan (Eds.)

Benchmarking, Measuring, and Optimizing

First BenchCouncil International Symposium, Bench 2018
Seattle, WA, USA, December 10–13, 2018
Revised Selected Papers

 Springer

Editors
Chen Zheng
Chinese Academy of Sciences
Beijing, China

Jianfeng Zhan
Chinese Academy of Sciences
Beijing, China

ISSN 0302-9743   ISSN 1611-3349   (electronic)
Lecture Notes in Computer Science
ISBN 978-3-030-32812-2   ISBN 978-3-030-32813-9   (eBook)
https://doi.org/10.1007/978-3-030-32813-9

LNCS Sublibrary: SL3 – Information Systems and Applications, incl. Internet/Web, and HCI

This Springer imprint is published by the registered company Springer Nature Switzerland AG
The registered company address is: Gewerbestrasse 11, 6330 Cham, Switzerland

BenchCouncil: Benchmarking and Promoting Innovative Techniques

The past decade witnessed many innovative techniques as they evolved our economy and society. The innovative techniques in Datacenter, AI, dedicated processors, and IoT are especially changing our world. For example, new wave AI techniques have changed every part of our daily life, such as facial recognition, self-driving cars, robots, financial services, personal assistants, etc. In recent years, this trend has accelerated, and there is an increasing interest in generating values from these emerging technologies. However, benchmarking and promoting innovative techniques are the very first steps in making the innovation successful, which is the mission of the International Open Benchmark Council (BenchCouncil).

BenchCouncil is a non-profit research institute, which aims to promote multi-disciplinary benchmarking research and practice and foster collaboration and interaction between industry and academia. The major goals of the BenchCouncil are as follows:

- Establish and maintain a repository of benchmark specifications for quantitative system and algorithm evaluation and analysis
- Review, shepherd, and release open-source benchmark implementations
- Organize conferences, workshops, and teleconferences fostering the transfer of knowledge between industry and academia in the areas of benchmarking
- Build a testbed to verify and promote the innovative techniques
- Organize challenges and competition using released benchmarks
- Publish the performance numbers to evaluate competitive techniques using the benchmarks

In order to fulfill its mission, the BenchCouncil organized the First International Symposium on Benchmarking, Measuring, and Optimizing (Bench 2018) (http://prof.ict.ac.cn/Bench18/), which was co-located with IEEE BigData 2018 (http://cci.drexel.edu/bigdata/bigdata2018/)—an IEEE International Conference on Big Data. The symposium solicits papers that address hot topical issues in benchmarking, measuring, and optimizing systems. This book includes 15 papers from the Bench 2018 conference, and 5 invited papers which report on the state-of-the-art AI benchmarking research and engineering efforts of the BenchCouncil. In addition, 6 Benchmark proposals were presented at the conference, but were not included in this book.

The call for papers for Bench 2018 attracted a number of high-quality submissions. During a rigorous review process, each paper was reviewed by at least three experts. In addition, we invited three keynote speakers:

- Prof. Geoffrey Fox (Indiana University): "Big Data Benchmarking: Applications and Systems"
- Prof. Vijay Janapa Reddi (Harvard University): "MLPerf: the Vision Behind an ML Benchmark Suite for Measuring the Performance of ML Software Frameworks, ML Hardware Accelerators, and ML Cloud and Edge Platforms"
- Dr. Arne Berre (SINTEF Digital): "Benchmarking for Digital Platforms with Big Data, IoT, AI, Cloud, HPC, and Cyber Security"

During the conference, we had 6 benchmark proposals covering the topics in Big Data, AI, Datacenter, Scalable Transaction, and Database. In order to discuss the implementation of benchmark and BenchCouncil workgroup specification, we also held the BenchCouncil Open Meeting to format the working groups.

We are very grateful for the efforts of all authors in relation to writing, revising, and presenting their papers at Bench 2018. We appreciate the indispensable support of the Bench 2018 Program Committee and thank them for their efforts and contributions in maintaining the high standards of the Bench 2018 Symposium.

June 2019   Chen Zheng
                                                                     Jianfeng Zhan

Organization

Program Chair

Jianfeng Zhan   ICT, Chinese Academy of Sciences, and University
                                 of Chinese Academy of Sciences, China

Program Committee

Lizy K. John   The University of Texas at Austin, USA
Vijay Janapa Reddi   University of Texas at Austin and Google, USA
Wenguang Chen   Tsinghua University, China
Woongki Baek   UNIST, South Korea
Yunji Chen   ICT, Chinese Academy of Sciences, China
Piotr Luszczek   University of Tennessee, USA
Rui Hou   Institute of Information Engineering, Chinese Academy
                                 of Sciences, China
Yueguo Chen   Renmin University of China, China
H. Peter Hofstee   IBM, USA
Cheqing Jin   East China Normal University, China
Trevor E. Carlson   National University of Singapore (NUS), Singapore
Jun-zhao Du   Xidian University, China
Hyogi Sim   Oak Ridge National Laboratory, USA
Weining Qian   East China Normal University, China
Zheng Cao   Alibaba, China
Matthias Nicola   IBM, Germany
Zhihui Du   Tsinghua University, China
Chunjie Luo   ICT, Chinese Academy of Sciences, China
Bin Ren   College of William and Mary, USA
Hua Chen   ICT, Chinese Academy of Sciences, China
Jiaquan Gao   Nanjing Normal University, China
Jiannan Ouyang   Facebook, USA
Xueming Si   Fudan University, China
Yanjun Wu   Institute of Software Chinese Academy of Sciences,
                                 China
Lucas Mello Schnorr   Federal University of Rio Grande do Sul (UFRGS),
                                 Brazil
Yunquan Zhang   ICT, Chinese Academy of Sciences, China
Shengzhong Feng   Shenzhen Institutes of Advanced Technology,
                                 Chinese Academy of Sciences, China
Zhen Jia   Princeton University, USA
Zhibin Yu   Shenzhen Institutes of Advanced Technology,
                                 Chinese Academy of Sciences, China

Dapeng Wang   Institute of Software Chinese Academy of Sciences,
                            China
Bo Wu   Colorado School of Mines, USA
Shaoliang Peng   National University of Defense Technology, China
Yong Qi   Xi'an Jiaotong University, China
Gwangsun Kim   Arm Inc., Austin, USA
Rui Ren   ICT, Chinese Academy of Sciences, China
Zujie Ren   Hangzhou Dianzi University, China
Xiaoyi Lu   The Ohio State University, USA
Lei Wang   ICT, Chinese Academy of Sciences, China
Jianhui Li   Computer Network Information Center,
                            Chinese Academy of Sciences, China
Jianwu Wang   University of Maryland, USA
Kenli Li   Hunan University, China
Suzanne Rivoire   Sonoma State University, USA
Rui Han   ICT, Chinese Academy of Sciences, China
Jungang Xu   Chinese Academy of Sciences, China
Xu Liu   College of William and Mary, USA
Tong Wu   National Institute of Metrology, China
Li Zha   University of the Chinese Academy of Sciences, China
Lei Liu   ICT, Chinese Academy of Sciences, China
Chen Zheng   ICT, Chinese Academy of Sciences, China

Contents

Big Data

Modelling and Prediction

Algorithm and Implementations

AI Benchmarking

AIBench: Towards Scalable and Comprehensive Datacenter AI Benchmarking

Wanling Gao[1,2,4], Chunjie Luo[1,2,4], Lei Wang[1,2,4], Xingwang Xiong[1,4],
Jianan Chen[1,4], Tianshu Hao[1,4], Zihan Jiang[1,4], Fanda Fan[1,4], Mengjia Du[1,4],
Yunyou Huang[1,4], Fan Zhang[1], Xu Wen[1,4], Chen Zheng[1,2,4], Xiwen He[1],
Jiahui Dai[2,3], Hainan Ye[2,3], Zheng Cao[5], Zhen Jia[6], Kent Zhan[7],
Haoning Tang[8], Daoyi Zheng[9], Biwei Xie[10], Wei Li[11], Xiaoyu Wang[12],
and Jianfeng Zhan[1,2,4(✉)]

[1] State Key Laboratory of Computer Architecture, Institute of Computing
Technology, Chinese Academy of Sciences, Beijing, China
{gaowanling,wanglei_2011,luochunjie,xiongxingwang,chenjianan,haotianshu,
jiangzihan,fanfanda,dumengjia,huangyunyou,zhangfan,wenxu,zhengchen,
zhanjianfeng}@ict.ac.cn
[2] BenchCouncil (International Open Benchmark Council), Dover, Delaware, USA
[3] Beijing Academy of Frontier Sciences and Technology, Beijing, China
{daijiahui,yehainan}@mail.bafst.com
[4] University of Chinese Academy of Sciences, Beijing, China
[5] Alibaba, Hangzhou, China
zhengzhi.cz@alibaba-inc.com
[6] Princeton University, Princeton, USA
zhenj@cs.princeton.edu
[7] Wuba, Zhuxi, China
zhankunlin@58.com
[8] Tencent, Shenzhen, China
haoningtang@tencent.com
[9] Baidu, Beijing, China
zhengdaoyi@baidu.com
[10] China RISC-V Alliance, Beijing, China
[11] Cambricon, Shenzhen, China
liwei1@cambricon.com
[12] Intellifusion, Shenzhen, China
wang.xiaoyu@intellif.com

Abstract. AI benchmarking provides yardsticks for benchmarking, measuring and evaluating innovative AI algorithms, architecture, and systems. Coordinated by BenchCouncil, this paper presents our joint research and engineering efforts with several academic and industrial partners on the datacenter AI benchmarks—AIBench. The benchmarks are publicly available from http://www.benchcouncil.org/AIBench/index.html. Presently, AIBench covers 16 problem domains, including image classification, image generation, text-to-text translation, image-to-text, image-to-image, speech-to-text, face embedding, 3D face

C. Zheng and J. Zhan (Eds.): Bench 2018, LNCS 11459, pp. 3–9, 2019.
https://doi.org/10.1007/978-3-030-32813-9_1

recognition, object detection, video prediction, image compression, recommendation, 3D object reconstruction, text summarization, spatial transformer, and learning to rank, and two end-to-end application AI benchmarks. Meanwhile, the AI benchmark suites for high performance computing (HPC), IoT, Edge are also released on the BenchCouncil web site. This is by far the most comprehensive AI benchmarking research and engineering effort.

Keywords: Datacenter · AI · Benchmark

1   Introduction

AIBench provides a scalable and comprehensive datacenter AI benchmark suite. In total, it includes 12 micro benchmarks, 16 component benchmarks, covering 16 AI problem domains: image classification, image generation, text-to-text translation, image-to-text, image-to-image, speech-to-text, face embedding, 3D face recognition, object detection, video prediction, image compression, recommendation, 3D object reconstruction, text summarization, spatial transformer, learning to rank, and two end-to-end application AI benchmarks: DCMix [1]—a datacenter AI application combination mixed with AI workloads, and E-commerce AI—an end-to-end business AI benchmark. The details of AIBench is introduced in our technical report [2].

We provide both training and inference benchmarks. The training metrics are the wall clock time to train the specific epochs, the wall clock time to train a model achieving a target accuracy [3], and the energy consumption to train a model achieving a target accuracy [3]. The inference metrics are the wall clock time, accuracy, and energy consumption. Additionally, the performance numbers are reported on the BenchCouncil web site (http://www.benchcouncil.org/numbers.html), to measure the training and inference speeds of different hardware platforms, including multiple types of NIVDIA GPUs, Intel CPUs, AI accelerator chips, and to measure the performance of different software stacks, including TensorFlow, PyTorch, and etc.

Using the benchmarks from AIBench, BenchCouncil is organizing the 2019 BenchCouncil International AI System and Algorithm Competition, including four tracks: AI System Competitions on RISC-V—an open-source chip, Cambricon—an AI accelerator Chip, and X86 processors, and 3D Face Recognition Algorithm Competition sponsored by Intellifusion.

2   Related Work

Much previous work focuses on datacenter AI benchmarking. Table 1 summarizes the differences between AIBench and the state-of-the-art and state-of-the-practise datacenter AI benchmarks. Previous work like MLPerf [4], Fathom [5], DAWNBench [3], and TBD suite [6] only targets at component benchmarks, while lacking of the micro and application benchmarks. On the contrary, benchmarks like DeepBench [7] and DNNMark [8] only provide several micro benchmarks, while lacking of the component and application benchmarks. Thus, previous work adopts a narrow vision of datacenter AI scenario, and fails to propose a comprehensive AI benchmark suite.

AIBench includes a series of micro, component and application benchmarks to benchmark the AI systems, architectures, and algorithms. Also, a wide variety of data types and data sources are covered, including text, images, street scenes, audios, videos, etc. The workloads are implemented not only based on mainstream deep learning frameworks like TensorFlow and PyTorch, but also based on traditional programming model like Pthreads, to conduct an apple-to-apple comparison. Meanwhile, the HPC AI benchmarks [9], IoT AI benchmarks [10], Edge AI benchmarks [11], and big data benchmarks [12–14] are also released on the BenchCouncil web site.

Table 1. The Summary of different AI Benchmarks.

	Micro benchmark	Component benchmark	Application benchmark	Dataset	Software stacks
AIBench	12	16	2	16	3
MLPerf [4]	N/A	7	N/A	3	2
Fathom [5]	N/A	8	N/A	6	1
DeepBench [7]	4	N/A	N/A	N/A	1
DNNMark [8]	8	N/A	N/A	N/A	1
DAWNBench [3]	N/A	2	N/A	3	2
TBD [6]	N/A	7	N/A	6	4

3 Datacenter AI Benchmark Suite—AIBench

Totally, AIBench covers 16 representative real-world data sets widely used in AI scenario and provides 12 AI micro benchmarks and 16 AI component benchmarks. Among them, each micro benchmark provides a neural network kernel implementation, consisting of a single unit of computation [15]; Each component benchmark provides a full neural network model to solve multiple tasks, each of which is a combination of multiple units of computation; Each application benchmark provides an end-to-end application scenario.

3.1 Datacenter AI Micro Benchmarks

Micro benchmarks in AIBench abstracts units of computation among a majority of AI algorithms, and covers 12 units of computation in total. The micro benchmarks are convolution, fully connected, relu, sigmoid, tanh, maximum pooling, average pooling, cosine normalization, batch normalization, dropout, elementwise operation, and softmax.

3.2 Datacenter AI Component Benchmarks

Component benchmarks in AIBench cover 16 problem domains and contain both training and inference. For both training and inference, TensorFlow and PyTorch implementations are provided.

Image classification uses ResNet neural network [16] and uses ImageNet [17] as data input to solve image classification task.

Image generation uses WGAN [18] algorithms and uses LSUN [19] dataset as data input to generate image data.

Text-to-Text Translation uses recurrent neural networks [20] and takes WMT English-German [21] as data input to translate text data.

Image-to-Text uses Neural Image Caption [22] model and takes Microsoft COCO dataset [23] as input to describe image using text.

Image-to-Image uses the cycleGAN [24] algorithm and takes Cityscapes [25] dataset as input to transform the image to another image.

Speech-to-Text uses the DeepSpeech2 [26] algorithm and takes Librispeech [27] dataset as input to recognize the speech data.

Face embedding uses the FaceNet [28] algorithm and takes the LFW (Labeled Faces in the Wild) dataset [29] or VGGFace2 [30] as input to convert image to an embedding vector.

3D face recognition uses 3D face modes to recognize 3D information within images. The input data includes 77,715 samples from 253 face IDs, which is published on the BenchCouncil web site.

Object detection uses the Faster R-CNN [31] algorithm and takes Microsoft COCO dataset [23] as input to detect objects in images.

Recommendation uses collaborative filtering algorithm and takes MovieLens dataset [32] as input to provide recommendations.

Video prediction uses motion-focused predictive models [33] and takes Robot pushing dataset [33] as input to predict video frames.

Image compression uses recurrent neural networks and takes ImageNet dataset as input to compression images.

3D object reconstruction uses a convolutional encoder-decoder network and takes ShapeNet Dataset [34] as input to reconstruct 3D object.

Text summarization uses sequence-to-sequence model [35] and takes Gigaword dataset [36] as input to generate summary description for text.

Spatial transformer uses spatial transformer networks and takes MNIST dataset [37] as input to make spatial transformations.

Learning to Rank uses ranking distillation algorithm [38] and uses Gowalla dataset [39] to generate ranking scores.

3.3 Application Benchmarks

The suite also provides two end-to-end application benchmarks: DCMix [1]—mixed datacenter workloads, and E-commerce AI—an end-to-end business AI benchmark. Among them, DCMix is to model the datacenter application scenario, and generate mixed workloads with different latencies, including AI workloads (i.e., image recognition, speech recognition), online service (e.g., Online search), etc.

E-commerce AI is to mimic complex modern Internet services workloads, which is a joint work with Alibaba. An AI-based recommendation module is included.

3.4 AI Competition

Using the benchmark implementations from AIBench as the baselines, Bench-Council is organizing the International AI System and Algorithm Competition, advancing the state-of-the-art or state-of-the-practice algorithms on different systems or architecture, like X86, Cambricon, RISC-V, and GPU. This year, there are four tracks, including AI System Competition based on RISC-V, Cambricon, and X86 chips, and Intellifusion 3D Face Recognition Algorithm Competition. The competition information is publicly available from http://www.benchcouncil.org/competition/index.html. Any companies and research institutes are welcomed to join and organize a competition track each year.

Among the four tracks., RISC-V and Cambricon-based AI System Competitions are to implement and optimize image classification on RISC-V and Cambricon, respectively. The X86-based AI System Competition is to implement and optimize the recommendation algorithm. The algorithm Competition is to develop innovative algorithms for 3D Face Recognition.

4   Conclusion

This paper proposes a comprehensive datacenter AI benchmarks—AIBench, covering 12 micro benchmarks, 16 component benchmarks, and 2 end-to-end application benchmarks. The benchmark suite is publicly available from http://www.benchcouncil.org/AIBench/index.html .

Acknowledgment. This work is supported by the Standardization Research Project of Chinese Academy of Sciences No.BZ201800001.

References

1. Xiong, X., et al.: DCMIX: generating mixed workloads for the cloud data center. In: BenchCouncil International Symposium on Benchmarking, Measuring and Optimizing (Bench18) (2018)
2. Gao, W., et al.: An industry standard internet service AI benchmark suite. Technical report, AIBench (2019)
3. Coleman, C., et al.: Dawnbench: an end-to-end deep learning benchmark and competition. Training **100**(101), 102 (2017)
4. Mlperf. https://mlperf.org

5. Adolf, R., Rama, S., Reagen, B., Wei, G.-Y., Brooks, D.: Fathom: reference workloads for modern deep learning methods. In: Workload Characterization (IISWC), pp. 1–10 (2016)
6. Zhu, H., et al.: TBD: Benchmarking and analyzing deep neural network training arXiv preprint arXiv:1803.06905 (2018)
7. Deepbench. https://svail.github.io/DeepBench/
8. Dong, S., Kaeli, D.: DNNMark: a deep neural network benchmark suite for GPUs. In: Proceedings of the General Purpose GPUs, pp. 63–72. ACM (2017)
9. Jiang, Z., et al.: HPC AI500: a benchmark suite for HPC AI systems. In: 2018 BenchCouncil International Symposium on Benchmarking, Measuring and Optimizing (Bench18) (2018)
10. Luo, C., et al.: AIoT Bench: towards comprehensive benchmarking mobile and embedded device intelligence. In: 2018 BenchCouncil International Symposium on Benchmarking, Measuring and Optimizing (Bench18) (2018)
11. Hao, T., et al.: Edge AIBench: towards comprehensive end-to-end edge computing benchmarking. In: 2018 BenchCouncil International Symposium on Benchmarking, Measuring and Optimizing (Bench18) (2018)
12. Gao, W., et al.: BigDataBench: a scalable and unified big data and AI benchmark suite. arXiv preprint arXiv:1802.08254 (2018)
13. Wang, L., et al.: BigDataBench: a big data benchmark suite from internet services. In: IEEE International Symposium On High Performance Computer Architecture (HPCA) (2014)
14. Jia, Z., Wang, L., Zhan, J., Zhang, L., Luo, C.: Characterizing data analysis workloads in data centers. In: 2013 IEEE International Symposium on Workload Characterization (IISWC), pp. 66–76. IEEE (2013)
15. Gao, W., et al.: Data Motifs: a lens towards fully understanding big data and AI workloads. In: 2018 27th International Conference on Parallel Architectures and Compilation Techniques (PACT) (2018)
16. He, K., Zhang, X., Ren, S., Sun, J.: Deep residual learning for image recognition. In: Proceedings of the IEEE Conference on Computer Vision and Pattern Recognition, pp. 770–778 (2016)
17. Deng, J., Dong, W., Socher, R., Li, L.-J., Li, K., Fei-Fei, L.: ImageNet: a large-scale hierarchical image database. In: 2009 IEEE Conference on Computer Vision and Pattern Recognition, CVPR 2009, pp. 248–255. IEEE (2009)
18. Arjovsky, M., Chintala, S., Bottou, L.: Wasserstein GAN arXiv preprint arXiv:1701.07875 (2017)
19. Yu, F., Seff, A., Zhang, Y., Song, S., Funkhouser, T., Xiao, J.: LSUN: construction of a large-scale image dataset using deep learning with humans in the loop arXiv preprint arXiv:1506.03365 (2015)
20. Vaswani, A., et al.: Attention is all you need. In: Advances in Neural Information Processing Systems, pp. 5998–6008 (2017)
21. https://nlp.stanford.edu/projects/nmt/
22. Vinyals, O., Toshev, A., Bengio, S., Erhan, D.: Show and tell: lessons learned from the 2015 MSCOCO image captioning challenge. IEEE Trans. Pattern Anal. Mach. Intell. 39(4), 652–663 (2017)
23. Lin, T.-Y., et al.: Microsoft COCO: common objects in context. In: Fleet, D., Pajdla, T., Schiele, B., Tuytelaars, T. (eds.) ECCV 2014. LNCS, vol. 8693, pp. 740–755. Springer, Cham (2014). https://doi.org/10.1007/978-3-319-10602-1_48
24. Zhu, J.-Y., Park, T., Isola, P., Efros, A.A.: Unpaired image-to-image translation using cycle-consistent adversarial networks. In: Proceedings of the IEEE International Conference on Computer Vision, pp. 2223–2232 (2017)

25. Cordts, M., et al.: The cityscapes dataset for semantic urban scene understanding. In: Proceedings of the IEEE Conference on Computer Vision and Pattern Recognition, pp. 3213–3223 (2016)
26. Amodei, D., et al.: Deep speech 2: end-to-end speech recognition in English and Mandarin. In: International conference on machine learning, pp. 173–182 (2016)
27. Panayotov, V., Chen, G., Povey, D., Khudanpur, S.: Librispeech: an ASR corpus based on public domain audio books. In: 2015 IEEE International Conference on Acoustics, Speech and Signal Processing (ICASSP), pp. 5206–5210. IEEE (2015)
28. Schroff, F., Kalenichenko, D., Philbin, J.: FaceNet: a unified embedding for face recognition and clustering. In: Proceedings of the IEEE Conference on Computer Vision and Pattern Recognition, pp. 815–823 (2015)
29. Huang, G.B., Mattar, M., Berg, T., Learned-Miller, E.: Labeled faces in the wild: a database for studying face recognition in unconstrained environments. In: Workshop on faces in 'Real-Life' Images: Detection, Alignment, and Recognition (2008)
30. Cao, Q., Shen, L., Xie, W., Parkhi, O.M., Zisserman, A.: VGGFace2: a dataset for recognising faces across pose and age. In: 2018 13th IEEE International Conference on Automatic Face & Gesture Recognition (FG 2018), pp. 67–74. IEEE (2018)
31. Ren, S., He, K., Girshick, R., Sun, J.: Faster R-CNN: towards real-time object detection with region proposal networks. In: Advances in Neural Information Processing Systems, pp. 91–99 (2015)
32. Harper, F.M., Konstan, J.A.: The movielens datasets: history and context. ACM Trans. Interact. Intell. Syst. (TiiS) **5**(4), 19 (2016)
33. Finn, C., Goodfellow, I., Levine, S.: Unsupervised learning for physical interaction through video prediction. In: Advances in Neural Information Processing Systems, pp. 64–72 (2016)
34. Chang, A.X., et al.: ShapeNet: an information-rich 3D model repository arXiv preprint arXiv:1512.03012 (2015)
35. Nallapati, R., Zhou, B., Gulcehre, C., Xiang, B., et al.: Abstractive text summarization using sequence-to-sequence RNNs and beyond arXiv preprint arXiv:1602.06023 (2016)
36. Rush, A.M., Harvard, S., Chopra, S., Weston, J.: A neural attention model for sentence summarization. In: ACLWeb. Proceedings of the 2015 Conference on Empirical Methods in Natural Language Processing (2017)
37. LeCun, Y., Cortes, C., Burges, C.: MNIST handwritten digit database, AT&T Labs, vol. 2, p. 18 (2010). http://yann.lecun.com/exdb/mnist
38. Tang, J., Wang, K.: Ranking distillation: learning compact ranking models with high performance for recommender system. In: Proceedings of the 24th ACM SIGKDD International Conference on Knowledge Discovery & Data Mining, pp. 2289–2298. ACM (2018)
39. Gowalla dataset. https://snap.stanford.edu/data/loc-gowalla.html

HPC AI500: A Benchmark Suite
for HPC AI Systems

Zihan Jiang[1,2], Wanling Gao[1,2,3], Lei Wang[1,3], Xingwang Xiong[1,2],
Yuchen Zhang[5], Xu Wen[1,2], Chunjie Luo[1], Hainan Ye[4], Xiaoyi Lu[6],
Yunquan Zhang[9], Shengzhong Feng[7], Kenli Li[8], Weijia Xu[10],
and Jianfeng Zhan[1,2,3(✉)]

[1] State Key Laboratory of Computer Architecture,
Institute of Computing Technology, Chinese Academy of Sciences, Beijing, China
{jiangzihan,gaowanling,wanglei_2011,xiongxingwang,
wenxu,luochunjie,zhanjianfeng}@ict.ac.cn
[2] University of Chinese Academy of Sciences, Beijing, China
[3] BenchCouncil (International Open Benchmark Council), Dover, Delaware, USA
[4] Beijing Academy of Frontier Sciences and Technology, Beijing, China
[5] State University of New York, Buffalo, USA
zhang232@buffalo.edu
[6] Department of Computer Science and Engineering, The Ohio State University,
Columbus, USA
luxi@cse.ohio-state.edu
[7] National Supercomputing Center in Shenzhen, Shenzhen, China
fengsz@nsccsz.cn
[8] National Supercomputing Center in Changsha, Changsha, China
lkl@hnu.edu.cn
[9] National Supercomputing Center in Jinan, Jinan, China
zyq@ict.ac.cn
[10] Texas Advanced Computing Center, The Texas University at Austin, Austin, USA
xwj@tacc.utexas.edu

Abstract. In recent years, with the trend of applying deep learning
(DL) in high performance scientific computing, the unique characteristics of emerging DL workloads in HPC raise great challenges in designing, implementing HPC AI systems. The community needs a new yard
stick for evaluating the future HPC systems. In this paper, we propose
HPC AI500—a benchmark suite for evaluating HPC systems that running scientific DL workloads. Covering the most representative scientific
fields, each workload from HPC AI500 is based on real-world scientific
DL applications. Currently, we choose 14 scientific DL benchmarks from
perspectives of application scenarios, data sets, and software stack. We
propose a set of metrics for comprehensively evaluating the HPC AI
systems, considering both accuracy, performance as well as power and
cost. We provide a scalable reference implementation of HPC AI500. The
specification and source code are publicly available from http://www.
benchcouncil.org/HPCAI500/index.html. Meanwhile, the AI benchmark
suites for datacenter, IoT, Edge are also released on the BenchCouncil
web site.

© Springer Nature Switzerland AG 2019
C. Zheng and J. Zhan (Eds.): Bench 2018, LNCS 11459, pp. 10–22, 2019.
https://doi.org/10.1007/978-3-030-32813-9_2

Keywords: HPC · Deep learning · Benchmarking

1   Introduction

The huge success of AlexNet [1] in the ImageNet [2] competition marks that deep learning(DL) is leading the renaissance of Artificial Intelligence (AI). Since then, a wide range of application areas have started using DL and achieved unprecedented results, such as image recognition, natural language processing, and even autonomous driving. In the commercial fields, many DL-based novel applications have emerged, creating huge economic benefits. In the fields of high performance scientific computing, similar classes of problems are faced, i.e., predicting extreme weather [21], finding signals of new particles [22], and estimating cosmological parameters [23]. These scientific fields are essentially solving the common class of problems that exist in commercial fields such as classifying images, predicting classes labels, or regressing a numerical quantity. In several scientific computing fields, DL has replaced traditional scientific computing methods and becomes a promising tool [24].

As an emerging workload in high performance scientific computing, DL has many unique features compared to traditional high performance computing. First, training a DL model depends on massive data that are represented by high-dimensional matrices. Second, leveraging deep learning frameworks such as Tensorflow [3] and caffe [4] aggravates the difficulty of the software and hardware co-design. Last but not least, the heterogeneous computing platform of DL is far more complicated than traditional scientific workloads, including CPU, GPU, and various domain-specific processor (e.g. Cambricon Diannao [5] or Google TPU [6]). Consequently, the community requires a new yardstick for evaluating future HPC AI systems. However, the diversity of scientific DL workloads raise great challenges in HPC AI benchmarking.

1. Dataset: Scientific data is often more complex than MINST or ImageNet data sets. First, the shape of scientific data can be 2D images or higher-dimension structures. Second, there are hundreds of channels in a scientific image, while the popular image data often consists of only RGB. Third, Scientific datasets are always terabytes or even petabytes in size.
2. Workloads: Modern scientific DL doesn't adopt off-the-shelf models, instead builds more complex model with domain scientific principles (e.g. energy conservation) [21].
3. Metrics: Due to the importance of accuracy, using a single performance metric such as FLOPS leads to insufficient evaluation. For a comprehensively evaluation, the selected metrics should not only consider the performance of the system, but also consider the accuracy of the DL model [8].
4. Scalability: Since the scientific DL workloads always run on the supercomputers, which are equipped with tens of thousands nodes, the benchmark program must be highly scalable.

Most of the existing AI benchmarks [7–10,28,29] are based on commercial scenarios. Deep500 [30] is a benchmarking framework aiming to evaluate high-performance deep learning. However, its reference implementation uses commercial open source data sets and simple DL models, hence cannot reflect real-world HPC AI workloads. We summary these major benchmarking efforts for AI and compare them with HPC AI500 as shown in the table below.

Table 1. Comparison of AI Benchmarking efforts.

Benchmark efforts	Datasets	Problem domains				Implementation	
		Scientific			Commercial	Standalone	Distributed
		EWA[a]	Cos[b]	HEP[c]			
HPC AI500	Scientific data	✓	✓	✓	×	✓	✓
TBD	Commercial data	×	×	×	✓	✓	×
MLPerf	Commercial data	×	×	×	✓	✓	×
DAWNBench	Commercial data	×	×	×	✓	✓	×
Fathom	Commercial data	×	×	×	✓	✓	×
Deep500	Commercial data	Framework, undefined				✓	✓

[a] Extreme Weather Analysis
[b] Cosmology
[c] High Energy Physics

Consequently, targeting above challenges, we propose HPC AI500—a benchmark suite for HPC AI systems. Our major contributions are as follows:

1. We create a new benchmark suite that covers the major areas of high performance scientific computing. The benchmark suite consists of micro benchmarks and component benchmarks. The workloads from component benchmarks use the state-of-the-art models and representative scientific data sets to reflect the real-world performance results. In addition, we select several DL kernels as the micro benchmarks for evaluating the upper bound performance of the systems.
2. We propose a set of metrics for comprehensively evaluating the HPC AI systems. Our metrics for component benchmarks include both accuracy and performance. For micro benchmarks, we provide metrics such as FLOPS to reflect the upper bound performance of the system.

Coordinated by BenchCouncil (http://www.benchcouncil.org), we also release the datacenter AI benchmarks [16,17], the IoT AI benchmarks [15], edge AI benchmarks [14], and big data benchmarks [12,13], which are publicly available from http://www.benchcouncil.org/HPCAI500/index.html.

2   Deep Learning in Scientific Computing

In order to benchmark HPC AI systems, the first step is to figure out how DL works in scientific fields. Although it is an emerging field, several scientific fields have applied DL to solve many important problems, such as extreme weather analysis [21,40–42], high energy physics [22,36–39], and cosmology [23,26,33–35].

2.1 Extreme Weather Analysis

Extreme Weather Analysis (EWA) poses a great challenge to human society. It brings severe damage to people health and economy every single year. For instance, the heatwaves in 2018 caused over 1600 deaths according to the UN report [44]. And the landfall of hurricane Florence and Michael caused about 40 billion dollars worth of damage to US economy [45]. In this context, understanding extreme weather life cycle and even predicting its future trend become a significant scientific goal. Achieving this goal always requires accurately identifying the weather patterns to acquire the insight of climate change based on massive climate data analysis. Traditional climate data analysis methods are built upon human expertise in defining multi-variate thresholds of extreme weather events. However, it has a major drawback: there is no commonly held set of criteria that can define a weather event due to the man-made subjectivism, which leads to inaccurate pattern extraction. Therefore, DL has become another option for climate scientists. Liu et al. [40] develop a relatively simple CNN model with two convolutional layers to classify three typical extreme weather events and achieve up to 99% accuracy. Racah et al. [42] implement a multichannel spatiotemporal CNN architecture for semi-supervised prediction and exploratory extreme weather data analysis. GlobeNet [41] is a CNN model with inception units for typhoon eye tracking. Kurth et al. [21] use variants of Tiramisu and DeepLabv3+ neural networks which are both built on Residual Network (ResNet) [20]. They deployed these two networks on Summit and firstly achieved exascale deep learning for climate analysis.

2.2 High Energy Physics

Particle collision is the most important experiment approach in High Energy Physics (HEP). Detecting the signal of new particle is the major goal in experimental HEP. Today's HEP experimental facility such as LHC creates particle signals with hundreds of millions channels with a high data rate. The signal data from different channels in every collision usually are represented as a sparse 2d image, so called a jet-image. In fact, accurately classifying these jet-images is the key to find signals of new particles. In recent years, due to the excellent performance in pattern recognition, DL has become the focus of the data scientists in HEP community and has a tendency to go mainstream. Oliveira et al. [38] use a CNN model with 3 convolutional layers to tag jet-images. They firstly demonstrated that using DL not only improve the discrimination power, but also gain new insights compared to designing physics-inspired features. Komiske et al. [39] adopt a CNN model to discriminate quark and gluon jet-image. Kurth et al. [22] successfully deploy CNN to analyze massive HEP data on the HPC system and achieve petaflops performance. Their work is the first attempt at scaling DL on large-scale HPC systems.

2.3 Cosmology

Cosmology is a branch of astronomy concerned with the studies of the origin and evolution of the universe, from the Big Bang to today and on into the future [49]. In 21st century, the most fundamental problem in cosmology is the nature of dark energy. However, this mysterious energy greatly affects the distribution of matter in the universe that is described by cosmological parameters. Thus, accurately estimating these parameters is the key to understand the insight of the dark energy. For solving this problem, Ravanbakhsh et al. [26] firstly propose a 3D CNN model with 6 convolutional layers and 3 fully-connected layers and opens the way to estimating the parameters with high accuracy. Mathuriya et al. propose CosmoFlow [23], which is a project aiming to process large 3D cosmology dataset on HPC systems. They extend the CNN model designed by Ravanbakhsh et al. [26]. Meanwhile, in order to guarantee the high fidelity numerical simulations and avoid the use of expensive instruments, generating high quality cosmological data is also important. Ravanbakhsh et al. [33] propose a deep generative model for acquiring high quality galaxy images. Their results show a reliable alternative for generating the calibration data of cosmological surveys.

2.4 Summary

After investigating the above representative scientific fields, we have identified the representative DL applications and abstracted these DL applications into classical AI tasks. As shown in Table 2, almost all the applications are essentially using CNN to extract the patterns of various scientific image data. From this perspective, *image recognition*, *image generation*, and *object detection* are the most important tasks in modern scientific DL. In our benchmark methodology (Sect. 3.1), we use these three classic AI tasks as the component workloads of the HPC AI500 Benchmark.

Table 2. Modern Scientific Deep Learning.

Scientific fields	DL applications	Classical DL tasks	Model type
Extreme weather analysis	Identify weather patterns	Object detection	CNN
High energy physics	Jet-images discrimination	Image recognition	CNN
Cosmology	Estimate parameters	Image recognition	CNN
	Galaxy image generation	Image generation	

3 Benchmarking Methodology and Decisions

3.1 Methodology

Our benchmarking methodology is shown in Fig. 1, similar to that [12]. As HPC AI is an emerging and evolving domain, we take an incremental and iterative

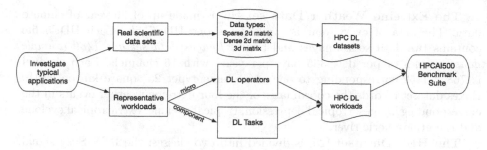

Fig. 1. HPCAI500 methodology

approach. First of all, we investigate the scientific fields that use DL widely. As mentioned in Sect. 2, *extreme weather analysis, high energy physics*, and *cosmology* are the most representative fields. Then, we pay attention to the typical DL workloads and data sets in these three application fields.

In order to cover the diversity of workloads, we focus on the critical tasks that DL has performed in the aforementioned fields. Based on our analysis in Sect. 2, we extracts three important component benchmarks that can represent modern scientific DL, namely *image recognition, image generation*, and *object detection*. This shows that CNN models play an important role. In each component, we choose the state-of-the-art model and software stack from the applications. We also select the hotspot DL operators as the micro benchmark for evaluating upper bound performance of the system.

We chose three real-world scientific data sets from aforementioned scientific fields and consider their diversity from the perspective of data formats. In modern DL, the raw data is always transformed into matrix for downstream processing. Therefore, we classify these matrices into three kinds of formats: 2D sparse matrix, 2D dense matrix, and 3 dimensional matrix. In each matrix format, we also consider the unique characteristics (e.g., multichannel that more than RGB, high resolution) in the scientific data.

3.2   The Selected Datasets

We investigate the representative data sets in our selected scientific fields and collect three data sets as shown in Table 3. Our selection guidelines follow the aforementioned benchmarking methodology.

Table 3. The Chosen Datasets

Dataset	Data format	Scientific features
Extreme weather dataset	2D dense matrix	High resolution, multichannel
HEP dataeset	2D sparse matrix	Multichannel
Cosmology dataset	3D matrix	Multidimensional

The **Extreme Weather Data set** [46] is made up of 26-year of climate data. The data of every year is available as one HDF5 file. Each HDF5 file contains two data sets: images and boxes. *Images data set has 1460 example dense images* (4 per day, 365 days per year) with 16 channels. Each channel is 768 * 1152 corresponding to one measurement per 25 square km on earth. Boxes dataset records the coordinates of the four extreme weather events in the corresponding images: tropical depression, tropical cyclone, extratropical cyclone and the atmospheric river.

The **HEP Data set** [25] is divided into two classes: the RPV-Susy signal and the most prevalent background. The training data set is composed of around 400 k jet-images. Each jet-image is represented as a 64*64 sparse matrix and has 3 channels. It also provides validation and test data. All the data are generated by using the Pythia event generator [51] interfaced to *the Delphes fast detector simulation* [38].

The **Cosmology Data set** [23] aims to predict the parameters of cosmology. It is based on dark matter N-body simulations produced using the MUSIC [52] and pycola [53] packages. Each simulation covers the volumes of $512h^{-1}Mpc^3$ and contains 512^3 dark matter particles.

3.3   The Selected Workloads

Component Benchmarks. Since object detection, image recognition, and image generation are the most representative DL tasks in modern scientific DL. We choose the following state-of-the-art models as the HPC AI500 component benchmarks.

Faster-RCNN [60] targets real-time object detection. Unlike the previous object detection model [61,62], it replaces the selective search by a region proposal network that achieves nearly cost-free region proposals. Further more, Faster-RCNN combines the advanced CNN model as their base network for extracting features and is the foundation of the 1st-place winning entries in ILSVRC'15 (ImageNet Large Scale Visual Recognition Competition).

ResNet [27] is a milestone in Image Recognition, marking the ability of AI to identify images beyond humans. It solves the degradation problem, which means in the very deep neural network the gradient will gradually disappear in the process of propagation, leading to poor performance. Due to the idea of ResNet, researchers successfully build a 152-layer deep CNN. This ultra deep model won all the awards in ILSVRC'15.

DCGAN [63] is one of the popular and successful neural network for GAN [50]. Its fundamental idea is replacing fully connected layers with convolutions and using transposed convolution for upsampling. The proposal of DCGAN helps bride the gap between CNNs for supervised learning and unsupervised learning.

Micro Benchmarks. We choose the following primary operators in CNN as our micro benchmarks.

Convolution. In mathematics, convolution is a mathematical operation on two functions to produce a third function that expresses how the shape of one is modified by the other [54]. In a CNN, convolution is the operation occupying the largest proportion, which is the multiply accumulate of the input matrix and the convolution kernel, and then produces feature maps. There are many convolution kernels distributed in different layers responsible for learning different level features.

Full-connected. The full-connected layer can be seen as the classifier of a CNN, which is essentially matrix multiplication. It is also the cause of the explosion of CNN parameters. For example, in AlexNet [1], the number of training parameters of fully-connected layers reaches about 59 million and accounts for 94% of the total.

Pooling. Pooling is a sample-based discretization process. In a CNN, the objective of pooling is to down-sample the inputs (e.g., feature maps), which leads to the reduction of dimensionality and training parameters. In addition, it enhances the robustness of the whole network. The commonly used pooling operations including max-pooling and average-pooling.

3.4 Metrics

Metrics for Component Benchmarks. At present, time-to-accuracy is the most well-received solution [8, 29]. For comprehensive evaluate, the training accuracy and validation accuracy are both provided. The former is used to measure

Table 4. The Summary of HPC AI500 Benchmark.

App scenarios	Workloads	Fields	Datasets	Data format	Software stack
Micro benchmarks	Convolution	HEP[a]	Matrix	Sparse 2D matrix	CUDA MKL
	Pooling	EWA[b]		Dense 2D matrix	
	Fully-connected	Cos[c]		3D matrix	
Image recognition	ResNet	HEP	HEP dataset	Sparse 2D matrix	TensorFlow
		Cos	Cos dataset	3D matrix	Pytorch
Object detection	Faster-RCNN	EWA	EWA dataset	Dense 2D matrix	TensorFlow
					Pytorch
Image generation	DCGAN	Cos	Cos dataset	3D matrix	TensorFlow
					Pytorch

[a] High Energy Physics
[b] Extreme Weather Analysis
[c] Cosmology

the training effect of the model, and the latter is used to measure the generalization ability of the model. The threshold of target accuracy is defined as a value according to the requirement of corresponding application domains. Each application domain needs to define its own target accuracy. In addition, cost-to-accuracy and power-to-accuracy are provided to measure the money and power spending of training the model to the target accuracy (Table 4).

Metrics for Micro Benchmarks. The metrics of the micro benchmarks is simple since we only measure the performance without considering accuracy. We adopt FLOPS and images per second (images/s) as two main metrics. We also consider power and cost related metrics.

4 Reference Implementation

4.1 Component Benchmarks

According to the survey [59] of NERSC (National Energy Research Scientific Computing Center, the most representative DL framework is TensorFlow, and the proportion of which is increasing year by year. Consequently, we adopt TensorFlow for preferred framework.

In order to evaluate large-scale HPC systems running scientific DL, scalability is the fundamental requirement. In modern distributed DL, synchronized training through data parallelism is the mainstream. In this training scheme, each training process gets a different portion of the full dataset but has a complete copy of the neural network model. At the end of each batch computation, all processes will synchronize the model parameters by *all_reduce* operation to ensure they are training a consistent model. TensorFlow implements *all_reduce* through a parameter server [32] and use the GRPC protocol for communication by default. The master-slave architecture and socket-based communication can not extend to large-scale clusters [55]. Horovod [56] irrespective a library originally designed for scalable distributed deep learning using TensorFlow. It implements *all_reduce* operation using ring-based algorithm [57] and MPI (Message Passing Interface) for communication. Due to the decentralized design and high effective protocol, the combination of TensorFlow and Horovod has successfully scaled to 27360 GPUs on Summit [21]. Therefore, we leverage Horovod to improve the scalability.

4.2 Micro Benchmarks

The goal of micro benchmarks is to determine the upper bound performance of the system. To do so, we implement it with succinct software stack. Every DL operator is written in C++ or call the low-level neural networks library (e.g. CuDNN) without any other dependencies.

5   Conclusion

In this paper, we propose HPC AI500—a benchmark suite for evaluating HPC system that running scientific deep learning workloads. Our benchmarks model real-world scientific deep learning applications, including extreme weather analysis, high energy physics, and cosmology. We propose a set of metrics for comprehensively evaluating the HPC AI systems, considering both accuracy, performance as well as power and cost. We provide a scalable reference implementation of HPC AI500. The specification and source code of HPC AI500 are publicly available from http://www.benchcouncil.org/HPCAI500/index.html.

Acknowledgments. This work is supported by the Standardization Research Project of Chinese Academy of Sciences No.BZ201800001.

References

1. Krizhevsky, A., Sutskever, I., Hinton, G.E.: ImageNet classification with deep convolutional neural networks. In: Advances in Neural Information Processing Systems (2012)
2. http://www.image-net.org/
3. Abadi, M., et al.: TensorFlow: a system for large-scale machine learning. In: OSDI, vol. 16 (2016)
4. Jia, Y., et al.: Caffe: convolutional architecture for fast feature embedding. In: Proceedings of the 22nd ACM International Conference on Multimedia. ACM (2014)
5. Chen, Y., et al.: DianNao family: energy-efficient hardware accelerators for machine learning. Commun. ACM **59**(11), 105–112 (2016)
6. Jouppi, N.P., et al.: In-datacenter performance analysis of a tensor processing unit. In: 2017 ACM/IEEE 44th Annual International Symposium on Computer Architecture (ISCA). IEEE (2017)
7. Robert, A., et al.: Fathom: reference workloads for modern deep learning methods. In: 2016 IEEE International Symposium on Workload Characterization (IISWC). IEEE (2016)
8. Coleman, C., et al.: DAWNBench: an end-to-end deep learning benchmark and competition. Training **100**(101), 102 (2017)
9. Zhu, H., et al.: TBD: benchmarking and analyzing deep neural network training arXiv preprint arXiv:1803.06905 (2018)
10. Shi, S., et al.: Benchmarking state-of-the-art deep learning software tools. In: 2016 7th International Conference on Cloud Computing and Big Data (CCBD). IEEE (2016)
11. Hennessy, J.L., Patterson, D.A.: Computer Architecture: A Quantitative Approach. Elsevier, Amsterdam (2011)
12. Wang, L., et al.: BigDataBench: a big data benchmark suite from internet services. In: 2014 IEEE 20th International Symposium on High Performance Computer Architecture (HPCA). IEEE (2014)
13. Jia, Z., Wang, L., Zhan, J., et al.: Characterizing data analysis workloads in data centers. In: 2013 IEEE International Symposium on Workload Characterization (IISWC), pp. 66–76. IEEE (2013)

14. Hao, T., Huang, Y., Wen, X., et al.: Edge AIBench: towards comprehensive end-to-end edge computing benchmarking. In: 2018 BenchCouncil International Symposium on Benchmarking, Measuring and Optimizing (Bench18) (2018)
15. Luo, C., Zhang, F., Huang, C., Xiong, X., Chen, J., et al.: AIoT Bench: towards comprehensive benchmarking mobile and embedded device intelligence. In: 2018 BenchCouncil International Symposium on Benchmarking, Measuring and Optimizing (Bench18) (2018)
16. Gao, W., Tang, F., Wang, L., Zhan, J., et al.: AIBench: an industry standard internet service AI benchmark suite. Technical report (2019)
17. Gao, W., Luo, C., Wang, L., Xiong, X., et al.: AIBench: towards scalable and comprehensive datacenter AI benchmarking. In: 2018 BenchCouncil International Symposium on Benchmarking, Measuring and Optimizing (Bench18) (2018)
18. Dean, J.: Keynote: Large Scale Deep Learning
19. Collobert, R., Bengio, S., Marithoz, J.: Torch: a modular machine learning software library, no. EPFL-REPORT-82802. Idiap (2002)
20. He, K., et al.: Deep residual learning for image recognition. In: Proceedings of the IEEE Conference on Computer Vision and Pattern Recognition (2016)
21. Kurth, T., Treichler, S., Romero, J., et al.: Exascale deep learning for climate analytics. In: Proceedings of the International Conference for High Performance Computing, Networking, Storage, and Analysis, p. 51. IEEE Press (2018)
22. Kurth, T., Zhang, J., Satish, N., et al.: Deep learning at 15pf: supervised and semi-supervised classification for scientific data. In: Proceedings of the International Conference for High Performance Computing, Networking, Storage and Analysis, p. 7. ACM (2017)
23. Mathuriya, A., Bard, D., Mendygral, P., et al.: CosmoFlow: using deep learning to learn the universe at scale. In: Proceedings of the International Conference for High Performance Computing, Networking, Storage, and Analysis, p. 65. IEEE Press (2018)
24. https://www.oreilly.com/ideas/a-look-at-deep-learning-for-science
25. Bhimji, W., Farrell, S.A., Kurth, T., et al.: Deep neural networks for physics analysis on low-level whole-detector data at the LHC. J. Phys.: Conf. Ser. **1085**(4), 042034 (2018)
26. Ravanbakhsh, S., Oliva J.B., Fromenteau, S., et al.: Estimating cosmological parameters from the dark matter distribution, pp. 2407–2416. In: ICML (2016)
27. He, K., Zhang, X., Ren, S., et al.: Deep residual learning for image recognition. In: Proceedings of the IEEE Conference on Computer Vision and Pattern Recognition, pp. 770–778 (2016)
28. Chen, T., Chen, Y., Duranton, M., et al.: BenchNN: On the broad potential application scope of hardware neural network accelerators. In: 2012 IEEE International Symposium on Workload Characterization (IISWC), pp. 36–45. IEEE (2012)
29. https://mlperf.org/
30. Ben-Nun, T., Besta, M., Huber, S., et al.: A modular benchmarking infrastructure for high-performance and reproducible deep learning. arXiv preprint arXiv:1901.10183 (2019)
31. Patton, R.M., Johnston, J.T., Young, S.R., et al.: 167-PFlops deep learning for electron microscopy: from learning physics to atomic manipulation. In: Proceedings of the International Conference for High Performance Computing, Networking, Storage, and Analysis, p. 50. IEEE Press (2018)
32. Li, M., Andersen, D.G., Park, J.W., et al.: Scaling distributed machine learning with the parameter server. In: 11th USENIX Symposium on Operating Systems Design and Implementation (OSDI 14), pp. 583–598 (2014)

33. Ravanbakhsh, S., Lanusse, F., Mandelbaum, R., et al.: Enabling dark energy with deep generative models of galaxy images. In: Thirty-First AAAI Conference on Artificial Intelligence (2017)
34. Mustafa, M., Bard, D., Bhimji, W., et al.: Creating virtual universes using generative adversarial networks. arXiv preprint arXiv:1706.02390 (2017)
35. Schmelzle, J., Lucchi, A., Kacprzak, T., et al.: Cosmological model discrimination with deep learning. arXiv preprint arXiv:1707.05167 (2017)
36. Peterson, C.: Track finding with neural networks. Nucl. Instrum. Methods Phys. Res. Sect. A: Accel. Spectrom. Detect. Assoc. Equip. **279**(3), 537–545 (1989)
37. Denby, B.: Neural networks and cellular automata in experimental high energy physics. Comput. Phys. Commun. **49**(3), 429–448 (1988)
38. de Oliveira, L., Kagan, M., Mackey, L., et al.: Jet-images-deep learning edition. J. High Energy Phys. **2016**(7), 69 (2016)
39. Komiske, P.T., Metodiev, E.M., Schwartz, M.D.: Deep learning in color: towards automated quark/gluon jet discrimination. J. High Energy Phys. **2017**(1), 110 (2017)
40. Liu, Y., Racah, E., Correa, J., et al.: Application of deep convolutional neural networks for detecting extreme weather in climate datasets. arXiv preprint arXiv:1605.01156 (2016)
41. Hong, S., Kim, S., Joh, M., et al.: GlobeNet: convolutional neural networks for typhoon eye tracking from remote sensing imagery. arXiv preprint arXiv:1708.03417 (2017)
42. Racah, E., Beckham, C., Maharaj, T., et al.: ExtremeWeather: a large-scale climate dataset for semi-supervised detection, localization, and understanding of extreme weather events. In: Advances in Neural Information Processing Systems, pp. 3402–3413 (2017)
43. Gmez-Bombarelli, R., Wei, J.N., Duvenaud, D., et al.: Automatic chemical design using a data-driven continuous representation of molecules. ACS Cent. Sci. **4**(2), 268–276 (2018)
44. https://www.ecowatch.com/un-extreme-weather-climate-change-2633131018.html
45. https://www.cbsnews.com/news/extreme-weather-events-2018-top-3-most-expensive-climate-driven-events-took-place-in-us/
46. https://extremeweatherdataset.github.io/
47. http://stanford.edu/group/stanford_atlas/
48. Spira, M., Djouadi, A., Graudenz, D., et al.: Higgs boson production at the LHC. Nucl. Phys. B **453**(1–2), 17–82 (1995)
49. https://en.wikipedia.org/wiki/Cosmology
50. Goodfellow, I., Pouget-Abadie, J., Mirza, M., et al.: Generative adversarial nets. In: Advances in Neural Information Processing Systems, pp. 2672–2680 (2014)
51. Sjstrand, T., Mrenna, S., Skands, P.: PYTHIA 6.4 physics and manual. J. High Energy Phys. **2006**(05), 026 (2006)
52. https://www-n.oca.eu/ohahn/MUSIC/
53. https://bitbucket.org/tassev/pycola/
54. https://en.wikipedia.org/wiki/Convolution
55. Mathuriya, A., Kurth, T., Rane, V., et al.: Scaling GRPC tensorflow on 512 nodes of cori supercomputer. arXiv preprint arXiv:1712.09388 (2017)
56. Sergeev, A., Del Balso, M.: Horovod: fast and easy distributed deep learning in TensorFlow. arXiv preprint arXiv:1802.05799 (2018)
57. Gibiansky, A.: Bringing HPC techniques to deep learning (2017). http://research.baidu.com/bringing-hpc-techniques-deep-learning. Accessed 6 Dec 2017

58. https://www.open-mpi.org/
59. https://www.jlab.org/indico/event/247/session/8/contribution/30/material/slides/0.pdf
60. Ren, S., et al.: Faster R-CNN: towards real-time object detection with region proposal networks. In: Advances in Neural Information Processing Systems (2015)
61. Girshick, R., et al.: Rich feature hierarchies for accurate object detection and semantic segmentation. In: Proceedings of the IEEE Conference on Computer Vision and Pattern Recognition (2014)
62. Girshick, R.: Fast R-CNN. In: Proceedings of the IEEE International Conference on Computer Vision (2015)
63. Radford, A., Metz, L., Chintala, S.: Unsupervised representation learning with deep convolutional generative adversarial networks. arXiv preprint arXiv:1511.06434 (2015)
64. Goodfellow, I., et al.: Generative adversarial nets. In: Advances in Neural Information Processing Systems, pp. 2672–2680 (2014)

Edge AIBench: Towards Comprehensive End-to-End Edge Computing Benchmarking

Tianshu Hao[1,2], Yunyou Huang[1,2], Xu Wen[1,2], Wanling Gao[1,3], Fan Zhang[1], Chen Zheng[1,3], Lei Wang[1,3], Hainan Ye[3,4], Kai Hwang[5], Zujie Ren[6], and Jianfeng Zhan[1,2,3(✉)]

[1] State Key Laboratory of Computer Architecture,
Institute of Computing Technology, Chinese Academy of Sciences, Beijing, China
{haotianshu,huangyunyou,wenxu,gaowanling,zhangfan,zhengchen,wanglei_2011,
zhanjianfeng}@ict.ac.cn
[2] University of Chinese Academy of Sciences, Beijing, China
[3] BenchCouncil (International Open Benchmark Council), Dover, Delaware, USA
[4] Beijing Academy of Frontier Sciences and Technology, Beijing, China
yehainan@mail.bafst.com
[5] Chinese University of Hongkong at Shenzhen, Shenzhen, China
hwangkai@cuhk.edu.cn
[6] Zhejiang Lab, Zhejiang, China
renzj@hdu.edu.cn

Abstract. In edge computing scenarios, the distribution of data and collaboration of workloads on different layers are serious concerns for performance, privacy, and security issues. So for edge computing benchmarking, we must take an end-to-end view, considering all three layers: client-side devices, edge computing layer, and cloud servers. Unfortunately, the previous work ignores this most important point. This paper presents the BenchCouncil's coordinated effort on edge AI benchmarks, named Edge AIBench. In total, Edge AIBench models four typical application scenarios: ICU Patient Monitor, Surveillance Camera, Smart Home, and Autonomous Vehicle with the focus on data distribution and workload collaboration on three layers. Edge AIBench is publicly available from http://www.benchcouncil.org/EdgeAIBench/index.html. We also build an edge computing testbed with a federated learning framework to resolve performance, privacy, and security issues.

Keywords: Edge computing · AI benchmarks · Testbed · Federated learning

1 Introduction

Cloud computing is a mature model to share computing resources by providing network access to users [1]. In cloud computing models, users communicate with

© Springer Nature Switzerland AG 2019
C. Zheng and J. Zhan (Eds.): Bench 2018, LNCS 11459, pp. 23–30, 2019.
https://doi.org/10.1007/978-3-030-32813-9_3

the data center to get hardware, software and other computing resources and store data. However, In recent years, the number of client-side devices (e.g. smart devices and monitors) grows rapidly. IoT Analytics [2] has reported the number of connected devices reached 17 billion in 2018 and Gartner says the IoT devices will install 26 billion units by 2020 [3]. These client-side devices produce a large amount of data to process. The overhead of data transmission and data encryption among devices and data centers becomes significant bottlenecks for many IoT scenarios, and hence it raises a daunting challenge for throughput, latency, and security guarantee.

Edge computing emerges as a promising technical framework to overcome the challenges in cloud computing. The edge computing framework adds a new layer, named the edge computing layer, on the basis of the traditional cloud computing framework. In the edge computing framework, only the real-time data processing is transferred to the edge computing layer, while other complicated data processing is still executed on the cloud server. Figure 1 shows a general edge computing framework, which includes three layers: cloud server, edge computing layer, and client-side devices.

In the edge computing scenarios, the distribution of data and collaboration of workloads on different layers are serious concerns for performance, security, and privacy issues. So for benchmarking, designing, and implementing edge computing systems or applications, we shall take an end-to-end view, considering all three layers. Unfortunately, the previous work, especially the previous benchmarking efforts [4,6,7,14] ignore this most important point.

In edge computing scenarios, AI techniques are widely used to augment device, edge and cloud intelligence, and they are most demanding in terms of computing power, data storage, and network. Typical application scenarios include smart city, smart home, autonomous vehicle, surveillance camera, smart medical, wearable devices and so on. These scenarios are complicated because of different kinds of client-side devices, a large quantity of heterogeneous data, privacy and security issues. Most of these scenarios have a high requirement for latency and network bandwidth. However, edge computing is in the initial stage and doesn't have a uniform standard for these scenarios. Therefore, a comprehensive end-to-end edge computing benchmark suite is needed to measure and optimize the systems and applications.

Meanwhile, edge computing is still in the initial stage with a lack of testbed. Because of the privacy issue, there is no incentive to share data. Because of the complexity, there is no end-to-end application scenario to validate the architectures, systems, or specific algorithms in certain settings.

Above all, it's necessary to develop a benchmark suite and testbed for edge computing. This paper reports the BenchCouncil's coordinated effort on edge AI benchmarks, named Edge AIBench, which is publicly available from http://www.benchcouncil.org/EdgeAIBench/index.html. Edge AIBench includes four typical application scenarios: ICU Patient Monitor, Surveillance Camera, Smart Home, and Autonomous Vehicle, which consider the complexity of all edge computing AI scenarios. Coordinated by BenchCouncil (http://www.benchcouncil.org), we are also building an edge computing testbed with a federated learning framework to resolve security and privacy issue, which can be accessed from http://www. benchcouncil.org/testbed/index.php. BenchCouncil also release datacenter AI benchmarks [8,9], HPC AI benchmarks [10], IoT AI benchmarks [11], and big data benchmarks [12,13], publicly available from the BenchCouncil website.

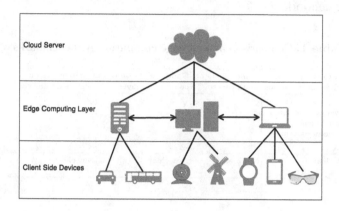

Fig. 1. A general edge computing framework.

2   Related Work

Since the edge computing AI applications have become more and more popular these years, benchmarks are needed to measure and optimize the systems and applications. There are several related benchmark suites. We summarize the state-of-the-art and state-of-the-practice work on edge AI benchmarking.

MLPerf [4] is a benchmark suite focusing on measuring Machine Learning(ML) performance. It provides the edge inference benchmarks, including eight ML tasks: image classification, object detection and so on [5]. But this benchmark suite just evaluates the edge computing layer with the lack of an end-to-end view.

EEMBC [6] develops an ML benchmark suite, named MLMark on embedded edge computing platforms. MLMark includes four AI applications: image classification, object detection, language translation, and speech recognition. However, only the licensees and members of EEMBC have the right to access these benchmarks and this benchmark suite is still in "beta" state now.

EdgeBench [14] compares two edge computing platforms–Amazon AWS Greengrass and Microsoft Azure IoT Edge. And it includes two AI applications: speech-to-text and image recognition. EdgeBench fails to provide an end-to-end application benchmarking framework.

AI Benchmark [7] is a benchmark suite for AI applications on smartphones, and it includes nine AI applications. It's an IoT benchmark suite and only focuses on the client-side devices (smartphones)' performance.

Table 1 compares the state-of-the-art and state-of-the-practice edge computing AI benchmarks. It shows many of them only focus on the edge computing layer instead of the whole edge computing framework. Our benchmark suite Edge AIBench provides an end-to-end application benchmarking framework, including train, validate and inference stages. Moreover, Edge AIBench includes four typical edge computing AI scenarios and measures the whole three-layer edge computing framework.

Table 1. Comparison among edge computing AI benchmarks

Benchmark name	End-to-end application scenarios	Components on cloud server	Components on edge computing layer	Components on client-side devices	Open-source
Edge AIBench	ICU patient monitor surveillance camera smart home autonomous vehicle	✓	✓	✓	✓
MLPerf	N/A	✗	✓	✗	✓
EEMBC MLMark	Not clear	Not clear	Not clear	Not clear	✗
EdgeBench	N/A	✓	✓	✓	✓
AI benchmark	N/A	✗	✗	✓	✓

3   The Summary of Edge AIBench

Edge AIBench includes four typical scenarios: Intensive care unit(ICU) patient monitor, surveillance camera, smart home, and autonomous vehicle. These four AI scenarios can present the complexity of edge computing AI scenarios from different perspectives.

3.1   ICU Patient Monitor

ICU is the treatment place for critical patients. Therefore immediacy is significant for ICU patient monitor scenario to notify doctors of the patients' status as soon as possible. The dataset we use is MIMIC-III [15]. MIMIC-III provides many kinds of patients data such as vital signs, fluid balance and so on. Moreover, we choose heart failure prediction [16] and endpoint prediction [17] as the AI benchmarks.

Heart failure prediction uses the MIMIC-III dataset and a two-level neural attention model. It collects the patients' data on the virtual client-side devices, trains on the cloud server (the data will be sent from the edge) and predicts the heart failure on the edge computing layer.

Endpoint prediction benchmark also uses the MIMIC-III dataset, and it uses an LSTM model. This benchmark collects patients' data on the virtual patient device generator and then transmit it to the edge to make the inference. Then the data will be sent to the cloud server to do more training.

3.2 Surveillance Camera

There are many surveillance cameras all over the world nowadays, and these cameras will produce a large quantity of video data at all times. If we transmit all of the data to cloud servers, the network transmission bandwidth will be very high. Therefore, this scenario focus on edge data preprocesses and data compression.

We choose the person re-identification application as the component benchmark. It collects data from the virtual camera devices and pre-process and infer these video data on the edge computing layer. Then the edge computing layer will send the compressed data to the cloud server. Moreover, the decompression and training process are on the cloud server.

3.3 Smart Home

Smart home includes a lot of smart home devices such as automatic controller, alarm system, audio equipment and so on. Thus, the uniqueness of the smart home includes different kinds of edge devices and heterogeneous data. We will choose two AI applications as the component benchmarks: speech recognition and face recognition. These two components have heterogeneous data and different collecting devices. These two component benchmarks both collect data on the client side devices(e.g. camera and smartphone), infer on the edge computing layer and train on the cloud server.

Speech recognition uses the DeepSpeech2 [18] model and the LibriSpeech dataset [19].

Face recognition uses the FaceNet [20] model and uses the LFW (Labeled Faces in the Wild) [21] dataset.

3.4 Autonomous Vehicle

The uniqueness of the autonomous vehicle scenario is that the high demand for validity. That is to say, it takes absolute correct action even without human intervention. This feature represents the demand of some edge computing AI scenarios. The automatic control system will analyze the current road conditions and make a corresponding reaction at once. We will choose the road sign recognition as the component benchmark.

The road sign recognition will collect the road signs data from the camera, train these data on the cloud and infer on the edge computing layer.

Table 2 shows the component benchmarks of Edge AIBench. Edge AIBench provides an end-to-end application benchmarking, consisting of train, inference, data collection and other parts using a general three-layer edge computing framework.

Table 2. The Summary of Edge AIBench

End-to-end application scenarios	AI component benchmarks	Cloud server	Edge computing layer	Client side device
ICU patient monitor	Heart failure prediction	Train	Infer send alarm	Generate data
ICU patient monitor	Endpoint prediction	Train	Infer	Generate data
Surveillance camera	Person re-identification	Decompress data train	Compress data infer	Generate data
Smart home	Speech recognition	Train	Infer	Generate data
Smart home	Face recognition	Train	Infer	Generate data
Autonomous vehicle	Road sign recognition	Train	Infer	Generate data

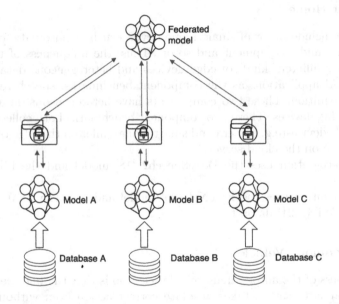

Fig. 2. An edge computing AI testbed with a federated learning framework

3.5   A Federated Learning Framework Testbed

We have developed an edge computing AI testbed to provide support for researchers and common users, which is publicly available from http://www.benchcouncil.org/testbed.html. Security and privacy issues become significant focuses in the age of big data, as well as edge computing. Federated learning is a distributed collaborative machine learning technology whose main target is to preserve the privacy [22]. Our testbed system will combine the federated learning framework.

At present, we are implementing the ICU scenario on the testbed. We are developing a "virtual patient" data generator and a federated machine learning training model. Doctors can train the model on the local server and transmit the encrypting parameter to the cloud server. Then the cloud server computes the overall parameter on the basis of these encrypting parameter from different hospitals. After all, the cloud server will send the overall parameter to the local server and the local server will decrypt it to update their models. Figure 2 shows our federated learning testbed framework.

4   Conclusion

This paper presents an edge computing AI benchmark, named Edge AIBench, which consists of four end-to-end application benchmarking framework and six component benchmarks. These scenarios we choose can present the complexity of edge computing scenarios from different perspectives. Also, we build an edge computing AI testbed with a federated learning framework.

Acknowledgment. This work is supported by the Standardization Research Project of Chinese Academy of Sciences No. BZ201800001.

References

1. Peter, M., Timothy, G.: The NIST definition of cloud computing, recommendations of the National Institute of Standards and Technology. In: National Institute of Standards and Technology (NIST) Special Publication 800–145. Technical report (2011)
2. IoT Analytics. https://iot-analytics.com/state-of-the-iot-update-q1-q2-2018-number-of-iot-devices-now-7b/
3. Gartner Says the Internet of Things Will Transform the Data Centre. https://prwire.com.au/pr/42679/gartner-says-the-internet-of-things-will-transform-the-data-centre
4. MLPerf. https://mlperf.org/
5. Vijay, J.R.: An ML benchmark suite for ML software frameworks and ML hardware accelerators in ML cloud and edge computing platforms. In: Report in BenchCouncil International Symposium on Benchmarking, Measuring and Optimizing (2018)
6. EEMBC. https://www.eembc.org/
7. Ignatov, A., et al.: AI benchmark: running deep neural networks on Android smartphones. In: Leal-Taixé, Laura, Roth, Stefan (eds.) ECCV 2018. LNCS, vol. 11133, pp. 288–314. Springer, Cham (2019). https://doi.org/10.1007/978-3-030-11021-5_19
8. Gao, W., et al.: AIBench: an industry standard internet service AI benchmark suite. Technical report (2019)
9. Gao W, et al.: AIBench: towards scalable and comprehensive datacenter AI benchmarking. In: BenchCouncil International Symposium on Benchmarking, Measuring and Optimizing (Bench 2018) (2018)
10. Jiang, Z., et al.: HPC AI500: a benchmark suite for HPC AI systems. In: BenchCouncil International Symposium on Benchmarking, Measuring and Optimizing (Bench 2018) (2018)

11. Luo, C., et al.: AIoT bench: towards comprehensive benchmarking mobile and embedded device intelligence. In: BenchCouncil International Symposium on Benchmarking, Measuring and Optimizing (Bench 2018) (2018)

12. Wang, L., et al.: BigDataBench: a big data benchmark suite from internet services. In: 2014 IEEE 20th International Symposium on High Performance Computer Architecture (HPCA), 15 February 2014, pp. 488–499. IEEE (2014)

13. Jia, Z., Wang, L., Zhan, J., Zhang, L., Luo, C.: Characterizing data analysis workloads in data centers. In: 2013 IEEE International Symposium on Workload Characterization (IISWC), 22 September 2013, pp. 66–76. IEEE (2013)

14. Das, A., Patterson, S., Wittie, M.: EdgeBench: benchmarking edge computing platforms. In: 2018 IEEE/ACM International Conference on Utility and Cloud Computing Companion (UCC Companion), 17 December 2018, pp. 175–180. IEEE (2018)

15. Johnson, A.E.W., et al.: MIMIC-III, a freely accessible critical care database. Sci. Data **3**, 160035 (2016)

16. Choi, E., Bahadori, M.T., Sun, J., Kulas, J., Schuetz, A., Stewart, W.: RETAIN: an interpretable predictive model for healthcare using reverse time attention mechanism. In: Advances in Neural Information Processing Systems, pp. 3504–3512 (2016)

17. Liu, L., Shen, J., Zhang, M., Wang, Z., Tang, J.: Learning the joint representation of heterogeneous temporal events for clinical endpoint prediction. In: Thirty-Second AAAI Conference on Artificial Intelligence, 25 April 2018

18. Amodei, D., et al.: Deep speech 2: end-to-end speech recognition in English and Mandarin. In: International Conference on Machine Learning, 11 June 2016, pp. 173–182 (2016)

19. Panayotov, V., Chen, G., Povey, D., Khudanpur, S.: Librispeech: an ASR corpus based on public domain audio books. In: 2015 IEEE International Conference on Acoustics, Speech and Signal Processing (ICASSP), 19 April 2015, pp. 5206–5210. IEEE (2015)

20. Schroff, F., Kalenichenko, D., Philbin, J.: FaceNet: a unified embedding for face recognition and clustering. In: Proceedings of the IEEE Conference on Computer Vision and Pattern Recognition, pp. 815–823 (2015)

21. Huang, G.B., Mattar, M., Berg, T., Learned-Miller, E.: Labeled faces in the wild: a database for studying face recognition in unconstrained environments. In: Workshop on Faces in 'Real-Life' Images: Detection, Alignment, and Recognition, October 2008

22. Yang, Q., Liu, Y., Chen, T., Tong, Y.: Federated machine learning: concept and applications. ACM Trans. Intell. Syst. Technol. (TIST) **10**(2), 12 (2019)

AIoT Bench: Towards Comprehensive Benchmarking Mobile and Embedded Device Intelligence

Chunjie Luo[1,2,4], Fan Zhang[1], Cheng Huang[1,2], Xingwang Xiong[1,2], Jianan Chen[1,2], Lei Wang[1,4], Wanling Gao[1,4], Hainan Ye[3,4], Tong Wu[5], Runsong Zhou[6], and Jianfeng Zhan[1,2,4(✉)]

[1] State Key Laboratory of Computer Architecture,
Institute of Computing Technology, Chinese Academy of Sciences, Beijing, China
`zhanjianfeng@ict.ac.cn`
[2] University of Chinese Academy of Sciences, Beijing, China
[3] Beijing Academy of Frontier Science and Technology, Beijing, China
[4] BenchCouncil (International Open Benchmarking Council), Dover, England
[5] China National Institute of Metrology, Beijing, China
[6] China Software Testing Center, Beijing, China

Abstract. Due to increasing amounts of data and compute resources, the deep learning achieves many successes in various domains. Recently, researchers and engineers make effort to apply the intelligent algorithms to the mobile or embedded devices. In this paper, we propose a benchmark suite, AIoT Bench, to evaluate the AI ability of mobile and embedded devices. Our benchmark (1) covers different application domains, e.g. image recognition, speech recognition and natural language processing; (2) covers different platforms, including Android and Raspberry Pi; (3) covers different development frameworks, including TensorFlow and Caffe2; (4) offers both end-to-end application workloads and micro workloads.

Keywords: AI · IoT · Benchmark

1 Introduction

Due to increasing amounts of data and compute resources, the deep learning achieves many successes in various domains. Recently, researchers and engineers make effort to apply the intelligent algorithms to the mobile or embedded devices, e.g. smart phone, self-driving cars, smart home. On one hand, the neural networks are made more lightweight to adapt the mobile or embedded devices by using simpler architecture, or by quantizing, pruning and compressing the networks. On the other hand, the mobile and embedded devices provide additional hardware acceleration using GPUs or NPUs to support the AI applications. Since AI applications on mobile and embedded devices get more and

© Springer Nature Switzerland AG 2019
C. Zheng and J. Zhan (Eds.): Bench 2018, LNCS 11459, pp. 31–35, 2019.
https://doi.org/10.1007/978-3-030-32813-9_4

more attention, the benchmarking of the AI ability of those devices becomes an urgent problem to be solved.

Benchmarking the AI ability of mobile and embedded devices is non-trivial. We consider that the benchmark should meet the following requirements. (1) It should cover typical AI application domains. Currently, the AI application mainly focuses on the image, speech, and text domain. The workloads should satisfy the diversity of the AI application domain. (2) It should cover the typical platforms of the IoT devices. Android devices and Raspberry Pi are the widely used in IoT environments. (3) It should consider the different development frameworks of the AI applications on the mobile and embed devices. (4) Beyond the end-to-end application workloads which can reflect the performance of the system comprehensively, we also need micro workloads to obtain the fine-grained analysis of the performance.

Recently, there are several AI related benchmarks have been proposed. For example, ETH Zurich AI benchmark [10] aim to benchmark the Android smartphone using different vision tasks implemented with TensorFlow Lite. Other AI related benchmarks have Fathom [2], DAWNBench [4]. The existing AI related benchmarks do not satisfy the requirements mentioned above.

In this paper, we propose a benchmark suite, AIoT Bench, to evaluate the AI ability of mobile and embedded devices. Our benchmark (1) covers different application domains, e.g. image recognition, speech recognition and natural language processing; (2) covers different platforms, including Android devices and Raspberry Pi; (3) covers different development tools, including TensorFlow and Caffe2; (4) offers both end-to-end application workloads and micro workloads. Coordinated by BenchCouncil, we also release AIBench [5,6], HPC AI500 [12], Edge AIBench [8] and BigDataBench [14,15].

2   Benchmarking Requirements

Here we will discuss the requirements of benchmarking mobile and embedded devices intelligence.

- **Domain Diversity.** Computer vision is the most active research area for AI applications, typical vision tasks include image classification, face recognition, and object detection. Speech recognition, to map an acoustic signal into the corresponding sequence of words, is another active area of AI research and application. Natural language processing (NLP) is one of the main AI areas. Natural language processing includes applications such as language model, machine translation, sentiment analysis and so on [7]. There are different features in different areas. The AI benchmarks should cover those typical application areas.
- **Platform Diversity.** Android is designed primarily for touchscreen mobile devices such as smartphones and tablets. In addition, Google has developed Android TV for televisions, Android Auto for cars, and Wear OS for wrist watches. Because of its openness, Android becomes the world's most popular

mobile platform. The Raspberry Pi is a series of small single-board computers. The Raspberry Pi is a powerful platform when it comes to AI. Because of its strong processing capability, the small form factor, and low power requirement, the Raspberry Pi is very popular for smart robotics and embedded projects.

– **Framework Diversity.** There are a number of popular deep learning frameworks. The benchmarks should cover the main frameworks, which are widely used on mobile and embedded devices. TensorFlow [1] is an open-source machine learning library, released by Google in 2015. TensorFlow Lite, designed for mobile and embedded devices, is presented in 2017. Caffe [11] is another popular open-source deep learning framework, developed at UC Berkeley. Facebooks releases Caffe2 in 2017, the mobile version for iOS and Android platforms.
– **Testing Hierarchy.** The end-to-end application benchmark can reflect the performance of the system comprehensively, while micro benchmark can get the fine-grained analysis of the performance. Both of them are useful for evaluating the mobile and embedded devices.

3   AIoT Bench

We propose a benchmark suite, AIoT Bench, to evaluate the AI ability of mobile and embedded devices. Our benchmark (1) covers different application domains, e.g. image recognition, speech recognition and natural language processing; (2) covers different platforms, including Android and Raspberry Pi; (3) covers different development frameworks, including TensorFlow and Caffe2; (4) offers both end-to-end application workloads and micro workloads.

Image Classification Workload. This is an end-to-end application workload of vision domain, which takes an image as input and outputs the image label. The model we use for image classification is MobileNet [9], which is a light weight convolutional network designed for mobile and embedded devices.

Speech Recognition Workload. This is an end-to-end application workload of speech domain, which takes words and phrases in a spoken language as input and converts them to the text format. The model we use is the DeepSpeech 2 [3], which consists of 2 convolutional layers, 5 bidirectional RNN layers, and a fully connected layer.

Transformer Translation Workload. This is an end-to-end application workload of NLP domain, which takes the text of one language as input and translates into another language. The model we use is transformer translation model [13], which solves sequence to sequence problems using attention mechanisms without recurrent connections used in traditional neural seq2seq models.

Micro Workloads. In our benchmarks, we provide the micro workloads, which are the basic operations to compose different networks. In detail, the micro workloads include convolutional operation, pointwise convolution, depthwise convolution, matrix multiply, pointwise add, ReLU activation, sigmoid activation, max pooling, average pooling.

The workloads in AIoT Bench are implemented using both TensorFlow Lite and Caffe 2 on the platform of Android as well as Raspberry Pi. We only include the prediction procedure since the training are usually carried out on datacenters.

4   Related Work

ETH Zurich AI benchmark [10] contains workloads covering the tasks of object recognition, face recognition, playing atari games, image deblurring, image super-resolution, bokeh simulation, semantic segmentation, photo enhancement. Those tasks are mainly focus on the vision application. The benchmark suite is implemented only using TensorFlow Lite and aims to evaluate the Android smartphones (Table 1).

Table 1. The comparison of AIoT Bench against ETH Zurich AI benchmark.

		AIoT bench	ETH Zurich AI benchmark
Domain diversity	Vision	Yes	Yes
	Speech	Yes	No
	NLP	Yes	No
Platform diversity	Android	Yes	Yes
	Raspberry Pi	Yes	No
Framework diversity	Tensorflow Lite	Yes	Yes
	Caffe2	Yes	No
Testing hierarchy	End-to-end	Yes	Yes
	Micro	Yes	No

5   Conclusion

In this paper, we analyze the requirements of benchmarking IoT devices intelligence. And to meet the requirements, we propose a benchmark suite, AIoT Bench, to evaluate the AI ability of mobile and embedded devices. Our benchmark covers different application domains, different platforms, different development frameworks. Moreover, we offer both end-to-end application workloads and micro workloads in our benchmark.

Acknowledgment. This work is supported by the Standardization Research Project of Chinese Academy of Sciences No.BZ201800001.

References

1. Abadi, M., et al.: TensorFlow: a system for large-scale machine learning. In: 12th {USENIX} Symposium on Operating Systems Design and Implementation ({OSDI} 16), pp. 265–283 (2016)
2. Adolf, R., Rama, S., Reagen, B., Wei, G.Y., Brooks, D.: Fathom: Reference workloads for modern deep learning methods. In: 2016 IEEE International Symposium on Workload Characterization (IISWC), pp. 1–10. IEEE (2016)
3. Amodei, D., et al.: Deep speech 2: end-to-end speech recognition in English and Mandarin. In: International Conference on Machine Learning, pp. 173–182 (2016)
4. Coleman, C., et al.: DAWNBench: an end-to-end deep learning benchmark and competition. Training **100**(101), 102 (2017)
5. Gao, W., et al.: AIBench: an industry standard internet service AI benchmark suite. Technical report (2019)
6. Gao, W., et al.: The report of datacenter AI benchmarks in BigDataBench: towards scalable and comprehensive AI and big data benchmarking. In: 2018 BenchCouncil Symposium on Benchmarking, Measuring and Optimizing (Bench 2018) (2018)
7. Goodfellow, I., Bengio, Y., Courville, A.: Deep Learning. MIT Press (2016)
8. Hao, T., et al.: Edge AIBench: towards comprehensive end-to-end edge computing benchmarking. In: 2018 BenchCouncil Symposium on Benchmarking, Measuring and Optimizing (Bench 2018) (2018)
9. Howard, A.G., et al.: MobileNets: efficient convolutional neural networks for mobile vision applications. arXiv preprint arXiv:1704.04861 (2017)
10. Ignatov, A.: AI benchmark: running deep neural networks on android smartphones. In: Leal-Taixé, L., Roth, S. (eds.) ECCV 2018. LNCS, vol. 11133, pp. 288–314. Springer, Cham (2019). https://doi.org/10.1007/978-3-030-11021-5_19
11. Jia, Y., et al.: Caffe: Convolutional architecture for fast feature embedding. In: Proceedings of the 22nd ACM International Conference on Multimedia, pp. 675–678. ACM (2014)
12. Jiang, Z., et al.: HPC AI500: a benchmark suite for HPC AI systems. In: 2018 BenchCouncil Symposium on Benchmarking, Measuring and Optimizing (Bench 2018) (2018)
13. Vaswani, A., et al.: Attention is all you need. In: Advances in Neural Information Processing Systems, pp. 5998–6008 (2017)
14. Wang, L., et al.: BigDataBench: a big data benchmark suite from internet services. In: IEEE International Symposium on High Performance Computer Architecture (HPCA) (2014)
15. Jia, Z., Wang, L., Zhan, J., Zhang, L., Luo, C.: Characterizing data analysis workloads in data centers. In: 2013 IEEE International Symposium on Workload Characterization (IISWC), 22 September 2013, pp. 66–76. IEEE (2013)

A Survey on Deep Learning Benchmarks: Do We Still Need New Ones?

Qin Zhang[1,2](✉), Li Zha[1], Jian Lin[3], Dandan Tu[3], Mingzhe Li[4], Fan Liang[5], Ren Wu[6], and Xiaoyi Lu[7]

[1] University of Chinese Academy of Sciences, Beijing, China
char@ict.ac.cn
[2] Institute of Computing Technology, Chinese Academy of Sciences, Beijing, China
zhangqin17s@ict.ac.cn
[3] Huawei Technologies Co., Ltd., Shenzhen, China
{linjian4,tudandan}@huawei.com
[4] Facebook, Inc., Menlo Park, USA
mingzhe0908@fb.com
[5] Cambricon, Inc., Beijing, China
liangfan@cambricon.com
[6] NovuMind, Inc., Santa Clara, USA
renw@novumind.com
[7] Department of Computer Science and Engineering, The Ohio State University, Columbus, USA
luxi@cse.ohio-state.edu

Abstract. Deep Learning has recently been gaining popularity. From the micro-architecture field to the upper-layer end applications, a lot of research work has been proposed in the literature to advance the knowledge of Deep Learning. Deep Learning Benchmarking is one of such hot spots in the community. There are a bunch of Deep Learning benchmarks available in the community already and new ones keep coming as well. However, we find that not many survey works are available to give an overview of these useful benchmarks in the literature. We also find few discussions on what has been done for Deep Leaning Benchmarking in the community and what are still missing. To fill this gap, this paper attempts to provide a survey on multiple high-impact Deep Learning Benchmarks with training and inference support. We share some of our insightful observations and discussions on these benchmarks. In this paper, we believe the community still needs more benchmarks to capture different perspectives, while these benchmarks need a way for converging to a standard.

Keywords: Deep Learning · Benchmark · Survey · Training · Inference

1 Introduction

Deep Learning (DL) is a rapidly moving area in terms of both software systems and hardware architectures. With the rapid evolution of Deep Learning, it is

C. Zheng and J. Zhan (Eds.): Bench 2018, LNCS 11459, pp. 36–49, 2019.
https://doi.org/10.1007/978-3-030-32813-9_5

very difficult to quickly evaluate the performance of a Deep Learning framework or a new DL model on new hardware platforms. However, such evaluation is vastly important in guiding framework and model developers, as well as hardware designers.

To help researchers and designers to perform meaningful studies, Deep Learning benchmarks are useful and vital tools to be adopted. Thus, a lot of Deep Learning benchmarks [3,8,13,14,21,51,52] have been proposed from both academia and industry areas and new ones keep coming as well.

Deep Learning training and inference is sometimes similar with High Performance Computing (HPC) tasks, and there has been a large number of benchmarks on HPC operations and systems [4,17,18,39,41]. However, we surprisingly find that not many survey works are available in the literature to give an overview of these useful benchmarks. Instead, multiple surveys have been done on Deep Learning methods and software tools or libraries [9,19,20,24,42,50,53]. We also find few discussions on what has been done for Deep Leaning Benchmarking in the community and what are still missing.

Therefore, we believe there is a need to have a survey paper on Deep Learning Benchmarking topic in the literature. To meet with this, this paper attempts to provide a comprehensive survey on multiple high-impact Deep Learning Benchmarks with training and inference support. Section 2 has summarized four Deep Learning benchmarks in detail. Two of them are chosen from the works proposed by research institutions and the other two are chosen from industry companies. In addition, some other related benchmarks are also discussed in Sect. 2.

Through our survey, we find the following important observations:

- Current-generation Deep Learning Benchmarks have covered many perspectives, such as performance, heterogeneity, power-consumption, accuracy, model density, precision requirement, cost, etc. But maybe more aspects can be considered, such as productivity.
- More benchmarks pay attention to training than inference so far. The community may need to start paying more attention to inference-centric benchmarks.
- The current-generation Deep Learning benchmarks are broadly designed with two methodologies. One way is proposing benchmarks with basic Deep Learning operations, while the other is collecting end-to-end Deep Learning models as benchmarks. Hybrid solutions are also available.
- The current status of Deep Learning Benchmark community is still in the "Warring States Period". There is no converged Deep Learning Benchmark standard yet in the community.

We share our thoughts and envisioned research directions on these observations in Sect. 3. We conclude this paper in Sect. 4 with many possible future works.

Through our survey, we believe that *the community still needs more benchmarks to capture different perspectives, while these benchmarks need a way to converge to a standard.*

2   A Survey on Deep Learning Benchmarks

In this section, we present a survey on related benchmarks in the literature and community.

2.1   Stanford DAWNBench

DAWNBench [12,13] is an open-source benchmark and competition for end-to-end deep learning training and inference. Measuring end-to-end performance of training such as time and cost, and inference such as latency. DAWNBench gives researchers an objective judgment standard of different computation frameworks, hardware, hyper-parameter settings, and optimization algorithms.

DAWNBench can measure the end-to-end time and cost to train a deep learning model to a specific accuracy together with its inference time. Specifically, DAWNBench measures the inference time to 93% validation accuracy for different hardware, frameworks, and model architectures. In their initial release, DAWNBench released benchmark specifications for image classification (ImageNet [15], CIFAR10 [35]) and question answering (SQuAD) [43]. Additional tasks and datasets may be included in their future releases.

The models in DAWNBench can be tested on both TensorFlow [1,2,44] and PyTorch [34], with four different types of hardware platforms, including one single NVIDIA Tesla K80 on Google Cloud and Amazon EC2, one single NVIDIA Tesla P100, and 16 vCPUs on Google Cloud.

Besides the official benchmarks, the DAWNBench project allows people to submit their benchmarking results for competition, which can push the community and promote the development of DAWNBench.

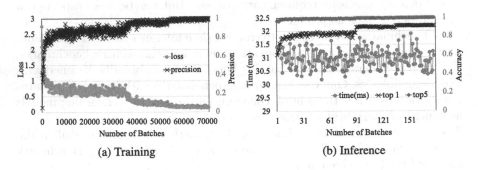

(a) Training   (b) Inference

Fig. 1. Training and inference performance of DAWNBench ResNet-20 using a single GPU

To demonstrate the capability of performing training and inference with DAWNBench, we perform a set of experiments with DAWNBench ResNet-20 [26] benchmark on our platform. Figure 1 shows our experimental results. Figure 1a presents the process of training the model with a batch size of 128. Figure 1b presents the inference results, which include Top-1 accuracy, Top-5 accuracy, and time cost. It is easy for us to observe the performance of the system and the characteristics of the model from these benchmark results. For example, we can find that in the process of training, other than increasing gradually, the accuracy of ResNet-20 increases in a ladder-shaped manner. The experiments above are finished on one compute node, which is equipped with one NVIDIA Tesla P100 GPU and two Intel Xeon Silver 4114 10-core CPUs.

The DAWNBench project largely relies on results uploaded by researchers and itself does not provide enough benchmark tools. It leads to the lack of detail profiling results of different experiments. When we need an in-depth understanding of different executions with varied models on different hardware platforms, it is not easy for developers to look for bottlenecks of the systems and models with DAWNBench.

2.2 Baidu DeepBench

DeepBench [14] from Baidu is an open-source benchmark covering both training and inference. DeepBench focuses on measuring the performance of basic operations in neural network libraries. It aims at determining the most suitable hardware for specific operations, and communicating requirements to hardware manufacturers. The benchmark has been adapted to both server-side and edge-side platforms. For example, DeepBench can run on top of mainstream GPU devices as well as mobile devices, such as iPhone.

DeepBench [14] focuses more on basic operations of Deep Learning inference rather than complete inferences. The key question DeepBench is trying to answer is – "Which hardware provides the best performance on the basic operations used in deep neural networks?".

Table 1. Operation benchmarks in DeepBench for inference

Operation	Applications
Dense Matrix Multiplication	DeepSpeech, Language Modeling
Sparse Matrix Multiplication	DeepSpeech
Convolution	DeepSpeech, Face Recognition, Vision
Recurrent Layers - LSTM	Language Modeling, Machine Translation
Recurrent Layers - GRU	DeepSpeech, Speaker ID

Table 1 shows the inference-related operations and devices supported by DeepBench. We can see that DeepBench can measure operations and layers like Dense Matrix Multiplication, Sparse Matrix Multiplication, Convolution [36,37], Long Short Term Memory [28] and Gated Recurrent Unit [11] layers. These operations and layers are widely used in applications like DeepSpeech [5,23], Language Modeing [7], Machine Translation, Speaker Identification [45], etc. Comparing with the training benchmark, the inference benchmark has some distinct

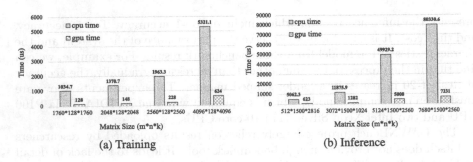

Fig. 2. Training and inference performance of DeepBench ResNet-20 using a single GPU

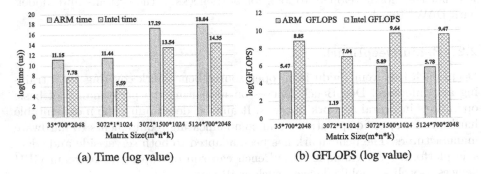

Fig. 3. Baidu DeepBench GEMM operation performance with Intel CPU and ARM CPU

designs. It provides a batching scheduler to improve the performance issue led by individual requests and provides kernels with different precisions to adapt diversified terminal devices. Sparse kernels are employed for benchmarking the optimized neural network operations on mobile devices.

In many deep learning models, the fully connected layer and convolution layer are basically implemented by General Matrix Multiplication (GEMM) operations, and about 90% of the network operations are in these two layers. Figure 2 shows the time cost of GEMM operation provided by DeepBench for train and inference with Intel CPU (Intel Xeon Silver 4114, 2.20 GHz) and NVIDIA GPU (P100, 12 GB). It can be seen that through using GPU, the time cost of GEMM operation can be reduced by about 90% in both training and inference scenarios. Figure 3 shows the time cost and GFLOPS values using x86 CPU (Intel Xeon Silver 4114, 2.20 GHz) and ARM CPU (ARMv8 (Atlas/A57), 2.4 GHz). The values are taken in the form of logarithm since the difference between values is too large. We can learn through these experiments that the performance difference between these two CPUs is big. The peak GFLOPS value of the ARM CPU is about 1/14 of that of Intel x86 CPU. But when the size of matrix gets smaller, the performance difference will become smaller at the same time. It is because small computation load cannot make full use of the ability of CPUs, and when running with small jobs, ARM CPUs can be totally competent. Experiments show that Baidu DeepBench can test Deep Learning operations on different hardware and architectures. Figures 2 and 3 are the typical example results which this benchmark can give us.

Although Baidu DeepBench can be run on different types of hardware platforms, it is not easy to use on some non-x86 architecture CPUs. For example, when we want to run DeepBench on ARM CPUs, we need to select the type of CPUs carefully because not all ARM CPUs are supported in DeepBench. We need to modify the code of DeepBench and the supporting libraries on ARM CPUs, because there may have some bugs. On the other hand, the datasets (e.g., the size of matrix) tested on different hardware are not exactly the same. It is inconvenient for users to compare the performance with different hardware.

2.3   Facebook AI Performance Evaluation Platform

Facebook AI Performance Evaluation Platform (i.e., FAI-PEP) [21] provides a way to compare Machine Learning or Deep Learning inference performance metrics on a set of models over different backends. This platform supports both mobile devices and server platforms.

Currently, FAI-PEP supports two platforms, TensorFlow Lite (TFLite) [38] and Caffe2 [31]. It includes 16 popular machine learning models including MobileNet [29,46], SqueezeNet [30], ShuffleNet [54], etc. This platform collects the total execution time, error rate, and power consumption of a model. It can also accept any ML or Deep Learning models given by users and reports any metrics defined by users.

The platform supports two modes of execution which are standalone benchmark run and continuous benchmark run. The standalone benchmark run mode reports the results for one benchmark run. Continuous benchmark run mode repeatedly pulls the framework and runs the benchmarks.

For model engineers, this platform provides an easy-to-use front-end that can get the performance of new Machine Learning or Deep Learning models on all existing backends. For Machine Learning or Deep Learning framework developers, this platform can be used to evaluate performance improvement and detect regression.

FAI-PEP provides a centralized model/benchmark specification, a benchmark driver for distributed execution, and a data consumption tool to compare the performance. The currently supported frameworks in FAI-PEP include Caffe2 and TFLite. FAI-PEP can test benchmarks with multiple different backends, including CPU, GPU, DSP, Android, iOS, and other Linux based systems.

2.4   ICT BigDataBench

BigDataBench [8,22] from Institute of Computing Technology, Chinese Academy of Sciences (ICT, CAS) is a comprehensive Big Data and AI benchmark suite. The core concept in BigDataBench is called *data motifs*, which considers any

Table 2. Operations, benchmarks, and data motifs in BigDataBench

Basic operation	Data motifs	Model benchmark	Data motifs
Convolution	Transform	Alexnet	Matrix, Transform, Sampling, Logic, Basic statistics
Fully Connectced	Matrix	Googlenet	Matrix, Transform, Sampling, Logic, Basic statistics
Relu	Logic	Resnet	Matrix, Transform, Sampling, Logic, Basic statistics
Sigmoid	Matrix	Inception Resnet V2	Matrix, Transform, Sampling, Logic, Basic statistics
Tanh	Matrix	VGG16	Matrix, Transform, Sampling, Logic, Basic statistics
MaxPooling	Sampling	DCGAN	Matrix, Transform, Sampling, Logic, Basic statistics
AvgPooling	Sampling	WGAN	Matrix, Transform, Sampling, Logic, Basic statistics
CosineNorm	Basic Statistics	GAN	Matrix, Sampling, Logic, Basic statistics
BatchNorm	Basic Statistics	Seq2Seq	Matrix, Sampling, Logic, Basic statistics
Dropout	Sampling	Word2vec	Matrix, Basic statistics, Logic

Big Data and AI workload as a pipeline of one or more classes of computation units performed on different input data sets.

The BigDataBench team has identified eight data motifs from a wide range of Big Data and AI workloads, including Matrix, Sampling, Logic, Transform, Set, Graph, Sort, and Statistic computation. Each data motif captures the common requirements of each class of computation units. The behaviors of each data motif are affected by the sizes, patterns, types, and sources of different data inputs. These data motifs can reflect not only computation patterns, memory access patterns, but also disk and network I/O patterns.

There are many benchmarks included in BigDataBench. The Deep Learning related basic operation and model benchmarks are summarized in Table 2. All of these operations and model benchmarks in BigDataBench can run on top of both TensorFlow and Caffe Deep Learning frameworks [33].

Figure 4 shows the time costs of five epochs and their average time costs of four deep learning models (AlexNet [36], GoogleNet [49], Inception-ResNet-v2 [48], VGG16 [47]) provided by BigDataBench v4.0 based on TensorFlow. We can test the training efficiency and time cost stability of different models and compare them with each other. The experiments are performed on a compute node with an Intel Xeon Silver 4114 10-core CPU.

2.5   Other Benchmarks

The community has many other Deep Learning related benchmarks as well. We can not discuss all of them in detail. Thus, we briefly summarize some of them in the following list.

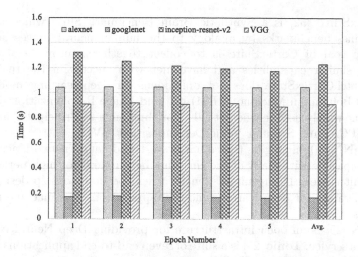

Fig. 4. Training performance of four benchmarks in BigDataBench. The bars represent the time costs of five epochs and the average time costs of four benchmarks provided by BigDataBench. The batch size is set to 64

MLPerf [40] is a synthetic benchmark suite for measuring the performance of software frameworks, hardware accelerators, and cloud platforms for machine learning. It is driven by a community supported by industry and academy. The basic approach of MLPerf is to measure the clock time of running the selected problem set with the standard dataset, and report a summarized score. With equivalent workloads, the performance of different software or hardware can be compared fairly. It also concerns the power cost of computation. MLPerf aims at enabling fair comparison of competing systems and promoting technological innovation. On the deep learning side, MLPerf covers problems like image classification, object detection, and speech recognition. As of now, the training benchmark of MLPerf is relatively mature, while the inference benchmark is still in its infancy.

Fathom [3] is a set of reference implementations of state-of-the-art deep learning models and has the ability to provide a quantitative analysis of the fundamental computational characteristics of these workloads. Fathom uses a custom and high-level analysis framework to identify the execution time of different types of operations and compares the performance of training and inference between different deep learning models. Furthermore, Fathom is able to measure the similarity between different deep learning models.

TensorFlow Benchmark [51] tests a selection of image classification models across multiple platforms. These tests are specially done to show the performance of TensorFlow in different environments. The models selected for TensorFlow Benchmark include InceptionV3 [32], ResNet50, ResNet152, VGG16, and AlexNet. All tests can be done with both NVIDIA GPGPUs and CPUs on native and cloud computing environments.

CortexSuite [52] is a Synthetic Brain Benchmark Suite which classifies and identifies benchmarks by analogy to the human neural processing functions. The goal of CortexSuite is to collect together man-made algorithms that have similar capabilities and have met with success in the real world. ioffe2015batchCortexSuite does not only focus on deep learning models like Restricted Boltzmann Machine (RBM) [27] and Image Recolonization, but also selects some widely used mathematical algorithms such as Principal Component Analysis (PCA) and Singular Value Decomposition (SVD).

BenchNN [10] highlights that a hardware-based neural network accelerator can be compatible with many of the emerging benchmarks for high-performance micro-architectures. The result of BenchNN will be used to help design hardware accelerators for deep learning models, applications and machine learning algorithms.

DjiNN [25] is an open infrastructure for providing Deep Neural Networks (DNN) as a service. **Tonic** [25] is a suite of seven end-to-end applications that are using DjiNN services. Tonic Suite provides image, speech, and natural language processing applications that can have a common DNN backend. The system measures the throughput, GPU occupancy, and latency of model training and inference.

Deep500 [6] is a customizable benchmarking infrastructure that enables a fair comparison of the plethora of deep learning frameworks, algorithms, libraries, and techniques. It supports distributed training on TensorFlow, Caffe and PyTorch and users can design different codes with its high-level APIs.

AIoT Bench [9] is a benchmark that is designed for mobile and embedded devices, from Android devices to Raspberry Pi. It supports both Tensorflow and Caffe2 and covers different application domains such as image recognition, speech recognition, and natural language processing. Besides end-to-end application workloads, AIoT Bench also offers micro workloads.

EdgeAI Bench [50] focuses on benchmarking artificial intelligence applications for edge computing scenarios. It takes four applications into consideration: ICU Patient Monitor, Surveillance Camera, Smart Home, and Autonomous Vehicle. Client-side devices, edge computing layer, and cloud servers are all included in this benchmark. EdgeAI Bench also builds an edge computing testbed to help the community to resolve performance, privacy, and security issues.

HPC AI500 [53] is a benchmark suite for testing Deep Leaning benchmarks on HPC systems. It selects several typical scientific fields to be the target scenes, e.g. extreme weather analysis, high energy physics, and cosmology. Workloads in this benchmark are made up of state-of-the-art DL models and representative scientific data sets instead of standard DL models (e.g., VGG and LSTM) and datasets (e.g., MNIST [16] and ImageNet).

3   Discussion

In this section, we provide a detailed comparison among many of the above-mentioned benchmarks. Based on our survey, experiments, and comparisons, we further discuss some interesting observations in this study.

3.1 Benchmark Comparison

To compare benchmarks introduced above, we build and test them (based on their code availability) on our platform. According to our experiments and literature survey, we summarize the capabilities of several typical benchmarks in Table 3. The column of **Time** represents whether the benchmark can give us the timing information of training and inference. Similarly, the column of **Loss** represents whether the benchmark can report training loss. The **Acc** column represents whether the benchmark can measure training accuracy. The **Cost** column represents whether the benchmark will report the execution cost (i.e., how many dollars to run the experiments.). The **Power** column represents whether the benchmark can report the power consumption. The column of **Util** represents whether the benchmark will report the usage of cache, memory, and processors (e.g., CPU or GPU). **Tput** represents whether the benchmark is designed for reporting system throughput. **Train** and **Infer** columns indicate whether the benchmark is designed mainly for training or inference. Column **Hete** represents whether this benchmark supports heterogeneous software and hardware platforms. Under this column, **S** means this benchmark supports software heterogeneity (i.e. supports different Deep Learning frameworks, like Tensorflow and PyTorch), while **H** means it supports hardware heterogeneity (i.e. supports different kinds of devices, like x86 processors, GPUs, and ARM processors).

Table 3. The capabilities of several typical deep learning benchmarks

Benchmark	Time	Loss	Acc	Cost	Power	Tput	Util	Train	Infer	Hete
DAWNBench	✓	×	✓	✓	×	×	×	✓	✓	S
DeepBench	✓	×	×	×	×	✓	×	✓	✓	H
FAI-PEP	✓	×	✓	×	✓	×	×	✓	✓	H/S
BigDataBench	✓	✓	✓	×	×	×	×	✓	×	S
Fathom	✓	×	×	×	×	✓	×	✓	✓	×
MLPerf	✓	✓	✓	✓	✓	×	×	✓	×	H/S
Deep500	✓	✓	✓	✓	×	✓	×	✓	✓	×

3.2 Observations

Even though we can not cover all the benchmarks in the community in this study, we believe the ones we have surveyed can represent the design philosophies for many other benchmarks as well. Through our survey and experiments, we have found the following interesting observations:

Observation-1: Current-generation Deep Learning benchmarks have covered many perspectives which are important for hardware and software system researchers as well as AI application designers. As shown in Table 3, almost all the benchmarks pay attention to performance, heterogeneity, and accuracy, which are the most important three properties for benchmarking Deep Learning systems and applications. Here, the heterogeneity means the benchmarks can support more than one type of Deep Learning frameworks as well as different hardware platforms, especially for both edge devices and cloud servers. Some benchmarks, such as Baidu DeepBench, start paying attention to more in-depth requirements, such as model density, precision requirement, etc. Some other interesting and important metrics, such as cost and energy consumption, are supported by Stanford DAWNBench and Facebook AI benchmarks.

Even though current-generation benchmarks can cover many aspects, we believe may be more aspects can be still considered, such as productivity, which means how fast a designer can propose a new model on a particular platform. This could be very interesting for Deep Learning algorithm researchers to have a way for comparing platforms and choosing a proper one to implement their ideas.

Observation-2: Many of current-generation benchmarks pay attention to measuring the training performance. Not all of them have a component for benchmarking inference process. However, some benchmarks start supporting inference benchmarking, such as Baidu DeepBench and Facebook AI benchmarks.

Observation-3: The current-generation Deep Learning benchmarks are broadly designed with two methodologies. In one way, designers are trying to propose benchmarks with basic Deep Learning operations, such as Baidu DeepBench, while the other way is collecting end-to-end Deep Learning models as benchmarks, such as ResNet, VGG, etc. Comprehensive solutions (like a hybrid approach) are also available, such as ICT BigDataBench.

Observation-4: The current status of Deep Learning Benchmark community is still in the "Warring States Period", which means the leading organizations of these projects are trying to propose their own benchmarks to the community and try to grow them stronger for the potential competition in the future. There is no converged and well-received single Deep Learning benchmark standard yet in the community. So far, it may not be easy for the community to define a clear and representative Deep Learning benchmark standard, but we believe this may happen in the future.

4   Conclusion and Future Work

This paper is an on-going work to survey the existing Deep Learning benchmarks in the community. We have covered multiple important ones, such as Stanford DAWNBench, Baidu DeepBench, Facebook AI Benchmarks, ICT BigDataBench, and many others. We have shared our experimental results, experience, and observations in this study. We wish our survey on these benchmarks can promote the evolution of Deep Learning benchmarks in the community.

In the future, we plan to do a comprehensive survey on more benchmarks. We also plan to perform systematical performance evaluations on these benchmarks and share more experience with the community.

Acknowledgments. This research is supported in part by the Strategic Priority Research Program of the Chinese Academy of Sciences, Grant No. XDA19020400.

References

1. Abadi, M., et al.: TensorFlow: large-scale machine learning on heterogeneous distributed systems. arXiv preprint arXiv:1603.04467 (2016)
2. Abadi, M., et al.: TensorFlow: a system for large-scale machine learning. In: 12th {USENIX} Symposium on Operating Systems Design and Implementation ({OSDI} 2016), pp. 265–283 (2016)
3. Adolf, R., Rama, S., Reagen, B., Wei, G.-Y., Brooks, D.M.: Fathom: reference workloads for modern deep learning methods. CoRR, abs/1608.06581 (2016)
4. Akioka, S., Muraoka, Y.: HPC benchmarks on Amazon EC2. In: 2010 IEEE 24th International Conference on Advanced Information Networking and Applications Workshops, pp. 1029–1034. IEEE (2010)
5. Amodei, D., et al.: Deep speech 2: end-to-end speech recognition in English and Mandarin. In: International Conference on Machine Learning, pp. 173–182 (2016)
6. Ben-Nun, T., Besta, M., Huber, S., Ziogas, A.N., Peter, D., Hoefler, T.: A modular benchmarking infrastructure for high-performance and reproducible deep learning. arXiv:1901.10183 (2019)
7. Bengio, Y., Ducharme, R., Vincent, P., Jauvin, C.: A neural probabilistic language model. J. Mach. Learn. Res. **3**(Feb), 1137–1155 (2003)
8. BigDataBench: A Big Data and AI Benchmark Suite (2018). http://prof.ict.ac.cn/
9. Huang, C., et al.: AIoT bench: towards comprehensive benchmarking mobile and embedded device intelligence. In: BenchCouncil International Symposium on Benchmarking, Measuring and Optimizing (Bench), Seattle, WA, USA (2018)
10. Chen, T., et al.: BenchNN: on the broad potential application scope of hardware neural network accelerators. In: Proceedings - 2012 IEEE International Symposium on Workload Characterization, IISWC 2012, pp. 36–45, November 2012
11. Cho, K., et al.: Learning phrase representations using RNN encoder-decoder for statistical machine translation. arXiv preprint arXiv:1406.1078 (2014)
12. Coleman, C., et al.: DAWNBench: an end-to-end deep learning benchmark and competition. In: Proceedings of ML Systems Workshop, Co-Located with 31st Conference on Neural Information Processing Systems (NIPS) (2017)
13. Stanford DAWNBench: An End-to-End Deep Learning Benchmark and Competition (2018). https://dawn.cs.stanford.edu/benchmark/
14. Baidu DeepBench: Benchmarking Deep Learning Operations on Different Hardware (2018). https://github.com/baidu-research/DeepBench
15. Deng, J., Dong, W., Socher, R., Li, L.-J., Li, K., Fei-Fei, L.: ImageNet: a large-scale hierarchical image database. In: 2009 IEEE Conference on Computer Vision and Pattern Recognition, pp. 248–255. IEEE (2009)
16. Deng, L.: The MNIST database of handwritten digit images for machine learning research. IEEE Sign. Process. Mag. **29**(6), 141–142 (2012)
17. Dongarra, J., Heroux, M.A., Luszczek, P.: HPCG benchmark: a new metric for ranking high performance computing systems. Technical report UT-EECS-15-736, Electrical Engineering and Computer Science Department, University of Tennessee (2015)
18. Dongarra, J.J., Luszczek, P., Petitet, A.: The LINPACK benchmark: past, present and future. Concurrency Comput.: Pract. Exp. **15**(9), 803–820 (2003)

19. Druzhkov, P.N., Kustikova, V.D.: A survey of deep learning methods and software tools for image classification and object detection. Pattern Recogn. Image Anal. **26**(1), 9–15 (2016)
20. Erickson, B.J., Korfiatis, P., Akkus, Z., Kline, T., Philbrick, K.: Toolkits and libraries for deep learning. J. Dig. Imaging **30**(4), 400–405 (2017)
21. Facebook AI Performance Evaluation Platform (2018). https://github.com/facebook/FAI-PEP
22. Gao, W., et al.: BigDataBench: a dwarf-based big data and AI benchmark suite, pp. 1–23 (2018)
23. Hannun, A., et al.: Deep speech: scaling up end-to-end speech recognition. arXiv preprint arXiv:1412.5567 (2014)
24. Hatcher, W.G., Yu, W.: A survey of deep learning: platforms, applications and emerging research trends. IEEE Access **6**, 24411–24432 (2018)
25. Hauswald, J., et al.: DjiNN and Tonic: DNN as a service and its implications for future warehouse scale computers. In: Proceedings of the 42nd Annual International Symposium on Computer Architecture (ISCA), ISCA 2015. ACM, New York (2015)
26. He, K., Zhang, X., Ren, S., Sun, J.: Deep residual learning for image recognition (2015)
27. Hinton, G.E.: A practical guide to training restricted boltzmann machines. In: Montavon, G., Orr, G.B., Müller, K.-R. (eds.) Neural Networks: Tricks of the Trade. LNCS, vol. 7700, pp. 599–619. Springer, Heidelberg (2012). https://doi.org/10.1007/978-3-642-35289-8_32
28. Hochreiter, S., Schmidhuber, J.: Long short-term memory. Neural Comput. **9**(8), 1735–1780 (1997)
29. Howard, A.G., et al.: MobileNets: efficient convolutional neural networks for mobile vision applications. arXiv preprint arXiv:1704.04861 (2017)
30. Iandola, F.N., Han, S., Moskewicz, M.W., Ashraf, K., Dally, W.J., Keutzer, K.: SqueezeNet: AlexNet-level accuracy with 50x fewer parameters and <0.5 MB model size. arXiv preprint arXiv:1602.07360 (2016)
31. Facebook Inc.: Caffe2. https://caffe2.ai/
32. Ioffe, S., Szegedy, C.: Batch normalization: accelerating deep network training by reducing internal covariate shift. arXiv preprint arXiv:1502.03167 (2015)
33. Jia, Y., et al.: Caffe: convolutional architecture for fast feature embedding. In: Proceedings of the 22nd ACM International Conference on Multimedia, pp. 675–678. ACM (2014)
34. Ketkar, N.: Introduction to PyTorch. Deep Learning with Python, pp. 195–208. Apress, Berkeley (2017). https://doi.org/10.1007/978-1-4842-2766-4_12
35. Krizhevsky, A., Hinton, G., et al.: Learning multiple layers of features from tiny images. Technical report, Citeseer (2009)
36. Krizhevsky, A., Sutskever, I., Hinton, G.E.: ImageNet classification with deep convolutional neural networks. In: Advances in Neural Information Processing Systems, pp. 1097–1105 (2012)
37. Lawrence, S., Giles, C.L., Tsoi, A.C., Back, A.D.: Face recognition: a convolutional neural-network approach. IEEE Trans. Neural Netw. **8**(1), 98–113 (1997)
38. Lee, J., et al.: On-device augmented reality with mobile GPUs (2019). https://mixedreality.cs.cornell.edu/s/10_CV4ARVR2019-jet-camera-ready.pdf
39. Luszczek, P.R., et al.: The HPC challenge (HPCC) benchmark suite. In: Proceedings of the 2006 ACM/IEEE Conference on Supercomputing, vol. 213. Citeseer (2006)

40. MLPerf: A Broad ML Benchmark Suite for Measuring Performance of ML Software Frameworks, ML Hardware Accelerators, and ML Cloud Platforms (2018). https://mlperf.org/
41. Nelson, M.T., et al.: NAMD: a parallel, object-oriented molecular dynamics program. Int. J. Supercomput. Appl. High Perform. Comput. 10(4), 251–268 (1996)
42. Ota, K., Dao, M.S., Mezaris, V., De Natale, F.G.B.: Deep learning for mobile multimedia: a survey. ACM Trans. Multimed. Comput. Commun. Appl. 13(3s), 34:1–34:22 (2017)
43. Rajpurkar, P., Zhang, J., Lopyrev, K., Liang, P.: SQuAD: 100,000+ questions for machine comprehension of text. arXiv preprint arXiv:1606.05250 (2016)
44. Rampasek, L., Goldenberg, A.: TensorFlow: biology's gateway to deep learning? Cell Syst. 2(1), 12–14 (2016)
45. Reynolds, D.A., Rose, R.C.: Robust text-independent speaker identification using Gaussian mixture speaker models. IEEE Trans. Speech Audio Process. 3(1), 72–83 (1995)
46. Sandler, M., Howard, A., Zhu, M., Zhmoginov, A., Chen, L.-C.: MobileNetV2: inverted residuals and linear bottlenecks. In: Proceedings of the IEEE Conference on Computer Vision and Pattern Recognition, pp. 4510–4520 (2018)
47. Simonyan, K., Zisserman, A.: Very deep convolutional networks for large-scale image recognition. arXiv preprint arXiv:1409.1556 (2014)
48. Szegedy, C., Ioffe, S., Vanhoucke, V., Alemi, A.A.: Inception-v4, inception-ResNet and the impact of residual connections on learning. In: Thirty-First AAAI Conference on Artificial Intelligence (2017)
49. Szegedy, C., et al.: Going deeper with convolutions. In: Proceedings of the IEEE Conference on Computer Vision and Pattern Recognition, pp. 1–9 (2015)
50. Wen, X., et al.: EdgeAI bench: towards comprehensive end-to-end edge computing benchmarking. In: BenchCouncil International Symposium on Benchmarking, Measuring and Optimizing (Bench), Seattle, WA, USA (2018)
51. TensorFlow Benchmarks (2018). https://www.tensorflow.org/performance/benchmarks
52. Thomas, S., et al.: CortexSuite: a synthetic brain benchmark suite. In: 2014 IEEE International Symposium on Workload Characterization (IISWC), pp. 76–79, October 2014
53. Wang, L., et al.: HPC AI500: a benchmark suite for HPC AI systems. In: BenchCouncil International Symposium on Benchmarking, Measuring and Optimizing (Bench), Seattle, WA, USA (2018)
54. Zhang, X., Zhou, X., Lin, M., Sun, J.: ShuffleNet: an extremely efficient convolutional neural network for mobile devices. In: Proceedings of the IEEE Conference on Computer Vision and Pattern Recognition, pp. 6848–6856 (2018)

Cloud

Benchmarking VM Startup Time
in the Cloud

Samiha Islam Abrita[1(✉)], Moumita Sarker[1], Faheem Abrar[2],
and Muhammad Abdullah Adnan[1]

[1] Bangladesh University of Engineering and Technology, Dhaka, Bangladesh
{0416052053.sia,0416052070.ms}@grad.cse.buet.ac.bd
adnan@cse.buet.ac.bd
[2] University of Saskatchewan, Saskatoon, Canada
faheem.abrar@usask.ca

Abstract. Elasticity is one of the primary reasons of the popularity of
cloud computing. However, a frequent problem is affecting this popularity - longer processing time for the acquired Virtual Machines (VM)
to be ready for usage. This problem hinders the advantages of elasticity.
This processing time, known as VM startup time, depends on various factors. VM startup time varies due to space-time trade-off. Comparing VM
startup time according to distinctive factors allows users to choose their
desirable VM. They have options to select among the VMs as per their
preferences. In this paper, we benchmark VM startup time in Amazon
EC2, Microsoft Azure and Google Cloud for factors like instance type,
time of the day, instance location, cluster creation and cluster resize.

Keywords: Elasticity · Cloud computing · VM startup time ·
Benchmarking

1 Introduction

Cloud Computing is a specialized distributed computing paradigm which delivers storage, platforms and services on demand to external customers over the
Internet [1]. It provides benefits such as elasticity, load balancing, low hardware
cost and high computing power. Elasticity means the degree to which a system is
able to adapt to workload changes by provisioning and de-provisioning resources
in an autonomic manner to match the current demand with available resources
as closely as possible [2]. This elasticity attracts many users to opt for cloud
computing services which can handle dynamic workload and reduce cost. However, elasticity is only helpful to the client when the acquired Virtual Machines
can be provisioned in time and ready to use within a reasonable time frame by
user [3].

Researchers found that although cloud users can request to start a Virtual
Machine (VM) at any time, it requires some time for the acquired VMs to be
ready for production use. This happens because cloud providers need some time

© Springer Nature Switzerland AG 2019
C. Zheng and J. Zhan (Eds.): Bench 2018, LNCS 11459, pp. 53–64, 2019.
https://doi.org/10.1007/978-3-030-32813-9_6

to find a spot to provision the VM in their data centers, to allocate resources to the VM and to copy/boot/configure the OS image. This processing time is known as VM startup time. As a result of the extended waiting time, users can get frustrated and lose their interest in using cloud computing services. The long waiting time can slow down user's progress and the performance of their applications. At this rate, the advantage of having elasticity makes no sense. Due to this problem, the cloud service providers can potentially lose a lot of customers. To solve this problem, it is important to benchmark VM startup time of existing cloud service providers and find out the bottlenecks causing the delays in startup.

A number of cloud computing services are providing VMs recently. Amazon Elastic Compute Cloud (EC2) [4], launched by Amazon.com in 2006, forms a central part of Amazon Web Services (AWS) by allowing users to rent virtual computers to run their own computer applications. It is a web service providing resizable compute capacity in the cloud and designed to make web-scale cloud computing easier for developers. The simple web interface provided by EC2 allows users to obtain and configure compute capacity with minimal friction. EC2 provides users significant control of their own computing resources and lets them run applications on Amazon's computing environment. Amazon claims that EC2 reduces the time required to obtain and boot new server instances to minutes, allowing users to quickly scale capacity both up and down. Using EC2, users will only need to pay for capacity that they will actually use. EC2 provides developers the tools to build fault tolerant applications and isolate themselves from common failure scenarios.

Microsoft Azure [5] is another cloud computing platform and infrastructure launched by Microsoft in 2010 for building, deploying and managing applications and services through a global network of Microsoft-managed data centers. It is a collection of integrated cloud services such as analytics, computing, database, mobile, networking, storage and web. Azure claims that users can deploy highly available and scalable applications and APIs as well as thousands of instances in minutes.

Similar to EC2 and Azure, Google Cloud Platform [6] is a cloud computing platform launched by Google in 2010 that offers hosting on the same support-ing infrastructure that Google uses internally for end-user products like Google Search. Cloud Platform gives users options for both computing and hosting. Users can choose to work with a managed application platform, leverage con-tainer technologies to gain flexibility or build their own cloud-based infrastruc-ture to have the most control and flexibility. With App Engine, Google han-dles most of the management of the resources. For example, if a user's appli-cation requires more computing resources because traffic to the user's website has increased, Google Cloud can automatically scale the system to provide those resources. If the software of a system needs a security update, that is handled for users as well.

In this paper, we calculate VM startup time across the cloud service providers mentioned above. To calculate VM startup time, we first create instances at different data center locations of the cloud service providers. Next, we stop these VM instances on cloud. After that, we restart the VM and calculate VM startup time which refers to the time it takes for a VM to go from stopped to running state. Then we compare the VM startup times among the cloud service providers chosen. Finally, we benchmark VM startup time for factors such as instance type, time of the day, instance location, cluster startup time and cluster resize time among the cloud service providers, as VM startup time depends on these factors.

The rest of the paper is organized as follows. Section 2 describes works related to this research. Section 3 details the methodology and the working process. Section 4 reports the performance analysis of the work. Section 5 provides a conclusion to the research.

2   Related Works

Although the performance of VM startup process is an important metric, very few studies have been done on VM startup time performance. These few studies focus on comparing VM startup time of different cloud service providers based on relative factors.

Mao and Humphrey [3] studied the startup time of cloud VMs across three real world cloud service providers - Amazon EC2, Windows Azure and Rackspace. They analyzed the relationship between the VM startup time and different factors such as time of the day, instance type, data center location and so on. They discovered that within each cloud provider, the VM startup time of both Linux and Windows machines are independent of time of the day. They also found that Rackspace has a higher failure rate (8 times) than EC2 (0.8 times) and Azure (0.4 times). Mao and Humphrey's research is the most comprehensive work done on VM startup time comparison so far, and we aim to extend this work by including different cloud providers in the experiments.

Ostermann et al. [7] conducts a performance analysis of EC2 services in which the duration of VM acquisition and release was evaluated using different methods. EC2 VMs of different sizes were used for the experiments. The experiments revealed that the time to acquire multiple instances can be more varied than acquiring a single instance and Amazon EC2 instances do not face system overload problems while instantiating VMs. The VM acquisition experiments were a small part of the overall research work, and it lacks details which can be useful to figure out how to make VM startup time faster.

Hill et al. [8] analyzed the startup time for WebRole and WorkRole in Azure. The study evaluated VM instantiating time as a critical metric for performance evaluation of dynamic scalability. The results of the study demonstrated an average startup time of 10 min for Azure machines. Hill et al. concluded that those who already chose Windows Azure as the target cloud are facing the challenge of architecting their cloud application to accommodate performance considerations and they do not consider the factors that affected VM startup time.

To the best of our knowledge, only Mao and Humphrey [3] extensively worked on comparing VM startup time. We wanted to extend their research and update their experiments to see what changes may have occurred in the meantime. As Rackspace has higher failure rate in Mao and Humphrey's [3] research, we decided to work with Google Cloud. The study of Mao and Humphrey defined the VM startup time as the time starting from VM instantiation to successful SSH login, but in our paper, VM startup time will refer to the time it takes for a VM to go from stopped to running state. The reason to choose this method to calculate the startup time is that it would provide a different perspective of the time it takes to start a VM. We also compare the VM startup time for two new factors - one is based on the cluster startup time and the other is based on the action of resizing a cluster and then restarting it.

3   Methodology

We chose three cloud service providers for our research - Amazon EC2, Microsoft Azure and Google Cloud Computing, as they are some of the top ranked cloud service providers [9]. A number of tools were used to calculate VM startup time for these cloud service providers. For Amazon EC2 we used Amazon Command Line Interface (CLI), for Microsoft Azure we used Azure REST API and for Google Cloud we used gcloud command line tool. Ruby Benchmark Module is used for benchmarking VM startup time. The module provides methods to measure and report the time used to execute Ruby code.

3.1   Environment Setup

During measurement of VM startup time, one factor is selected as variable and other factors as constant. For all of the considering factors, the operating system is Linux. Using Graphical User Interface (GUI) we create the VMs and select SSH for secure login. Each of these VMs has an unique ID. We pass the ID as parameter during script launch.

We run the script in a terminal and the data is saved in Comma-Separated Values (CSV) format. For experiments based on time of a day, Batch (BAT) file are assigned to task scheduler which executes at one hour interval. Finally, we save all the startup times in CSV format.

3.2   Algorithm

For accurate measurement of starting up a VM from stopped state, an algorithm has been developed to calculate the VM startup time. The algorithm is as follows:

Before the measurement starts, the machine is in stopped state. The startup time is set to zero. The status of the VM is initially set as stopped. When the start request is sent to the cloud provider, the status of the VM is set to pending. At the same time, a time counter is initialized using the benchmark module. After that, a request is sent to the cloud provider continuously to check if the machine has started. Once the machine is confirmed to be running, the counter is stopped and the startup time is recorded.

Algorithm 1. startup_time_measurement

1: $startup\_time \leftarrow 0$
2: $time \leftarrow 0$
3: $status\_stopped \leftarrow -1$
4: $status\_pending \leftarrow 0$
5: $status\_running \leftarrow 1$
6: $vm\_status \leftarrow status\_stopped$
7: SEND START REQUEST TO VIRTUAL MACHINE
8: $time\_counter \doteq Benchmark.realtime$
9: $vm\_status \leftarrow status\_pending$
10: **while** $vm\_status = status\_pending$ **do**
11:    **if** $vm\_status = status\_running$ **then**
12:       $startup\_time \leftarrow time\_counter$
13:       **break**
14:    **end if**
15: **end while**

---

4 Result

We benchmark VM startup time for instance type, time of the day, instance location, cluster create time and cluster resize time among Amazon EC2, Microsoft Azure and Google Cloud. The experimental results are presented in this section.

4.1 By Instance Type

In our first experiment, we calculate VM startup time based on VM instance types. Cloud service providers provide different types of instances to fulfill user demand. Amazon EC2 provides twenty types of instances, Microsoft Azure provides six types of instances and Google Cloud provides eighteen types of instances. In Table 1 we list the instance types we have worked on.

In this experiment, the data center locations are in Singapore and the operating system is Linux for the instances of the cloud service providers. Table 2 shows the experiment results and Fig. 1 shows the results in a bar plot.

As can be seen from Fig. 1, for Amazon EC2, m4.large takes lowest time to start (17.046 s) and t2.micro takes highest time (19.194 s) to start. On average, instances of Amazon EC2 take around 19.5 s to startup. Furthermore, standard-f1 takes lowest time (29.709 s) to start and basic-A0 takes highest time (36.744 s) to start for Microsoft Azure. Finally, Google Cloud n1-standard-1 takes the lowest time (27.152 s) and f1-micro takes the highest time (32.842 s) to start. Amazon EC2 has the lowest startup time on average, while Microsoft Azure and Google cloud are quite close, with Google Cloud having a slight advantage.

4.2 By Time of the Day

In our second experiment, we calculate VM startup time based on time of the day. From 12AM to 12PM, we take thirteen hours of measurement of VM startup

Table 1. VM types for EC2, Azure and Google Cloud

Cloud provider	Instance type	CPU	Memory	Disk
Amazon EC2	t2.nano	1CU	0.5 GB	EBS
	t2.micro	1CU	1 GB	EBS
	m4.large	2CU	6 GB	EBS
Microsoft Azure	basic A0	1CU (shared)	0.75 GB	20 GB
	standard-A0	2CU	0.75 GB	20 GB
	standard-A1	1CU	1.75 GB	70 GB
Google Cloud	f1-micro	1CU	0.60 GB	3 TB
	g1-small	1CU	1.70 GB	3 TB
	n1-standard-1	1CU	3.75 GB	64 TB

Table 2. VM startup time by instance type

Cloud provider	Instance type	Startup time (second)
Amazon EC2	t2.nano	18.681
	t2.micro	19.194
	m4.large	17.046
Microsoft Azure	basic-A0	36.744
	standard-A0	36.278
	standard-A1	29.709
Google Cloud	f1-micro	32.842
	g1-small	27.264
	n1-standard-1	27.152

time. During these thirteen hours, we restart the instances in interval of an hour and calculate the VM startup time for each interval. In this experiment, the location of the data centers is Singapore and the operating system for the instances of the cloud service providers is Linux. We use t2.micro for Amazon EC2, basic-A0 for Microsoft Azure and f1-micro for Google cloud. Table 3 shows the experiment results and Fig. 2 shows the results in a bar plot.

Figure 2 shows that for Amazon EC2, t2.micro takes the lowest time (15.945 s) to start at 9AM and highest time (42.815 s) to start at 12AM. From 12AM to 1AM, there is a major startup time difference of 24.589 s. The instance takes half the time to start at 4AM (17.647 s) compared to startup time at 5AM (34.979 s), at 6AM (16.191 s) compared to startup time at 5AM (34.979 s) and at 9AM (15.945 s) compared to startup time at 10AM (31.058 s).

For Microsoft Azure, basic-A0 takes lowest time (23.202 s) to start at 2AM and highest time (89.678 s) to start at 8AM. From 7AM to 8AM, there is a major startup time difference of 58.4 s. The instance takes one third the time to start

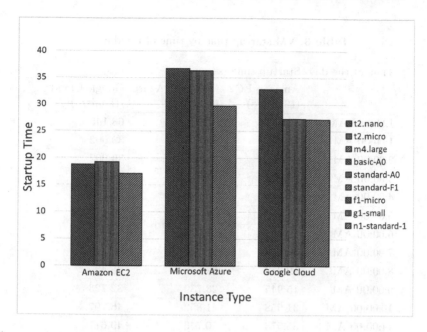

Fig. 1. VM startup time by instance type

at 9AM (23.739 s) compared to startup time at 8AM (89.678 s) and half the time to start at 9AM (23.739 s) compared to startup time at 10AM (41.852 s).

For Google Cloud, f1-micro takes lowest time (27.710 s) to start at 12PM and highest time (68.839 s) to start at 3AM. From 3AM to 4AM, there is a major startup time difference of 39.429 s. The instance takes half the time to start at 1AM (33.002 s) compared to startup time at 12AM (68.145 s), at 4AM (29.410 s) compared to startup time at 3AM (68.839 s) and at 9AM (15.945 s) compared to startup time at 10AM (31.058 s). From 1AM to 2AM, the instance take almost equal time (33.002 s) to start.

We can conclude that VM startup time changes during each part of a day from the result of this experiment. This can be an indication that there is a relation between the time of a day and the startup time of a VM.

4.3   By Instance Location

In our third experiment, we calculate VM startup time based on VM instance location. There are six regions for Amazon EC2, twenty six regions for Microsoft Azure and five regions for Google. Each region consists of several locations. We create and start instances in different locations and measure the startup time of the instances based on these locations. We take t2.micro for Amazon EC2, basic-A0 for Microsoft Azure and f1-micro for Google cloud. The operating system is Linux for the instances. Table 4 shows the experiment results and Fig. 3 shows the results in a bar plot.

Table 3. VM startup time by time of the day

Time of the day	Startup time (second)		
	Amazon EC2 (t2.micro)	Microsoft Azure (basic-A0)	Google Cloud (f1-micro)
12:00:00 AM	42.815	38.324	68.145
1:00:00 AM	18.226	23.953	33.002
2:00:00 AM	24.175	23.202	33.002
3:00:00 AM	30.067	24.145	68.839
4:00:00 AM	17.647	31.128	29.410
5:00:00 AM	34.979	23.533	48.015
6:00:00 AM	16.191	31.277	38.771
7:00:00 AM	22.846	31.278	32.414
8:00:00 AM	19.232	89.678	35.425
9:00:00 AM	15.945	23.739	32.723
10:00:00 AM	31.058	41.852	46.797
11:00:00 AM	35.973	30.746	49.617
12:00:00 PM	28.900	23.626	27.710

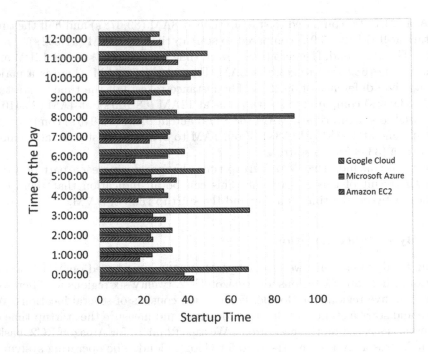

Fig. 2. VM startup time by time of the day

From Fig. 3, it can be seen that Amazon EC2 takes the lowest time (26.147 s) to start instances on ap-south-1 and Google Cloud takes the highest time (32.842 s) to start instances on asia-east1-a; both of these instances are located in Asia. Microsoft Azure takes moderate time (29.709 s) to start instances on southeast-asia which is located in Asia. If we compare the instances of each providers, we can see that for Amazon EC2, the t2.micro instance located in sa-east-1 takes the highest time to startup (30.321 s). For Microsoft Azure, the Basic-A0 instance located in south-central-us takes the lowest time (27.346 s) to startup and the instance located in east-asia takes the highest time to startup (33.734 s). Finally, for Google Cloud, the f1-micro instance located in us-east1-c takes the lowest time to startup (29.539 s) and the instance located in us-west1-a takes the highest time to startup (36.098 s). On average, the instances of Google Cloud take slightly longer to startup than the other two cloud providers.

Table 4. VM startup time by instance location

Cloud provider	Instance location	Startup time (second)
Amazon EC2	ap-south-1	26.147
	eu-west-1	29.025
	sa-east-1	30.321
	us-east-1	27.594
	us-west-2	30.241
Microsoft Azure	southeast-asia	29.709
	east-asia	33.734
	north-central-us	31.028
	south-central-us	27.346
Google Cloud	asia-east1-a	32.842
	us-east1-c	29.539
	europe-west1-c	32.969
	us-west1-a	36.098

4.4   By Cluster

In our fourth experiment, we calculate the time to startup and resize clusters. The cluster consists of instances from the same service providers. The clusters are resized up to two instances. We take m4.medium and m3.xlarge instances for Amazon EC2, standard-A0 and standard-F1 instances for Microsoft Azure and f1.micro and g1.small instances for Google Cloud. Table 5 shows the result of startup time and resize time of the clusters. Figure 4 shows the result of startup time of the clusters and Fig. 5 shows the result of resize time of the clusters in bar plot.

Figure 4 shows that m3.xlarge cluster takes around 1.4 times less time than m4.medium cluster to start up for Amazon EC2. It also shows that standard-A0 cluster is 2.5 times faster than standard-F1 cluster to start up for Microsoft

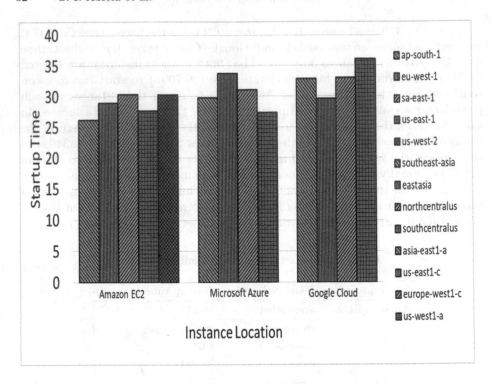

Fig. 3. VM startup time by instance location

Table 5. Cluster startup and resize time

Cloud provider	Cluster type	Startup time (second)	Resize time (second)
Amazon EC2	m4.medium	506.441	3.388
	m3.xlarge	373.515	3.855
Microsoft Azure	standard-A0	69.565	69.019
	standard-F1	178.308	83.533
Google Cloud	f1-micro	240.597	240.597
	g1-small	245.241	1639.302

Azure. For Google Cloud startup time, the difference between f1-micro cluster and g1.small cluster is 5 s. Overall, the instances in the cluster of Microsoft Azure took the lowest time on average, while the cluster of Amazon EC2 took the highest time on average.

Figure 5 shows that the resize time difference between m4.medium and m3.xlarge instances is 0.467 s for Amazon EC2. Moreover, the resize time difference between standard-A0 and standard-F1 instances is 14.514 s for Microsoft Azure. Finally, f1-micro cluster takes 6.3 times less than g1-small cluster to resize for Google Cloud. On average, Amazon EC2 has the fastest resize time while Google Cloud has the slowest resize time.

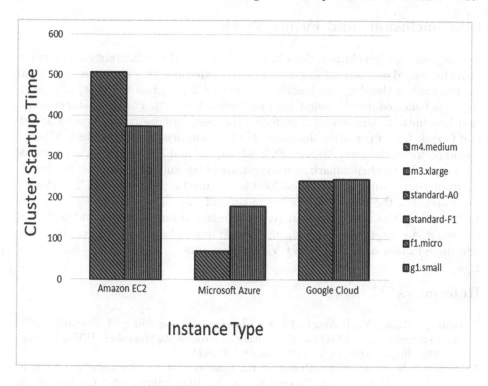

Fig. 4. Cluster startup time

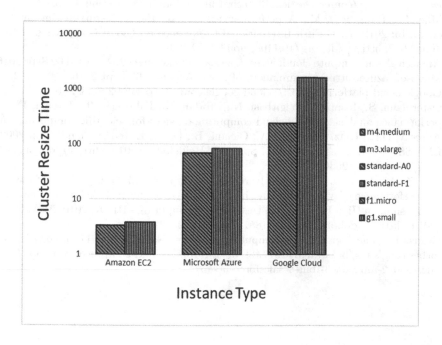

Fig. 5. Cluster resize time

5   Conclusions and Future Work

In this paper, we benchmark the VM startup time of three different cloud service providers based on different factors. From our experiments, we can conclude that for the time of the day benchmark, Amazon EC2 performs the best, Microsoft Azure is balanced and Google Cloud performs the worst. For the instance location benchmark, Amazon EC2 performs the best, Microsoft Azure is balanced and Google Cloud performs the worst. For the instance type benchmark, Google Cloud performs the best, Amazon EC2 is balanced and Microsoft Azure performs the worst. For the benchmark of startup time of instances in a cluster, Microsoft Azure performs the best, Google Cloud is balanced and Amazon EC2 performs the worst. For the benchmark of resize time of instances in a cluster, Amazon EC2 performs the best, Microsoft Azure is balanced and Google cloud performs the worst. In the future, we plan to include more cloud service providers and add more factors which can affect VM startup time.

References

1. Foster, I., Zhao, Y., Raicu, I., Lu, S.: Cloud computing and grid computing 360-degree compared. In: 2008 Grid Computing Environments Workshop. IEEE, November 2008. https://doi.org/10.1109/gce.2008.4738445
2. Herbst, N.R., Kounev, S., Reussner, R.: Elasticity in cloud computing: what it is, and what it is not. In: Proceedings of the 10th International Conference on Autonomic Computing (ICAC 2013), pp. 23–27. USENIX, San Jose (2013). https://www.usenix.org/conference/icac13/technical-sessions/presentation/herbst
3. Mao, M., Humphrey, M.: A performance study on the VM startup time in the cloud. In: 2012 IEEE Fifth International Conference on Cloud Computing. IEEE, June 2012. https://doi.org/10.1109/cloud.2012.103
4. Amazon elastic compute cloud. https://aws.amazon.com/ec2. Accessed 02 Sept 2016
5. Microsoft azure. https://azure.microsoft.com. Accessed 02 Sept 2016
6. Google cloud platform. https://cloud.google.com. Accessed 02 Sept 2016
7. Ostermann, S., Iosup, A., Yigitbasi, N., Prodan, R., Fahringer, T., Epema, D.: A performance analysis of EC2 cloud computing services for scientific computing. In: Avresky, D.R., Diaz, M., Bode, A., Ciciani, B., Dekel, E. (eds.) CloudComp 2009. LNICSSTE, vol. 34, pp. 115–131. Springer, Heidelberg (2010). https://doi.org/10.1007/978-3-642-12636-9_9
8. Hill, Z., Li, J., Mao, M., Ruiz-Alvarez, A., Humphrey, M.: Early observations on the performance of windows Azure. In: Proceedings of the 19th ACM International Symposium on High Performance Distributed Computing - HPDC 2010. ACM Press (2010). https://doi.org/10.1145/1851476.1851532
9. Evans, B.: The top 5 cloud-computing vendors, November 2017. https://www.forbes.com/sites/bobevans1/2017/11/07/the-top-5-cloud-computing-vendors-1-microsoft-2-amazon-3-ibm-4-salesforce-5-sap/

An Open Source Cloud-Based NoSQL and NewSQL Database Benchmarking Platform for IoT Data

Arjun Pandya[✉], Chaitanya Kulkarni, Kunal Mali, and Jianwu Wang

Department of Information Systems, University of Maryland, Baltimore County,
Baltimore, MD 21250, USA
{apandya1, chai2, kunal.mali, jianwu}@umbc.edu

Abstract. Internet of Things (IoT) is continually expanding, and the information being transmitted through IoT is often in large-scale in both volume and velocity. With its evolution, IoT raises new challenges such as throughput and scalability of software and database working with it. This is the reason that traditional techniques for data management and database operations cannot adopt the new challenges from IoT data. We need an efficient database system that can handle, store, and retrieve continuous, high-speed, and large-volume data, perform various database operations, and generate quick results. Recent developments of database technologies such as NoSQL and NewSQL database provides promising solutions to IoT. This paper proposes an extensible cloud-based open-source benchmarking framework on how these databases could work with IoT data. Using the framework, we compare the performances of VoltDB NewSQL and MongoDB NoSQL database systems on IoT data injection, transactional operations, and analytical operations.

Keywords: NoSQL · NewSQL · IoT · Big Data · MongoDB · VoltDB · Cloud computing · Benchmarking

1 Introduction

In the last few years, there has been an incredible rise in the amount of data that is being generated. Big data is the term, used to describe such a massive volume of data, which can be structured, semi-structured, and unstructured. According to the Gartner group, Big Data can be defined by 3Vs: volume, velocity, and variety [1]. Processing such vast amounts of data requires speed, flexible schemas, and distributed databases [2]. As a typical Big Data, we are now seeing more and more Internet of Things (IoT) data, which could be large in both volume and velocity that needs to be stored and processed efficiently.

Meanwhile, database systems are also evolving quickly in recent years, especially with new generations of database systems such as NewSQL and NoSQL. Although these database systems claim to be more efficient and scalable than many traditional database systems, it is still an open challenge on which database system can work better

© Springer Nature Switzerland AG 2019
C. Zheng and J. Zhan (Eds.): Bench 2018, LNCS 11459, pp. 65–77, 2019.
https://doi.org/10.1007/978-3-030-32813-9_7

with IoT data. To deal with the challenge, this paper compares two entirely different types of database systems, NewSQL and NoSQL, on Amazon Web Service AWS cloud. These databases are designed to address the 3Vs (Velocity, Volume, Variance) challenge of Big Data processing. Several tests have been performed for two popular database systems: MongoDB representing the NoSQL category and VoltDB representing NewSQL. Both are configured as multi-node cluster/shard on AWS.

The contributions of this paper are two folds. First, we propose an extensible cloud open-source benchmarking framework on how well different database systems could work with respect to the IoT data which has been tested on both AWS and Microsoft Azure cloud. Second, using the framework, we compare the performances of a NewSQL database system, namely VoltDB, and a NoSQL database system, namely MongoDB, on IoT data injection and database operations.

The paper is organized as follows. Section 2 focuses on the background of each system. Section 3 covers the benchmarking framework we developed to compare these databases. Section 4 covers the experimental setup. Section 5 covers the analysis and results. Section 6 eventually draws a conclusion and mentions future research.

2   Background

2.1   NewSQL

NewSQL describes new database architectures, deviating from the way relational DBMS are implemented. In contrast to the NoSQL databases, they aim to maintain characteristics of relational databases, similar to SQL as a query language, which has support for the relational model and ACID transactions. At the same time, they provide additional performance, scalability, and distribute-ability. This is done by leveraging modern hardware and deploying improved algorithms which have not been available yet when older existing DBMS had been designed. NewSQL databases rewrite the core of the database system from scratch to remove legacy code that hinders distribute-ability and performance due to its assumptions being outdated [3]. Operating in-memory is often mentioned as a key property of NewSQL, making relational databases like Google Spanner and VoltDB.

2.2   NoSQL

NoSQL stands for "not only SQL". In a broader sense, it includes all non-relational DBMS (which may or may not use a querying language). In contrast with RDBMS conforming to ACID (Atomicity, Consistency, Isolation, Durability), NoSQL DBMS follow the CAP (Consistency, Availability, Partition Tolerance) theorem (Eric Brewer) and thus their transactions conform to the BASE principle [4]. DBMS based on CAP, instead of having their transactions conform to ACID, conform to BASE (Basically, Available, Soft State, and Eventually Consistent) properties. NoSQL systems are distributed, non-relational databases designed for large-scale data storage and for massively-parallel data processing across a large number of commodity servers.

2.3 MongoDB

MongoDB is a document-based database which stores data in JSON like documents. MongoDB provides flexibility of storing data, meaning the fields within a collection can vary from document to document and can be changed over time without altering the previously stored data. This schema-free type of design is suitable when the incoming data is highly unstructured. Each document within MongoDB can be mapped with objects within the application code which makes data easy to work with. Although the documents may vary within the same collection, this feature does not compromise the MongoDB features like Ad hoc queries, indexing, and real-time aggregation to access and analyze your data. Since it is a distributed database at its core high availability, horizontal scaling, and geographical distribution are built in an easy to use [5].

2.4 VoltDB

VoltDB is an in-memory, scale-out SQL database built to power a new generation of applications that thrive on fast, smart data. VoltDB is a fully ACID-compliant transactional database, relieving the application developer from having to develop code to perform transactions and manage rollbacks within their own application [6]. VoltDB is designed to take full advantage of the modern computing environment, VoltDB uses in-memory storage to maximize throughput, avoiding costly disk access. Further performance gains are achieved by serializing all data access, avoiding any of the time-consuming functions of traditional databases such as locking, latching, and maintaining transaction logs. Scalability, reliability, and high availability are achieved through clustering and replication across multiple servers and server farms (Table 1).

Table 1. Conceptual comparison between VoltDB and MongoDB.

	VoltDB	MongoDB
Scaling	Yes	Yes
Partitioning	Yes	Yes
Flexible schema	No	Yes
Replication	Yes	Yes
Primary data store	Relation store	Document store
Note	Distributed with In-Memory new SQL RDBMS	Document store, schema-free database

2.5 Apache Kafka

Apache Kafka is a distributed streaming platform. Initially, it was started as a messaging queue system and quickly evolved into a "publish and subscribe", streaming platform [7]. Being a streaming platform, Apache Kafka provides services like publish and subscribe, to stream and consume records like a message queue system, store the messages with fault tolerance capabilities and records can be streamed as they occur. It provides the connection with customer front-end applications and a downstream system with data in real-time.

2.6 Cloud Computing

Cloud computing includes on-demand computing resources, such as virtual machines, storage, or an application as a utility rather than having them in-house. Everything is available over the internet on a pay-to-use basis. Here, security and maintenance are not the user concerns as it is taken care of by the vendor. Some of the benefits of cloud computing are self-service provisioning, elasticity, pay-per-use, workload resilience, and migration flexibility. Cloud computing service can be private, public, or a combination of both [8, 9].

3   Benchmarking Framework

Following Infrastructure as a service (IaaS), our benchmarking environment consists of three types of virtual servers: IoT data generators, Stream messaging middleware, and Database clusters/shards. Our open-source benchmarking framework is available at [18]. We have tested our benchmarking environment on both Microsoft Azure and AWS clouds.

3.1   Framework Components

IoT Data Generator. We generated synthetic IoT sensor data by executing the java code on dedicated servers. Synthetic data generator provided us with the flexibility of controlling the volume and velocity of sensor data. These data generators implemented a Kafka Simple Producer API to send data to Kafka servers. Further, it produced sensor data in two different formats CSV and JSON.

Stream Messaging Middleware. Since the location where IoT data is generated is also different from the location of the database, it often requires a stream messaging middleware to make sure IoT data is injected to the database in real-time and with fault-tolerance support.

We have selected Apache Kafka to be our stream messaging middleware which is a distributed streaming platform. Kafka publishes and subscribes to streams of records, similar to a message queue or enterprise messaging system. It is used in building real-time streaming data pipelines that reliably get data between systems or applications. All the sensors are pushing data to Kafka servers, for the experiments we set up 3 node Kafka server to ensure fault tolerance.

Database Clusters/Shards. Database sharding can be simply defined as a "shared-nothing" partitioning scheme for large databases across a number of servers, enabling new levels of database performance and scalability achievable [10]. A database cluster is a collection of databases that is managed by a single instance of a running database server [11]. MongoDB and VoltDB use different mechanisms to achieve scalability. In VoltDB we can simply add database servers to create an elastic cluster. Whereas in MongoDB we need an additional configuration server to create a MongoDB sharded cluster and a Mongos server to run queries in distributed mode.

3.2   Architecture

Figure 1 represents the conceptual architecture our framework supports. This architecture is divided into 3 tiers: (1) IoT Data Generators, (2) Stream messaging middleware and (3) Database cluster.

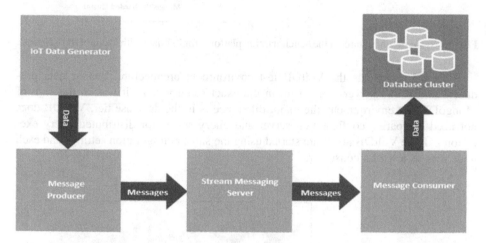

Fig. 1. Conceptual architecture diagram for the database benchmarking platform for IoT data.

Our test setup had a dedicated environment for each database with 3, 6, and 9 nodes cluster. This was done to ensure the performance of any database should not be affected.

The architecture of the MongoDB test environment is represented in Fig. 2. The following figure represents 6 node MongoDB sharded cluster, similarly, we had 3 node and 9 node clusters. In the following MongoDB test environment, sensor data producer, and Kafka server are running on the same virtual machines, the database is running with 2 replication sets on 6 nodes. In addition to data nodes, MongoDB requires a configuration server which has information about all the available nodes, and a MongoDB's server which executes queries in distributed mode.

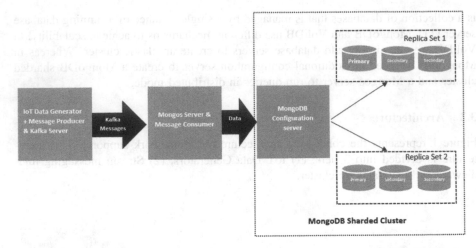

Fig. 2. System architecture for the benchmarking platform for IoT data with MongoDB (6 Nodes).

Figure 3 represents the VoltDB test environment architecture. Sensor data producers and Kafka servers are set up in the exact same way as it was in the case of MongoDB test environment, the major difference is in the database tier, VoltDB does not need a separate configuration server and query server for distributed query execution. All the VoltDB nodes are started using the same configuration settings and each node acts as a Kafka consumer.

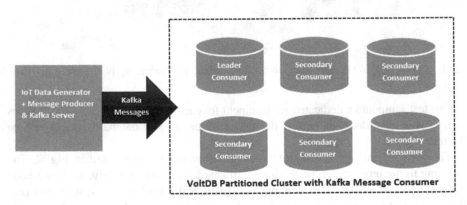

Fig. 3. System architecture for the benchmarking platform for IoT data with VoltDB (6 nodes).

3.3   Data Generation and Consumption Algorithms

We implemented the Apache Kafka Producer API [12] to develop sensor data producer. For synthetic sensor data generation, we used a Random Java class [13]. To consume messages from Kafka server into MongoDB we implemented Kafka Consumer API [14] and for the VoltDB, we used VoltDB Kafka importer utility.

Algorithm 1. Sensor Data Producer

Input: **N** *Number of sensors*, **T** *Execution Time*, **R** *Number of records per second*
Output: Message post on Kafka Server under the specific topic

---
Step 1: Create Kafka Producer using Kafka API
Step 2: Generate random sensor data
Step 3: Send the data as a message to Kafka server
Step 4: Repeat steps 2 and 3 **R** times per second till **T** seconds

---

The above process is performed in parallel for N number of sensors. Each database test environment had its own set of sensor data producer which generates the data in the database's required format.

Algorithm 2. Sensor Data Consumer

Input: **S** *Kafka Server name*, **T** *Kafka Topic Name*, **P** *Number of message partitions*
Output: Record insertion in MongoDB database

Step 1: Create Consumer using Kafka Consumer API
Step 2: Create database connector using MongoDB connector API
Step 3: Open Database connection
Step 4: Read message from Kafka Server **S**, topic **T** and partition **P**
Step 5: Insert the message as the BSON document in the database
Step 6: Get next message
Step 7: Repeat steps 4 to 6 till the end of messages in Kafka topic T
Step 8: Close database connection

We developed a consumer program only for MongoDB. The consumer program was executed in N (Number of producers) × P (Number of message partitions) parallel threads i.e., we will have 10 × 4 parallel consumers for 10 sensor data producers and 4 Kafka message partitions. This program was executed on MongoDB's server to execute queries in distributed mode.

4   Experiments

Questions we want to answer through the experiments are as follows:

1. Which database can ingest and scale high-velocity IoT data more efficiently?
2. Which database can ingest and scale high volume IoT data more efficiently?
3. Which database is more suitable for fast transactional data processing on the high volume of data?
4. Which database is more suitable for the fast analytical data processing on the high volume of data?

To answer these questions, we performed three different experiments on 3 and 6 node partitioned/sharded database clusters hosted on the AWS cloud.

Experiment I consists of 6 different tests and will help us answer questions 1 and 2. Experiment II consists of 2 tests which help us answer to question 3. Experiment III helps us answer the last question.

4.1   System Configuration, Sensor Data Structure, and Formats

For these experiments, we used the same system configuration for all the servers. These servers are deployed on Linux Ubuntu virtual machines on AWS cloud (Table 2).

Table 2. Hardware and software information used in our experiments.

Hardware		Software	
Operating system	Linux Ubuntu 16.04 LTS	Mongo DB	3.6 community edition
Memory	8 GBs	Volt DB	8.1.2 community edition
Storage	200 GBs	Kafka	2.11
Processors	8 vCPUs	Java	1.8

Table 3 lists the IoT sensor data structure; this structure was common among the databases. However, both the databases handle the storage of this data separately.

Table 3. IoT sensor data structure used in our experiments.

Name	Type
SENSOR_ID	INTEGER
CLOCK_TIME	TIMESTAMP
AIR_TEMP	VARCHAR
WIND SPEED	VARCHAR
SURFACE_TEMP	VARCHAR
LATITUDE	VARCHAR
LONGITUDE	VARCHAR
RECEIVED_TIME	TIMESTAMP

4.2   Experiment I: Data Injection with Different Volume and Velocity

Under the data injection experiment, we performed 6 tests to ensure we cover different volume and velocity. Following tests are performed on 3 and 6 node database cluster hosted on AWS (Table 4).

Table 4. Tests for data injection with different volume and velocity.

Test	Sensors	Experiment time (Hrs.)	Velocity (records/sec)	Volume (GBs)
1	1	4	100	~1
2	10	4	100	3
3	20	4	100	6
4	1	4	1000	3
5	10	4	1000	30
6	20	4	1000	60

Figure 4 shows 3 node injection time comparison of VoltDB and MongoDB, On 3 node setup, VoltDB was unable to complete injection tests 3, 5, and 6 because the server went out of memory, remember VoltDB is an in-memory database so the total memory of 3 nodes with (8 GB memory) was not sufficient to store a high volume of data. On the other hand, the MongoDB was able to complete all the injection tests on 3 node setup. VoltDB was slightly fast in the injection for the tests it was able to finish.

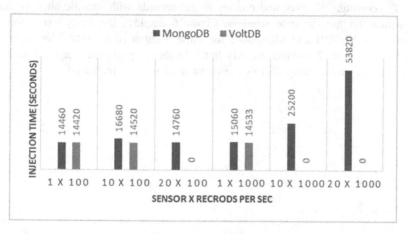

Fig. 4. Injection time comparison on 3 node MongoDB and VoltDB cluster.

Figure 5 shows Injection time comparison on 3 and 6 node cluster for the same amount of data for VoltDB (left) and MongoDB (right). Data injection timings of both the databases were slightly improved with the increase in the number of nodes in the database cluster. In the case of VoltDB, an increase in the number of nodes leads to an increase in the amount of data stored. The following figure represents the comparison between the injection time on 3 nodes and 6 nodes cluster for the same number of records. The left graph shows VoltDB injection timings for 3 and 6 nodes, and the right graph shows MongoDB injection timings. We can notice from the left graph that VoltDB does not have results for 3 nodes.

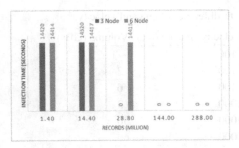
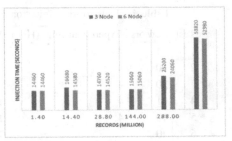

Fig. 5. Injection time comparison on 3 and 6 node cluster for the same amount of data for VoltDB (left) and MongoDB (right)

4.3 Experiment II: Transactional Data Processing on High Volume of Data

In this experiment, we conducted two transactional functions, namely query and indexing, on the whole dataset.

Query Processing. We executed queries to get records with specific air temperature value within the specific time window. Figure 6 displays the query execution time comparison of VoltDB and MongoDB for same number of records. The experiment shows for less than 2 million records both databases performed equally well, but VoltDB outperformed MongoDB as the number of records increased.

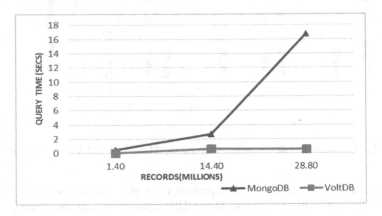

Fig. 6. Query time comparison on high volume data.

Indexing. Index on the field "AIR_TEMP" of our data structure. Figure 7 shows the indexing time comparison for same number of records in millions. VoltDB performed consistently, on the other hand with an increase in the number of records MongoDB took much more time to index the data. Again, VoltDB outperformed MongoDB in data indexing.

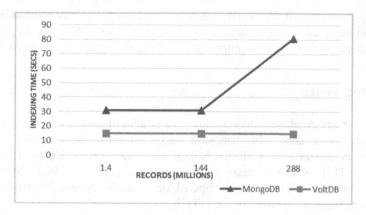

Fig. 7. Indexing time comparison on high volume data.

4.4 Experiment III: Analytical Data Processing on High Volume of Data

We executed three analytical aggregation functions, namely sum, count, and average, on the whole dataset. Figure 8 shows the comparison of the average time taken by the 3 aggregation operations listed above on the given number of records. Initially, the performance of MongoDB and VoltDB varies slightly but as the number of records increases, the performance varies considerably. In overall aggregation performance comparison, VoltDB performed better.

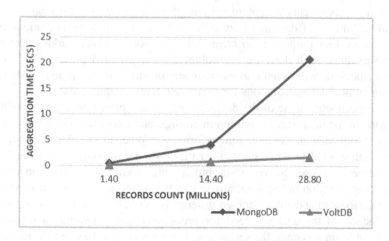

Fig. 8. Data aggregation time comparison on high volume data.

4.5 Findings from Experiments

Based on the above results, we can answer the questions we had at the starting of these experiments. When it comes to efficiently handle the high velocity of data, both the databases performed well. MongoDB was able to manage better than VoltDB in storing a high volume of data on comparative smaller environments. In fast data processing and aggregation section, VoltDB outperformed MongoDB that makes it a better choice.

5 Related Work

There are various database solutions now available which offers an adaptable data model, scale-out on commodity hardware for existing and future applications, thus various survey papers were published NoSQL databases were evaluated for different use cases in [15]. Numerous comparison papers are published, SQL, NoSQL and NewSQL Databases for IoT was compared on a single system in [16]. Different NewSQL databases were compared in [17].

To our best knowledge, our work is unique and different from existing work in the following three aspects. First, we developed a benchmarking framework which can be used to compare this new generation of databases on distributed networks. Second, our framework uses IoT middleware to ensure zero percent data loss over the networks. Third, instead of using simple client-server architecture to test database performance, our architecture is cloud-based in which we can scale our databases. Our paper compares NoSQL and NewSQL database systems on the basis of IoT transaction processing performance on the cloud-based environment like AWS.

6 Conclusion

We performed experiments to explore not only the storage ability of databases but also horizontal scalability of data and how efficiently we can perform operations on the distributed data. Our purpose is to create an open source benchmarking framework which can evaluate such database technologies on distributed systems. This benchmarking framework will benefit users who are planning to setup IoT systems and looking for right database solutions for their customized requirements.

In our experiments, none of the databases came as a clear winner, MongoDB was able to store all the data with the minimum configuration provided but got hit in terms of database processing and aggregation performance. Whereas, VoltDB was not able to store the volume of data we generated on the system configuration for the VoltDB database servers we used for our tests, but it outperformed MongoDB in data processing and aggregation in the scenarios where the memory was enough for VoltDB.

These databases handle data storage differently, VoltDB uses main memory of the system to store all the data we need for processing which requires a considerable amount of RAM on a system, the secondary storage is not used except for storing data snapshots. The processing time of operations on VoltDB is impressive. On the other hand, MongoDB stores data on secondary storage, which enables it to store huge data on systems with less main memory, but it takes longer to process and aggregate the same amount of data which VoltDB can handle.

Acknowledgment. This work is supported in part by the National Natural Science Foundation of China (No. 61462076).

References

1. Beyer, M.A., Laney, D.: The Importance of 'Big Data': A Definition. Gartner, Stamford (2012)
2. Li, Y., Manoharan, S.: A performance comparison of SQL and NoSQL databases. In: Proceedings of 2013 IEEE Pacific Rim Conference on Communications, Computers and Signal Processing (PACRIM), pp. 15–19. IEEE (2013)
3. Stonebraker, M., Madden, S., Abadi, D.J., Harizopoulos, S., Hachem, N., Helland, P.: The end of an architectural era: (it's time for a complete rewrite). In: Proceedings of the 33rd International Conference on Very Large Data Bases, pp. 1150–1160. VLDB Endowment (2007)
4. Guy, H.: Next Generation Databases: NoSQL, NewSQL, and Big Data. Apress, New York City (2015)
5. MongoDB. https://www.mongodb.com/what-is-mongodb. Accessed 14 Feb 2019
6. VoltDB. https://docs.voltdb.com/UsingVoltDB/. Accessed 14 Feb 2019
7. Apache Kafka. https://kafka.apache.org/intro. Accessed 14 Feb 2019
8. Kafka. https://www.confluent.io/what-is-apache-kafka/. Accessed 14 Feb 2019
9. Cloud Computing. https://www.ibm.com/cloud/learn/what-is-cloud-computing. Accessed 14 Feb 2019
10. Database Sharding. http://www.agildata.com/database-sharding. Accessed 14 Feb 2019
11. Database Cluster,. https://www.postgresql.org/docs/9.0/static/creating-cluster.html. Accessed 14 Feb 2019
12. Apache Kafka Producer API. https://kafka.apache.org/0110/javadoc/index.html?org/apache/kafka/clients/producer/KafkaProducer.html. Accessed 14 Feb 2019
13. Java Random Class. https://docs.oracle.com/javase/8/docs/api/java/util/Random.html. Accessed 14 Feb 2019
14. Apache Kafka Consumer API. https://kafka.apache.org/0100/javadoc/index.html?org/apache/kafka/clients/consumer/KafkaConsumer.html. Accessed 14 Feb 2019
15. Hecht, R., Jablonski, S.: NoSQL evaluation: a use case oriented survey. In: 2011 International Conference on Cloud and Service Computing (CSC), pp. 336–341. IEEE (2011)
16. Haleemunnisa, F., Wasnik, K.: Comparison of SQL, NoSQL and NewSQL databases for Internet of Things. In: Bombay Section Symposium (IBSS), pp. 1–6. IEEE (2016)
17. Kaur, K., Sachdeva, M.: Performance evaluation of NewSQL databases. In: 2017 International Conference on Inventive Systems and Control (ICISC), pp. 1–5. IEEE (2017)
18. Open Source IoT Database Benchmarking Framework. https://github.com/big-data-lab-umbc/IoT-database-benchmarking. Accessed 14 Feb 2019

Scalability Evaluation of Big Data Processing Services in Clouds

Xin Zhou[1,2], Congfeng Jiang[1,2](✉), Yeliang Qiu[1,2], Tiantian Fan[1,2],
Yumei Wang[1,2], Liangbin Zhang[3], Jian Wan[4], and Weisong Shi[5]

[1] Key Laboratory of Complex Systems Modeling and Simulation,
Ministry of Education, Hangzhou Dianzi University, Hangzhou 310037, China
cjiang@hdu.edu.cn
[2] School of Computer Science and Technology, Hangzhou Dianzi University,
Hangzhou 310037, China
[3] College of Big Data and Software Engineering, Zhejiang Wanli University,
Ningbo, China
[4] School of Information and Electronic Engineering,
Zhejiang University of Science and Technology, Hangzhou 310023, China
[5] Department of Computer Science, Wayne State University,
Detroit, MI 48202, USA

Abstract. Currently, many cloud providers deploy their big data processing systems as cloud services, which helps users conveniently manage and process their data in clouds. Among different service providers' big data processing services, how to evaluate and compare their scalability is an interesting and challenging work. Most traditional benchmark tools focus on performance evaluation of big data processing systems, such as aggregated throughput and IOPS, but fail to conduct a quantitative analysis of their scalability. In this paper, we propose a measurement methodology to quantify the scalability of big data processing services, which makes the cloud services scalability comparable. We conduct a group of comparative experiments on AliCloud E-MapReduce and Baidu MRS, and collect their respective scalability characteristics under Hadoop and Spark workloads. The scalability characteristics observed in our work could help cloud users choose the best cloud service platform to set up an optimized big data processing system to achieve their specific goals more successfully.

Keywords: Big data · Benchmark · Scalability · AliCloud · Baidu cloud

1 Introduction

In the past decade, a variety of big data processing platforms, such as Hadoop [1] and Spark [2] have been proposed to accelerate the processing of large-scale data. Today many giant cloud providers move big data processing systems to the clouds, forming as public cloud services. Typical examples include Amazon EMR

© Springer Nature Switzerland AG 2019
C. Zheng and J. Zhan (Eds.): Bench 2018, LNCS 11459, pp. 78–90, 2019.
https://doi.org/10.1007/978-3-030-32813-9_8

[3], AliCloud E-MapReduce [4], and Baidu MRS [5]. As more and more SaaS products of big data processing become available, the demand of benchmarking and evaluating these cloud services rises continuously because cloud users need to compare these services and choose the best one according to their requirements. Moreover, cloud system designers and operators also need to understand the system performance and scalability to improve the systems deployment and workload placement.

However, most of today's cloud system benchmarks focus on the performance of the system, such as the job response time and system throughput. There is a lack of study on the scalability characteristics of big data processing services in clouds. Generally better scalability means that the system can handle larger workloads as the amount of additional resources available increases. Given a specific budget, how to build a high performance platform is a non-trivial problem. On the other hand, the workloads in clouds are also diverse, in terms of required resources types and resource capacities. The workloads may also require specific resources temporally or spatially. For example, CPU-intensive or IO-intensive, or mixed workloads may require different resource deployment. Therefore, given a group of workload, should user scale-up or scale-out their deployed cluster?

To address these problems, in this paper we propose a measurement approach to quantify the scalability of data processing services in clouds. A group of experiments are conducted on AliCloud E-MapReduce and Baidu MRS using various workloads. We collect the comparative results regarding horizontal scalability and vertical scalability with workloads on Hadoop and Spark platforms. Some observations are derived from the experimental results, which can help users build a more scalable data processing system.

The reminder of this paper is organized as follows. Section 2 presents some related work on big data processing benchmarks and their scalability evaluation. Section 3 describes our quantitative measurement method. In Sect. 4 we conduct a group of experiments to analyze the scalability of two cloud services. Section 5 concludes this paper and directs our future work.

2 Related Work

In the fields of big data benchmarks, researchers have taken a lot of research efforts and designed several benchmarks for big data. In this section, we briefly introduce some existing works close to ours.

2.1 Big Data Benchmarks

With the advent of big data techniques, there have been plenty of benchmarks developed to evaluate the performance of big data systems. These benchmarks are mainly designed for two kinds of systems: *benchmarks for big data management systems* and *benchmarks for big data processing systems*.

For example, YCSB (Yahoo! Cloud Serving Benchmark) [6], was proposed to compare the performance of transactional processing systems including Cassandra [7], HBase [8], PNUTS [9], and a simple sharded MySQL implementation.

YCSB supplies several workloads with different combinations of insert, read, update and scan on database tables. Similarly, Shi *et al.* [10] developed two benchmarks with a collection of structured queries, to compare the performance of Cassandra, HBase, Hive and HadoopDB.

In addition, dozens of benchmarks have been proposed for big analytical processing systems, such as CloudSuite [11], Bigdatabench [12], DCBench [13], Hibench [14], GraySort [15], CloudRank-D [16], and several other research work in [17–20], and so on. These benchmarks supply a set of analytical jobs to benchmark the performance to MapReduce systems. Besides, Pavlo *et al.* [21] proposed a general benchmark with a collection of analytical jobs to compare the performance between Hadoop and parallel DBMS.

Generally, these benchmarks can be effectively utilized to evaluate the performance of standalone transactional or analytical processing systems hosted in a cloud platform. Unfortunately, there is a lack of study on how to conduct a comparable experiment.

2.2   Scalability Evaluation of Big Data Processing Systems

Scalability is the ability to describe a process, network, software, or organization to cope with increased demand and load. A system, business, or software that is described as being extensible is generally a favorable condition, because it will be more adaptable to the needs of its users. Scalability is usually a synonym for stability, which means that networks, systems, software, or organizations have the ability to deal with changes in demand, increased productivity and even competition from other challengers.

Since the time scalability has been proposed, a series of scalability definitions and measurement methods have been proposed. Rizzelli *et al.* proposed a novel approach to assess wavelength switched optical network scalability and efficiency. This method takes into account the routing constraints of reconfigurable optical add/drop multiplexers, a variety of coherent transmission systems, different amplification schemes and types of fibre [22]. Badia *et al.'* paper [23] includes a comprehensive performance and scalability study of the resulting codes when they are applied to the solution of the Poisson problem on a large-scale multicore-based distributed-memory machine with up to 4096 cores.

Unlike the scalability discussed in the literature [22,23], this paper examines the relationship between big data process tools in extending and performance, that is, how to quantify the scalability of big data processing tools. Gunther [24] referred to a generic model USL (Universal Scalability Law), and made the following definition, M_p stands for speed-up ratio, that can represent the scalability:

$$M_p = T_1/T_p \tag{1}$$

In Eq. 1, T_p represents the execution time that is measured on the $p = 1, 2, 3, \ldots$ processor or cluster node. This method measures the execution time of the task and derives the speed-up ratio. But this method is used only from the Scale-out metric, relatively simple, and this model cannot directly quantify the scalability, just to observe the scalability from the figures.

Gao *et al.* [25] utilized the radar map to assess the scalability of the Sass application on the cloud. This paper measures the performance of many Sass applications, the system load, throughput, response time, etc., and show the area of the radar map for each metric, then add all the area value, obtain the corresponding performance or capacity value. Ultimately by subtracting the best performance and worst performance, derived scalability range. Giant cloud providers tend to mix online and batch services on the same cluster to save energy costs. Jiang [26] analyzed the actual tracking data of the production cluster containing 1.3k servers in Alibaba Cloud. The findings and insights can help researchers better understand the workload characteristics and achieve more efficient cluster expansion. Jiang and Qiu [27–29] proposed a virtual machine scheduling framework based on energy efficiency and proportional awareness, EASE. EASE correlates the server's EP and EE preferences with the VM's workload type to schedule the VM to the most proper server to ensure performance growth during cluster expansion.

In the field of big data processing tools, the above methods are difficult for comparing the scalability of different tools, do not use a scalability measurement model about big data processing tool. Therefore, we have done the following work.

3   Evaluation Model

Through the analysis of the previous quantitative method, we think the USL [24] is worthy of reference. The method only quantifies the scalability from scale-out metric, but we can also apply this method to quantify the scalability of big data processing by scale-up.

Traditionally, evaluating the performance of a scaled system is to measure the amount of performance changes within unit resources of system, and this calculation is monotonously rising or declining functional relationships. In the cloud environment, the relationship of resource changes and system performance is not monotonous.

In the model, the resources of the cloud environment are extended by the approach of horizontal extension and vertical extension. After each extension, the performance of the test system is collected, and the performance parameters are collected.

We have made the following definition by extending generic model USL [24], S_p represents the speed-up ratio:

$$S_p = M_1/M_p \tag{2}$$

Where p ($p = 1, 2, 3, 4, 5...$), p is not only node nums, but also is resource change, so we can apply this method to quantify the scalability of scale-up, and M is the task running time. Since the multi-node's time is expected to be less than the single-node, the scalability usually is a discrete concave function about p. According to the relationship, scalability can be divided into three categories:

1. Linear acceleration: If M_p is equal to M_1/p, then S_p will equal 1, 2, 3 ... so appear linearly.
2. Sub-linear acceleration: For each node of the cluster or every resource change, $M_p > M_1/p$, the speed-up ratio will be lower than the linear acceleration. For example, if p = 2 and $M_2 = 3M_1/4$, then $S_2 = 1.33$. Since S_2 less than 2, scalability is sub-linear.
3. Super linear acceleration: If $M_p < M_1/p$, the speed-up ratio will be better than the linear, that is, super linear expansion. For instance, if M = 2 and $M_2 = M_1/3$, then $S_2 = 3$, which is bigger than linear acceleration.

Figure 1 shows the scalability of three acceleration models, including super linear acceleration, linear acceleration, and sub-linear acceleration. In order to further quantify the scalability of a certain stage, we fit the speed-up ratio curve, the relationship we use the following formula:

$$S = f(P) \tag{3}$$

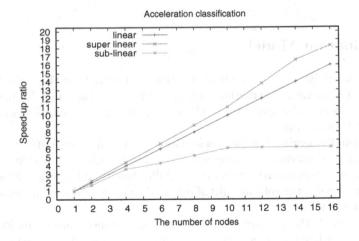

Fig. 1. Acceleration classification.

P is the resource change value, and S is the speed-up ratio. Since the relationship between S and P is not monotonic, in order to accurately express the scalability, set p = ΔP, q = ΔS, and by integrating ΔP, and get the area, then measure the scalability of the system by the value Q:

$$Q = \int f(p)dp \tag{4}$$

The bigger the Q, the better the scalability of the system. For comparison, we also calculate the scalability of linear acceleration, the value is Q_{linear}. Through the ratio of Q and Q_{linear}, the final scalability of the target system is obtained:

$$V_{scalability} = Q/Q_{linear} \tag{5}$$

4   Experiments

In this section, we use Hadoop and Spark to execute a group of big data tasks, by running Terasort [30] and WordCount [31], and applying the evaluation model which is proposed in this paper, to obtain scalability of Hadoop and Spark. Terasort is used to test the data processing capabilities of distributed big data processing tools. Internationally, there are Terasort games with big data tools each year. Therefore we think it can reflect the scalability of the system.

Terasort is a CPU-intensive task, and for the usual tasks, in addition to CPU-intensive tasks, there are a lot of IO-intensive tasks, and only conducting the CPU-intensive task are relatively simple and unacceptable, so we pick a representative IO-intensive tasks: WordCount. We apply the random 50G text data, to compare Hadoop with Spark in the IO-intensive tasks.

Due to the heterogeneity of the workload in the cloud environment, a single experiment is hard to guarantee the validity and accuracy of the results. This section will design the experiment firstly, then conduct the experiment, to find the corresponding speed-up ratio, and try to analyze experiments. Then we introduce the experimental environment, system parameters and experimental process. Finally, the experimental results are analyzed, the scalability of the system is evaluated, and the optimization proposal is given.

With the rapid development of cloud computing, more and more companies will choose the cloud environment, which is the trend. Therefore, we chose to do comparative experiments about big data processing services, to compare the advantages and disadvantages of different cloud providers' processing tools and the scalability of different processing tools.

4.1   Experiment Environment

According to the analysis of the architecture about AliCloud and Baidu cloud, the experimental test cluster is initially a namenode node and a datanode node. Our initial configuration is three-nodes, a namenode node, two datanode nodes. Then, we use the Teragen [32] (Terasort data generator) to produce disordered data, and then conduct experiment. In the course of the experiment, recording the task execution time. Table 1 shows the hardware configuration for the cloud host:

Table 1. Configuration for the cloud host.

Configuration	NameNode	DataNode
CPU	4core	4core
Memory	16 GB	16 GB
Disk	SATA	SATA

4.2   Scale-Out Analysis

AliCloud Scale-Out Experiment. On the AliCloud E-MapReduce platform, we used Teragen [32] to generate 50G disordered data, followed by Terasort experiment. During the sorting process, recorded the sort execution time. We measured the experiment data about Hadoop cluster and Spark cluster that were extended from 2 data nodes to 16 data nodes, respectively, and the experiment execution time is shown in Fig. 2. Then we used the evaluation model to calculate the speed-up ratio of different nodes under the scale-out, and by making the figure to show the speed-up ratio, as showed in Fig. 3:

From Fig. 3, we found that after the implementation of same Terasort task, Spark execution time was significantly less than Hadoop, which proves the fact that Spark is faster than Hadoop, in fact, it is a victory of memory calculation. In the comparison of the speed-up ratio, spark in the front 8 nodes, scalability is better than Hadoop, then the scalability is smaller than Hadoop. By fitting the curves of Hadoop and Spark, we obtained the corresponding fitting functions, respectively:

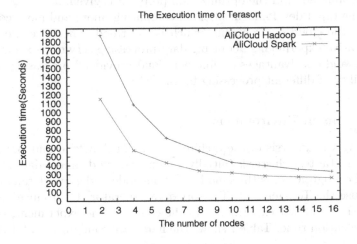

Fig. 2. AliCloud Terasort execution time.

$$S_1 = -0.000798271p^3 + 0.0131687p^2 + 0.343683p + 0.241379 \tag{6}$$

$$S_2 = 0.000693182p^3 - 0.0340611p^2 + 0.670093p - 0.197714 \tag{7}$$

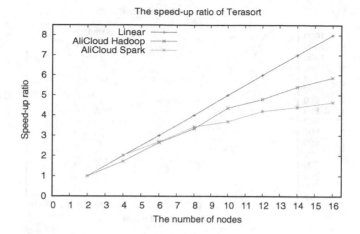

Fig. 3. AliCloud Terasort speed-up ratio.

We integrated on the S_1 and S_2, the resulting area were:

$$Q_{alihadoop} = 51.552 \tag{8}$$

$$Q_{alispark} = 46.604 \tag{9}$$

We also integrated the linear acceleration, the area obtained is:

$$Q_{linear} = 63 \tag{10}$$

Further, we obtained the scalability of 0.818 and 0.739, respectively, which showed on the AliCloud. When Hadoop and Spark scale out to 16 nodes, the scale-out performance is good, and Hadoop overall performance is better than the Spark.

On AliCloud, we also used WordCount to do 50G text data's word statistics, the result of different nodes are shown in Figure 4:

Through the evaluation model, we made the chart when the nodes were extended, as showed in Fig. 5, respectively, integrated on Hadoop and Spark, we found the scalability of Hadoop and Spark were 0.77 and 0.504. In the IO-intensive tasks, the scalability of Hadoop is still good, but the scalability of Spark is not so good.

Baidu Cloud Scale-Out Experiment. In the Baidu cloud platform, we also used the cloud server with same configuration to execute Hadoop Terasort, the execute time and speed-up ratio shown in Fig. 6. The Spark version in Baidu cloud is 1.6, and the Spark version in AliCloud is 2.1. So, we didn't compare Baidu BMR with AliCloud on Spark.

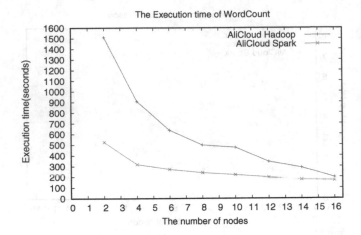

Fig. 4. WordCount execution time.

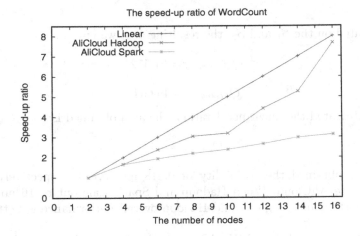

Fig. 5. The speed-up ratio for WordCount job.

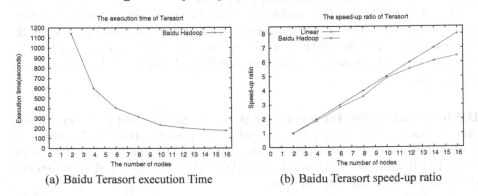

(a) Baidu Terasort execution Time   (b) Baidu Terasort speed-up ratio

Fig. 6. Baidu Terasort experiment.

4.3   Scale-Up Experiment

It's only one important aspect to measure the scalability from scale-out. In order to analyze the scalability of the big data processing system, we had done four different configurations' experiment on two datanodes, the configuration is as Table 2. The same, starting from the Terasort, the experimental results are as Table 3.

Table 2. Configuration for scale-up.

Experimental group	CPU	Memory
1	4core	16 GB
2	8core	32 GB
3	16core	64 GB
4	32core	128 GB

Table 3. Execution time for scale-up.

Experimental group/Task execution time	Hadoop	Spark
4core, 16 GB	1872 s	1151 s
8core, 32 GB	940 s	870 s
16core, 64 GB	457 s	810 s

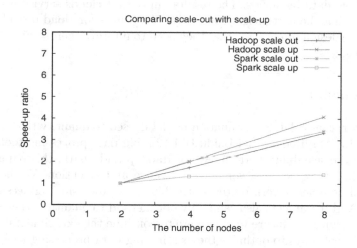

Fig. 7. A comparison between scale-out and scale-up.

We made a figure to show the speed-up ratio by extending the nodes and increasing the configuration, respectively. Here we think 8-core 32 GB configuration is equivalent to two 4-core 16 GB nodes, and so on. So scale-up can be compared with scale-out, the result is shown at Fig. 7.

4.4   Experimental Results

Through the AliCloud E-MapReduce and Baidu cloud BMR experiment, firstly, we find that the scalability of Hadoop and Spark are good on AliCloud and Baidu cloud, because the cloud platform, subject to different factors, but also can represent basic performance of the two cloud platform, when users get confused in the selection of big data processing tools, they can learn from. From the performance of Hadoop and Sparks on AliCloud E-MapReduce, we can see Hadoop's scalability is slightly better than Spark. For Hadoop users, they can use big data processing service by adding nodes, and do not need to consider scalability with relatively few nodes. Spark's speed is faster than Hadoop, memory computing reflects the advantages, and users that speed seeking can give priority to Spark. On Baidu cloud, the scalability of Hadoop is better than AliCloud at some stage.

Secondly, comparing scale-out with scale-up, each has its own advantages and disadvantages. Extended configuration, for Hadoop, the performance is better than increase nodes, but for Spark, it's not so good. The scalability of Spark is bad when enhancing the configuration of the server. We think users that use big data processing service, if you want to enhance your configuration on Spark, it will not a better choice than add nodes. And though our observation, adding nodes isn't expensive relative to enhance configuration. But for Hadoop, you should take this choice, when we upgrade configuration on Hadoop, its scalability is even more better than scale-out.

Thirdly, as shown by the significant variance of every big data processing service, this work enhances the understanding of the risks and rewards when processing big data by clouds. The results imply that clouds service need to be analysed so that the user picks them easily. The results for cloud provider could be a valuable design implication that they need to improve their services to avoid loss of customers.

5   Conclusion

In this paper, the scalability evaluation model is used to quantity the scalability of AliCloud E-MapReduce and Baidu BMR on big data processing tools. Compared with the scalability performance of Hadoop and Spark, this paper draws some conclusions which are worthy of reference and attention. We hope that readers will be able to work better on the big data processing services through our work. And researchers also can apply our method to quantify other big data processing service. As future work, we are to continue the experimental analysis and we will seek ways to optimize the existing big data processing tool.

Acknowledgement. This work is supported by Natural Science Foundation of China (No. 61472109, No. 61572163 and No. 61472112) and Key Research and Development Program of Zhejiang Province (No. 2018C01098,2019C01059 and 2019C03134). This work is also supported in part by National Science Foundation (NSF) grant CNS-1205338 and CNS-1561216, and by the Introduction of Innovative R&D team program of Guangdong Province (No. 201001D0104726115). This work is supported by Alibaba

Group through Alibaba Innovative Research (AIR) Program. This work is partially supported by Visiting Scholarship of Teachers' Professional Development Program (No. FX2018050).

References

1. Hadoop. http://hadoop.apache.org/
2. Spark. https://spark.apache.org/
3. Amazon EMR. https://aws.amazon.com/cn/emr/
4. AliCloud E-MapReduce. https://www.aliyun.com/product/emapreduce?utm_med ium=text&utm_source=baidu&utm_campaign=emr&utm_content=se_331947
5. Baidu BMR. https://cloud.baidu.com/product/bmr.html?track=cp:nsem|pf:pc|pp: bmr|pu:brand|ci:|kw:50293
6. Cooper, B.F., Silberstein, A., Tam, E., Ramakrishnan, R., Sears, R.: Benchmarking cloud serving systems with YCSB. In: SoCC, pp. 143–154 (2010)
7. Lakshman, A., Malik, P.: Cassandra: a decentralized structured storage system. Spec. Interest Group Oper. Syst. Oper. Syst. Rev. **44**(2), 35–40 (2010)
8. George, L.: HBase - The Definitive Guide. O'Reilly, Newton (2011)
9. Cooper, B.F., et al.: PNUTS: Yahoo!'s hosted data serving platform. Proc. VLDB Endow. **1**(2), 1277–1288 (2008)
10. Shi, Y., Meng, X., Zhao, J., Hu, X., Liu, B., Wang, H.: Benchmarking cloud-based data management systems. In: Proceedings of the Second International Workshop on Cloud Data Management, pp. 47–54. ACM (2010)
11. Ferdman, M., et al.: Clearing the clouds: a study of emerging scale-out workloads on modern hardware. In: ACM SIGARCH Computer Architecture News, vol. 40, pp. 37–48. ACM (2012)
12. Jia, Z., et al.: Understanding big data analytics workloads on modern processors. IEEE Trans. Parallel Distrib. Syst. **28**(6), 1797–1810 (2017)
13. Jia, Z., Wang, L., Zhan, J., Zhang, L., Luo, C.: Characterizing data analysis workloads in data centers. In: IISWC, pp. 66–76. IEEE (2013)
14. Huang, S., Huang, J., Dai, J., Xie, T., Huang, B.: The HiBench benchmark suite: characterization of the MapReduce-based data analysis. In: 2010 IEEE 26th International Conference on Data Engineering Workshops (ICDEW), pp. 41–51. IEEE (2010)
15. Gray, J.: Graysort benchmark. Sort Benchmark. http://sortbenchmark.org
16. Luo, C., et al.: CloudRank-D: benchmarking and ranking cloud computing systems for data processing applications. Front. Comput. Sci. **6**(4), 347–362 (2012)
17. Jia, Z., et al.: The implications of diverse applications and scalable data sets in benchmarking big data systems. In: Rabl, T., Poess, M., Baru, C., Jacobsen, H.-A. (eds.) WBDB -2012. LNCS, vol. 8163, pp. 44–59. Springer, Heidelberg (2014). https://doi.org/10.1007/978-3-642-53974-9_5
18. Baru, C., Bhandarkar, M., Nambiar, R., Poess, M., Rabl, T.: Benchmarking big data systems and the bigdata top100 list. Big Data **1**(1), 60–64 (2013)
19. Dede, E., Fadika, Z., Govindaraju, M., Ramakrishnan, L.: Benchmarking MapReduce implementations under different application scenarios. Future Gener. Comput. Syst. **36**, 389–399 (2014)
20. Ming, Z., et al.: BDGS: a scalable big data generator suite in big data benchmarking. arXiv preprint arXiv:1401.5465 (2014)
21. Pavlo, A., et al.: A comparison of approaches to large-scale data analysis. In: Special Interest Group on Management Of Data, pp. 165–178. ACM (2009)

22. Rizzelli, G., Maier, G., Quagliotti, M., Schiano, M., Pattavina, A.: Assessing the scalability of next-generation wavelength switched optical networks. J. Lightwave Technol. **32**(12), 2263–2270 (2014)
23. Badia, S., Martín, A.F., Principe, J.: Implementation and scalability analysis of balancing domain decomposition methods. Arch. Comput. Methods Eng. **20**(3), 239–262 (2013)
24. Gunther, N., Puglia, P., Tomasette, K.: Hadoop superlinear scalability. Queue **13**(5), 20 (2015)
25. Gao, J., Pattabhiraman, P., Bai, X., Tsai, W.T.: Saas performance and scalability evaluation in clouds. In: 2011 IEEE 6th International Symposium on Service Oriented System Engineering (SOSE), pp. 61–71. IEEE (2011)
26. Jiang, C., Han, G., Lin, J., Jia, G., Shi, W., Wan, J.: Characteristics of co-allocated online services and batch jobs in internet data centers: a case study from alibaba cloud. IEEE Access **7**, 22495–22508 (2019)
27. Jiang, C., et al.: Energy efficiency comparison of hypervisors. Sustain. Comput.: Inf. Syst. **22**, 311–321 (2019)
28. Jiang, C., et al.: Interdomain I/O optimization in virtualized sensor networks. Sensors **18**(12), 4395 (2018)
29. Qiu, Y., Jiang, C., Wang, Y., Ou, D., Li, Y., Wan, J.: Energy aware virtual machine scheduling in data centers. Energies **12**(4), 646 (2019)
30. Terasort. https://hadoop.apache.org/docs/current/api/org/apache/hadoop/examples/terasort/package-summary.html
31. WordCount. https://hadoop.apache.org/docs/current/hadoop-mapreduce-client/hadoop-mapreduce-client-core/MapReduceTutorial.html#Example:_WordCount_v1.0
32. OMalley, O.: Terabyte sort on apache Hadoop. Yahoo, pp. 1–3, May 2008. http://sortbenchmark.org/Yahoo-Hadoop.pdf

PAIE: A Personal Activity Intelligence Estimator in the Cloud

Yingjie Shi[1](✉), Fang Du[2], Yanyan Zhang[3], Zhi Li[4], and Tao Zhang[4]

[1] School of Information Engineering, Beijing Institute of Fashion Technology,
Beijing, China
20150015@bift.edu.cn
[2] School of Information Engineering, Ningxia University, Yinchuan, China
dfang@ruc.edu.cn
[3] Rural Development Institute, Chinese Academy of Social Sciences, Beijing, China
zhang_yy1900@163.com
[4] Internet Finance Department, Agricultural Bank of China, Beijing, China
{lizhi,zhangtaoo}@abchina.com

Abstract. Personal Activity Intelligence (PAI) is a recently proposed metric for physical activity tracking, which takes into account continuous heart rate and other physical parameters. PAI plays an important role to inform users of the risk of premature cardiovascular disease, and helps to promote physical activity. However, the PAI computing is too expensive to provide feedback in time, which restricts its practical value in disease warning. In this paper, we present PAIE, a Personal Activity Intelligence Estimator based on massive heart rate data in the cloud. PAIE provides approximate PAI with desired accuracy of statistical significance, which costs much less time than that used to provide the exact value. We design the PAI estimate framework in the cloud, and propose a novel estimate mechanism to leverage the efficiency and accuracy. We analyze the PAI algorithm, and formulate the statistical foundation that supports block-level stratified sampling, effective estimation of PAI and error bounding. We experimentally validate our techniques on Storm, and the results demonstrate that PAIE can provide promising physical activity estimate for massive heart rate data in the cloud.

Keywords: Personal Activity Intelligence · Cloud · Estimate · Storm

1 Introduction

Cardiovascular disease (CVD) is the leading cause of death in the world [4], and the corresponding studies have shown that high levels of moderate intensity physical activity (PA) is helpful to reduce the risk of cardiovascular disease mortality [8,9]. Moreover, it's a general belief that physical activity and exercise can enhance the quality of life and bring positive health outcomes, which is also proven by scientific evidences [17]. Nowadays, as people pay more and more attention to health, numberous devices and applications are designed to track

© Springer Nature Switzerland AG 2019
C. Zheng and J. Zhan (Eds.): Bench 2018, LNCS 11459, pp. 91–104, 2019.
https://doi.org/10.1007/978-3-030-32813-9_9

physical activity, which always take step number, walk distance or exercise time as the metric. However, the measurements based directly on these physiological variables can only detect the body's behaviour changing without reflecting the body's response to each activity. So they can not provide evidence-based recommendations nor risk of premature diseases. Monitoring a person's heart rate is suggested to track body's response as a predictor for future health, and the Nord-Trodelag Health (HUNT) study develops a new single metric called Personal Activity Intelligence (PAI) that can be integrated in self-assessment heart rate devices. PAI takes into account sex, age and continuous heart rate to reflect the body's response to PA, and it's an important tool to determine the sufficient amount of PA required to produce significant health benefit in an individual from the general population [12]. It is proven that PAI is closely associated with risk of cardiovascular disease mortality in all age-groups [22]. PAI has a huge potential to motivate people to become and stay active, what's more, it can be used to prevent or predict premature cardiovascular disease. However, the PAI algorithm may cost long time, on the one hand, it requires complex mathematical calculations with expensive computing resource, on the other hand, the continuous heart rate data gotten from monitoring devices can be huge. As a predictor of person's health, the PAI's practice value decreases as the running time increases. Since computing the precise PAI on massive data is expensive, getting the approximate PAI within a given error range of statistical significance is a more feasible solution.

Approximate query processing (AQP) is proposed and studied in the data management field to provide approximate results with desired accuracy. However, the PAI compute mechanism is different from query processing: the PAI computation conducts algebraic calculus on continuous heart rate data, while query processing executes relational operations on the tuples. So the techniques of AQP can not be used directly in PAI estimation. Motivated by the requirements and challenges, we propose and develop a system called PAIE to estimate PAI in the cloud. The main contributions of our work include:

1. We design the architecture for estimating PAI based on massive heart rate data in the cloud, which includes sampling phase and estimating phase. PAIE retrieves random sampling from distributed data, and provide progressive approximate answers with bounded error.
2. We analyze the PAI computing algorithm and the characteristics of collected heart rate data, and transform the definite integral into the sum of rectangle areas, then we model the PAI estimation into estimating the average of specified random variable.
3. We formulate a statistical framework to support PAI estimation in the cloud. We design a block-level stratified sampling method to make best use of transmitted sampling data, based on which we develop the estimation mechanisms to provide approximate results and bound the estimation error.
4. We implement PAIE on Storm and conduct comprehensive experiments, the results show PAIE's efficiency in PAI estimating, and we also verity it's scalability as both data volume and cluster scale increase.

The rest of the paper is organized as follows. In Sect. 2 we summarize the related work in physical activity tracking and approximate query processing. In Sect. 3 we introduce the main framework and workflow of PAIE. Section 4 discusses the problem modeling and statistical issues, which includes the sampling mechanism and PAI estimation algorithm. The implementing details of PAIE based on Storm is described in Sect. 5. The performance evaluation is given in Sect. 6, followed by the conclusions.

2   Related Work

It's widely recognized that physical activity is associated with enhanced health, and numerous studies have proven that physical activity is a mean of preventing chronic diseases and reducing the risk of all-cause mortality [7,10,17,20]. As people pay more and more attention to health associated with physical activity, many devices and applications are designed to tracking physical activity. According to [11], there are 23,490 and 17,756 applications in the Apple store and Google Play respectively categorized in the health and fitness section. Most of the applications track physiological variables such as step number, activity time, distance walked, heart rate changes and so on [16]. Though these applications are designed to guide people towards healthy lifestyle, the variables provided do not reflect the body's response to different activity, and they are not scientifically proven metrics that could inform users of physical activity needed to reduce the risk of chronic diseases or prevent the premature diseases. The HUNT study proposed a new single metric called Personal Activity Intelligence (PAI), which is computed comprehensively based on age, sex, and changing heart rate [12]. The PAI is proven to be closely associated with cardiovascular disease mortality risk, and can be used to offer individuals with recommended physical activity quantity and to predict cardiovascular disease risk [22]. However, the PAI algorithm is too expensive to provide realtime feedback, which limits its practical value in disease warning. Approximate query processing provides estimated results with bounded errors of statistical significance, which provides a more feasible solution.

Approximate query processing (AQP) is proposed in the database field [2], which guarantees results at interactive speeds during the data exploration process. The AQP technique preprocesses the original data, and construct auxiliary data structure for estimate, including wavelets [6], histograms [21], and sampling technique [18,19]. The above work is implemented on traditional database, BlinkDB provides approximate query results on very large data, and is implemented on Spark [14]. Though the AQP technique is well studied during the data management field, it can not be used directly to estimate the PAI metric, which is computed through complex mathematical calculation. We analyze the computing mechanism of PAI, and model the estimation into estimating the population average of specified random variable.

3   Overview of PAIE

PAIE estimates the PAI based on the changing heart rate data and provides the corresponding accuracy, which significantly reduce the time it takes to get the PAI value over large data sets. However, providing approximate PAI in the cloud requires to solve the following challenging problems. First, computing the PAI requires complex mathematical computing, the random variable and population should be carefully designed to guarantee the statistical significance. Secondly, the heart rate data distributed in the cloud should be sampled randomly to guarantee the estimation accuracy, and data in the cloud is always organized into blocks. Sampling on the tuple level is expensive on the block-organized data set, while sampling on block brings correlation into the estimation. We design a block-level stratified sampling mechanism to provide online random samples, which adapts to the data correlation of tuples in one block. Thirdly, the estimate error should be determined during the online processing, in order to verify whether the estimate result satisfies the desired accuracy.

In order to provide online feedback, we implement PAIE on Storm [1], which is a realtime processing system for big data flow. Figure 1 illustrates the workflow of PAIE, and the architecture includes two phases: sampling phase and online processing phase. The collected heart rate data is distributed on the cluster, and PAIE conducts random sampling on each node to generate one strata of the stratified sampling. The stratified sampling is put into a scheduling queue, and the data is then retrieved randomly from this queue to the Kafka spout, which manages the data into topics, and transfers the data to the online processing phase as a data pipeline. The KafkaReader of the online processing phase gets the data flow through subscribing the corresponding topic. There are three bolts in the Storm processing phase. The AlgebraComputer spans the sample data, computes the intensity score, and accumulates the corresponding variables of one block. The StatisticalComputer computes the estimated activity score and bounds the error of every user. The FinalReducer collects the estimate results of all the users, and show them at fixed time intervals. In order to decrease the compute cost and network data transmission, we design a spout called SignalSpout, which broadcasts timing signals to all the bolts to trigger the data emission.

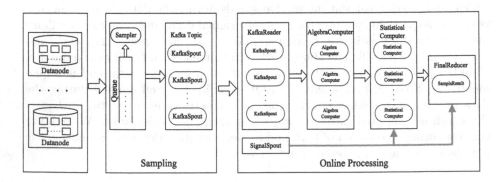

Fig. 1. Architecture of PAIE

4   Statistic Issues

In this section, we analyze the PAI computing algorithm and model the estimation into a statistical problem, based on which we discuss the statistical issues. First we introduce the computing mechanism of PAI.

4.1   PAI Computing Mechanism

The HUNT study invites 4,631 participants aged 20–74 as derivation cohort to construct the offset and decay level coefficients of the mathematical model to derive PAI, which is based on the comprehensive analysis including sex, age, body mass index, hypertension status, smoke status, physical activity habits, etc. [13]. They also invite 39,298 participants as the validation cohort to verify the PAI's efficiency on prevention of premature cardiovascular disease and promotion of physical activity. The PAI algorithm includes three steps. First, it computes the normalized intensity $\bar{y}(t)$ based on $y(t)$, which represents the heart rate value at time t:

$$\bar{y}(t) = \frac{y(t) - y_{th}}{y_{max} - y_{th}} \tag{1}$$

y_{max} is the maximum heart rate and y_{th} is the threshold of heart rate less than which the intensity does not contribute to increased cardiorespiratory fitness. Both y_{max} and y_{th} are different for various person categories of different sexes, ages, physical habits, etc. Then $\bar{y}(t)$ is further scaled with an exponential function containing two coefficients $c1$ and $c2$, which are derived based on the analysis of the derivation cohort:

$$z(t) = c_1(e^{c_2 y(t)} - 1) \tag{2}$$

$z(t)$ is referred to as the intensity score, then the activity score is calculated:

$$P = \int_{-T}^{0} z(t)dt \tag{3}$$

T is the time when the heart rate data begins to be gotten. Finally, a health-predictive activity score is calculated based on P and then scaled ranging from 0 for convenience and readability. The first two steps conduct direct algebraic calculus on each variable, and the third step requires integration on the variables during the time of interest. The third step costs most of the computation time, and the estimation of PAIE is conducted on this step.

4.2   Statistical Modeling

The heart rate data $y(t)$ is gotten at specific time interval, so the $z(t)$ function curve is like Fig. 2. According to the geometric definition of definite integral, the value of P is the area of the region of the xy-plane bounded by the graph of $z(t)$, the x-axis and the vertical lines of x = $-$T and x = 0. Set Δt to represent the time interval, $z(t_i)$ to represent the intensity score of the ith time interval, and set R to represent the number of heart rate records, then the activity score P can be modeled as the accumulation of all the rectangle areas:

$$P = \sum_{i=1}^{R} z(t_i) * \Delta t \tag{4}$$

We construct a random variable: $X_i = R * z(t_i) * \Delta t$, then the average of random variable X_i in the population μ is the exact activity score:

$$\mu = \frac{1}{R} \sum_{i=1}^{R} X_i \tag{5}$$

Consequently the problem of estimation can be transformed to estimating the average value of X_i over all the heart rate data.

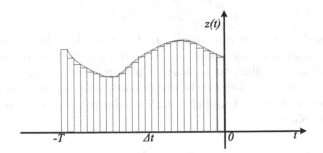

Fig. 2. Function curve of $z(t)$

4.3 PAI Estimating and Error Bounding

The approximate computation requires uniform sampling over the population, however, the record-level uniform sampling is very inefficient in the cloud. Recall that data in the cloud is organized into blocks, so retrieving n records under this organization may cause a full scan of n blocks in the worst case. Let $\tilde{\mu}_b$ and $\tilde{\mu}_r$ represent the estimated result on block-level uniform sampling and record-level sampling respectively. According to the analysis of [15], both $\tilde{\mu}_b$ and $\tilde{\mu}_r$ are unbiased estimates of μ, and $\tilde{\mu}_b$ provides more accurate estimate than $\tilde{\mu}_r$ under the same data transmission cost. PAIE adopts block-level uniform sampling from each node in the cluster, which constructs the stratified sample data from the population. The stratified sampler of PAIE retrieves blocks according to the data size on each node. Set N_i to represent the number of data blocks on the ith node, and set p to represent the sampling proportion on each node, then $N_i * p$ blocks are sampled on the ith node. Set N to represent the total number of blocks, and each block size is B.

We adopt $relative\_err$ to measure the accuracy of the estimated result, which is defined as: $relative\_err = \frac{|\tilde{\mu}_b - \mu|}{\tilde{\mu}_b}$. Let $z(B_i)$ represent the accumulation of intensity scores during the ith block. Based on the n blocks sampled from the cluster, we propose the unbiased estimation and error bounding method in Theorem 1:

Theorem 1. *Set σ^2 to represent the variance of sampled data, then $\tilde{\mu}_b = \frac{1}{n}\sum_{i=1}^{n} N * z(B_i) * \Delta t$ is the unbiased estimate of the activity score, and the bound of the error can be computed through:$err\_bound = \frac{z_p \sigma_n}{\sqrt{n}\tilde{\mu}_b}$.*

Proof. After the sampling phase, $N_i * p$ blocks are retrieved randomly from each node, and construct one strata of the stratified sampling. According to the stratified sampling property [3], the unbiased estimate of P on the sample data from c nodes can be computed as:

$$\tilde{\mu}_b = \sum_{k=1}^{c} \frac{N_k}{N} * \frac{1}{N_k pB} * \sum_{m=1}^{N_k p} \sum_{n=1}^{B} X_{mn}$$

$$= \frac{1}{Np} \sum_{k=1}^{c} \sum_{m=1}^{N_k p} \frac{1}{B} \sum_{n=1}^{B} X_{mn}$$

$$= \frac{1}{Np} \sum_{k=1}^{c} \sum_{m=1}^{N_k p} \frac{1}{B} \sum_{n=1}^{B} NB * z(t_{mn}) * \Delta t$$

$$= \frac{1}{n} \sum_{i=1}^{n} N * z(B_i) * \Delta t \tag{6}$$

According to Eq. 6, the final activity score can also be considered as the average of Θ_i, where $\Theta_i = N * z(B_i) * \Delta t$. The sampled blocks are retrieved in random order from each node, so the observations of Θ_i from each node are identical distributed and independent. According to the analysis based on CLT (Central Limit Theorem) of [5], the average of Θ_i obeys the normal distribution: $\tilde{\mu}_b \sim Normal(\mu, \sigma^2/n)$, during which μ is the average of the normal distribution, and it is also the actual activity score. The distribution can be standardized as: $Z = (\tilde{\mu}_b - \mu)/(\frac{\sigma}{n}) \sim Normal(0, 1)$. Given the confidence level p, we can get $P\{-z_p \le Z \le z_p\} = p$, where z_p is the p-quantile in the standard normal distribution. Then it can be derived as: $P\{\tilde{\mu}_b - z_p\sigma/\sqrt{n} \le \mu \le \tilde{\mu}_b + z_p\sigma/\sqrt{n}\} = p$. It means that with probability p, we have: $| \mu - \tilde{\mu}_b | \le z_p\sigma/\sqrt{n}$. In most cases, the variance of the population is not available, we adopt the variance on the sample data σ_n^2 to compute the err_bound, where $\sigma_n^2 = \frac{1}{n}\sum_{i=1}^{n}(\Theta_i - \tilde{\mu}_b)^2$. According to the property of stratified sampling, σ_n^2 is a consistent estimation of σ^2 [3].

Algorithm 1. AlgebraComputer Function

---
input : record r
output: text key, double z_sum, double z_quad
1 // key: user ID
2 // z_sum: accumulation of intensity score
3 //z_quad: accumulation of intensity score's square
4 $cols = r.split()$;
5 **if** $cols.length()!=1$ **then**
6 | $key.set(col[0])$;
7 | $y=(col[3]-y_{th})/(y_{max}-y_{th})$;
8 | $z=c_1(\text{Math.pow}(e,c_2y)-1)$;
9 | $z\_sum+=z$;
10 | $z\_quad+=z*z$;
11 **end**
12 **else**
13 | $collector.emit(key, z\_sum, z\_quad)$;
14 **end**

---

5   Implementing over Storm

Storm supports realtime computing through data stream in the cloud, so it supports online data processing naturally. PAIE is implemented on Storm to provide online estimate result and error bound at fixed time interval. When the estimate reaches the desired accuracy, the computing can be stopped. We designed two spouts and three bolts in the Storm processing topology, which is illustrated in Fig. 3. The KafkaReader reads the sampled data from the subscribed topic of Kafka, and then sends it to the AlgebraComputer with random grouping. The other spout called SignalSpout broadcasts signals to StatisticalComputer and FinalReducer at fixed time interval. The StatisticalComputer and FinalReducer only emit output results when getting the SignalSpout's signal. Before getting the signal, the StatisticalComputer only accumulates the intermediate statistical variables based on the received data. This mechanism is designed to reduce the data transmission cost in the network.

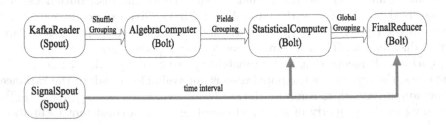

Fig. 3. Topology design on storm

Algorithm 2. StatisticalComputer Function

---

    input : text *key*, double list *zsum_list*, double list *zquad_list*
    output: double $\tilde{\mu}$, double *err*
1 // $\tilde{\mu}$: estimated result
2 // *err*: bounded error
3 //*n*: number of sampled blocks
4 //*sum$_l$*: sum of the intensity score of the last iteration
5 //*quadsum$_l$*: quadratic sum of the intensity score of the last iteration
6 **while** *zsum_list.hasNext()* **do**
7 | double *zsum* = *zsum_list*.getNext();
8 | double *zquad* = *zquad_list*.getNext();
9 | *sum* += *zsum*;
10 | *quadsum*+= *zquad*;
11 **end**
12 *sum=sum+sum$_l$*;
13 *quadsum=quadsum+quadsum$_l$*;
14 *variance* = *quadsum/n* - *sum* * *sum/n* * *n*;
15 μ = *sum**N*Δt/*n*;
16 *err* = z_p*N*Δt*sqrt(*variance*)/(sqrt(*n*)*μ);

The AlgebraComputer splits the received records, and conducts the algebra computing on the heart rate data to compute the intensity score, then it accumulates the intensity score and its square, and emits the key-value pairs to the next bolt. The implementation is illustrated in Agorithm1. If the record input is not the end of one data block, AlgebraComputer computes the intensity score according to Eqs. 1 and 2 (7–8). Then the intensity score and its square is summed with the other record's corresponding variables of the same block respectively (9–10). When all the records of one block are processed, Algebra-Computer emits the key-value pair, during which the key is set as the userID, and the value includes the intensity score's sum and its quadratic sum (13).

The outputs of AlgebraComputer are transmitted to StatisticalComputer through "fields grouping", which guarantees that the values of the same key are sent to the same bolt task. The StatisticalComputer function is designed as Algorithm 2 illustrates. The output pairs belonging to the same userID are sent to the same StatisticalComputer bolt task, which accumulates the intensity score and its square (6–11). The new intensity score's sum and square sum are then accumulated with the values of the last iteration (12–13), and then the variance of the samples are computed (14). At last, the estimated value and the bounded error are computed based on the statistical parameters (15–16). All the estimate results are sent to the FinalReducer in the manner of "global grouping", which shows the results of all the users at fixed time interval.

6   Performance Evaluation

In this section, we evaluate the performance of PAIE in terms of running time to get an estimate result with desired accuracy and the required sample size.

We compare PAIE's block-level stratified sampling with tuple-level sampling on different block sizes, and evaluate the scalability of PAIE on data size and cluster scale.

6.1   Experiment Methodology

Our experiment platform is a cluster of 11 nodes connected by a 1Gbit Ethernet switch. One node serves as the nimbus (master node), and the other nodes serve as the supervisors (worker nodes). Every node has a 3.3 GHz quad-core CPU and 4 GB of RAM, and the disk size of every node is 1 TB. The cluster coordination is Zookeeper 3.4.7, and the Storm version is 0.10.0. We set two workers on each supervisor of Storm. The parallel degree of KafkaReader, AlgebraComputer, and StatisticalComputer is configured to 15, and FinalReport's parallel degree is configured to 1.

We adopt two metrics to evaluate the performance: *avgRestime* and *sampling size*. AvgRestime is the average of time cost for different users to get the estimated result of desired accuracy, and *sampling size* is the number of records processed before getting the final estimate. We compare the performance of PAIE with TUPLE, which is an estimator adopting record-level sampling mechanism.

We monitor the heart rate changings of eight participants through wearable wristbands, and the participants' age ranges from 18 to 60. We also analyze their heart rate data during different stages, which include sedentary behavior, sleeping, physical activity of different intensities. Based on the collecting data and the analysis, we generate the experiment data sets of different scales by randomly choosing different stages for different persons. Each record of the data includes four columns: userID, date, time, heart rate. We set the confidence interval of bounding the error at 95%, and set the specified error at 0.05. The result updating interval is set to 5 s.

6.2   Performance Analysis

In the cloud data organization, the block size is set according to the data set scale. We evaluate the performance of PAIE and TUPLE on four kinds of block sizes: 5 MB, 10 MB, 20 MB and 40 MB. The total data size of the experiment is 200 GB. During our experiment data set, the records of the same hour are ordered by the user ID, so the data correlation is between random layout and the fully ordered layout. The sample size of PAIE is actually the number of blocks, in order to compare the two sampling mechanisms more directly, we show the number of records in the experiment results. As Fig. 4 illustrated, the PAIE required more samples than TUPLE, while its avgResTime is much shorter than TUPLE in general. The sample variance of PAIE is generally larger than that of TUPLE, so given the desired estimate accuracy, it requires more sampled records according to the error bounding theorem. However, during the sampling phase, TUPLE scans the total data block to retrieve some of records with uniform sampling. So it costs more time than the PAIE's sampling phase, which conducts block-level uniform sampling directly. What's more, during the online processing phase, the AlgebraComputer bolt of PAIE emits one output result each block. While TUPLE emits one output result each record on the corresponding bolt, which requires more data transmission and sends more computer burden on the following bolt.

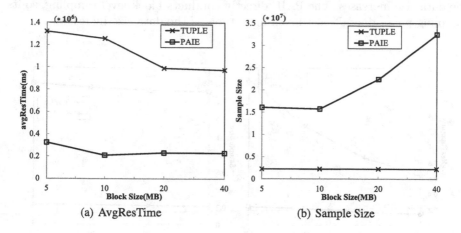

(a) AvgResTime   (b) Sample Size

Fig. 4. Performance on different block size

The block size doesn't affect the sample size of TUPLE because of its sampling level. Given the data set, larger data block results in less number of blocks. During the sampling phase of TUPLE, it requires less tasks to retrieve sampling records, and at the same time, each sampling task costs more time, so there is a tradeoff between the block size and avgResTime of TUPLE.

During the experiment data set, records according to one hour is stored in a file, whose size is about 10 MB. As a result, the data correlation during one block of 5 MB is larger than the other three block sizes, so it requires more sampling blocks for PAIE. When the block is larger than 10 MB, the data correlation decreases gradually as the block size increases, so the number of required sampling blocks of PAIE decreases correspondingly. As the block size increases, the time to process one block of the AlgebraComputer bolt gets longer, so there is also a tradeoff between the block size and avgResTime of PAIE. In our experiment results, PAIE gets the shortest avgResTime when the block size is 10 MB.

6.3   Scalability Evaluation

We evaluate the scalability from both data size and cluster scale on the data size of 200 GB, and we set the block size to 10 MB. Figure 5 illustrates the avgResTime and sampling size of the estimators on the 10-worker node cluster with different data sizes. As analyzed in Theorem 1, the bounded error is not affected directly by the data size, but associated with the variance and the sample size. During our experiment data set, the variance doesn't change a lot as the data size increases. So given the desired error, the sample size doesn't increase proportionally to the data size for neither PAIE nor TUPLE. Though the sample size changes little for TUPLE, its avgResTime increases as the data size increases. This is because that the sample phase of TUPLE has to access more blocks as the data size increases. The PAIE directly conducts block-level sampling, so its sampling phase doesn't cost much more time as the data size increases.

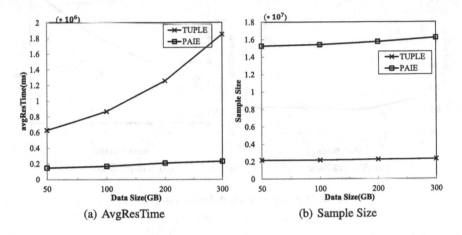

Fig. 5. Scale-up with data size

The scalability on cluster scale is evaluated by varying the number of workers. The cluster scale doesn't affect the sample size, so we only show the results of avgResTime in Figure 6. As the number of worker nodes increases, the running time decreases, and the speedup mainly originates from the distributed sampling phase and the online processing phase on Storm. Generally speaking, PAIE has scalability both on data size and cluster scale.

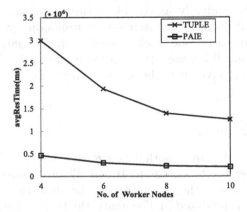

Fig. 6. Scale-up with cluster scale

7 Conclusions

As people's concern for health increases rapidly, to track the body's physical activity and reflect the health status timely have attracted more and more attentions. PAI is a recently proposed metric based on continuous heart rate and other physical parameters, and it is validated in the general HUNT population aged 20–74 that PAI helps to prevent cardiovascular disease and promote physical activity. However, the complex computing algorithm and huge continuous heart rate data affect its timeliness to flect the body's health status. In this paper, we propose a novel PAI estimator called PAIE, which focuses on estimating the PAI based on massive heart rate data in the cloud. Based on the analysis of PAI algorithm and characteristics of data organization in the cloud, we propose the stratified block-level sampling mechanism, and design the algorithm of PAI estimating and error bounding. The evaluation results of our technique on Storm show that PAIE can provide promising estimate on massive heart rate data in the cloud.

Acknowledgment. This research was supported by the grants from the Natural Science Foundation of China (No. 61502279), the General Program of Science and Technology Development Project of Beijing Municipal Education Commission (No. KM201710012008), the Special Funds for High-level Teacher's Building of Beijing Institute of Fashion Technology (No. BIFTQG201803), the Ningxia Natural Science Foundation (No. 2018A0899). We would like to thank Yadong You, Guangyao Guo, Yongpeng Sun and Tianchen Xiong from Beijing Institute of Fashion Technology, who gave much help in the experiment.

References

1. Apache storm (2018). http://storm.apache.org
2. Barbara, D., Dumouchel, W., Faloutsos, C., et al.: The New Jersey data reduction report. Data Eng. Bull. **20**(4), 3–45 (1997)
3. Cochran, W.G.: Sampling Techniques. Wiley, New York (1977)
4. GBD 2013 Mortality and Causes of Death Collaborators: Global, regional, and national agecsex specific all-cause and cause-specific mortality for 240 causes of death, 1990–2013: a systematic analysis for the global burden of disease study 2013. Lancet **385**(9963), 117–171 (2015)
5. Hellerstein, J.M., Haas, P.J., Wang, H.J.: Online aggregation. In: Proceedings of the SIGMOD 1997 Conference, pp. 171–182 (1997)
6. Kaushik, C., Minos, N., Rajeev, R., et al.: Approximate query processing using wavelets. Proc. VLDB Endow. **10**(2), 199–223 (2001)
7. Kruk, J.: Physical activity in the prevention of the most frequent chronic diseases: an analysis of the recent evidence. Asian Pac. J. Cancer Prevent. **8**, 325–338 (2007)
8. Lavie, C., Arenaand, R., Blair, S.: A call to increase physical activity across the globe in the 21st century. Future Cardiol. **12**, 605–607 (2016)
9. Lavie, C., Arenaand, R., Swift, D., et al.: Exercise and the cardiovascular system: clinical science and cardiovascular outcomes. Circ. Res. **117**, 207–219 (2015)

10. Lebrun, C.E.I., Van der Schouw, Y.T., De Jong, F.H., et al.: Relations between body composition, functional and hormonal parameters and quality of life in healthy postmenopausal women. Maturitas **55**, 82–92 (2006)
11. Middelweerd, A., Mollee, J.S., Natalie, C., et al.: Apps to promote physical activity among adults: a review and content analysis. Int. J. Behav. Nutr. Phys. Activ. **11**(1), 97 (2014)
12. Nes, B., Gutvik, C., Lavie, C., et al.: Personalized activity intelligence (PAI) for prevention of cardiovascular disease and promotion of physical activity. Am. J. Med. **130**(3), 328–336 (2017)
13. Nes, B., Janszky, I., Vatten, L., et al.: Estimating V.O2 peak from a nonexercise prediction model: the HUNT study, Norway. Med. Sci. Sports Exerc. **43**(11), 2024–2030 (2011)
14. Sameer, A., Barzan, M., Aurojit, P., et al.: BlinkDB: queries with bounded errors and bounded response times on very large data. In: Proceedings of the Eighth Eurosys Conference, pp. 29–42 (2013)
15. Shi, Y., Meng, X., Wang, F., Gan, Y.: HEDC++: an extended histogram estimator for data in the cloud. J. Comput. Sci. Technol. **28**(6), 973–988 (2013)
16. Silva, B.M., Rodrigues, J.J., et al.: Mobile-health: a review of current state in 2015. J. Biomed. Inform. **56**, 265–272 (2015)
17. Strohle, A.: Physical activity, exercise, depression and anxiety disorderss. J. Neural Transm. **116**(6), 777–784 (2009)
18. Surajit, C., Rajeev, M., Vivek, R.: On random sampling over joins. In: Proceedings of the 1999 ACM SIGMOD International Conference on Management of Data, pp. 263–274 (1999)
19. Swarup, A., Phillip, B., Viswanath, P.: Congressional samples for approximate answering of group-by queries. In: Proceedings of the 2000 ACM SIGMOD International Conference on Management of Data, pp. 487–498 (2000)
20. Wen, C.P., Wai, J.P.M., Tsai, M.K., et al.: Minimum amount of physical activity for reduced mortality and extended life expectancy: a prospective cohort study. Lancet **378**(9798), 1244–1253 (2011)
21. Yannis, E., Viswanath, P.: Histogram-based approximation of set-valued query-answers. In: Proceedings of 25th International Conference on Very Large Data Bases, pp. 174–185 (1999)
22. Zisko, N., Skjerve, K., Tari, A., et al.: Personal Activity intelligence (PAI), sedentary behavior and cardiovascular risk factor clustering-the HUNT study. Prog. Cardiovasc. Dis. **60**(1), 89–95 (2017)

DCMIX: Generating Mixed Workloads for the Cloud Data Center

Xingwang Xiong[1], Lei Wang[1], Wanling Gao[1], Rui Ren[1], Ke Liu[1],
Chen Zheng[1], Yu Wen[2], and Yi Liang[3(✉)]

[1] Institute of Computing Technology, Chinese Academy of Sciences, Beijing, China
{xiongxingwang,wanglei_2011,gaowanling,renrui,liuke19g,zhengchen}@ict.ac.cn
[2] Institute of Information Engineering, Chinese Academy of Sciences, Beijing, China
[3] College of Computer Science, Beijing University of Technology, Beijing, China
yliang@bjut.edu.cn

Abstract. To improve system resource utilization, consolidating multitenants' workloads on the common computing infrastructure is a popular way for the cloud data center. The typical deployment of the modern cloud data center is co-locating online services and offline analytics applications. However, the co-locating deployment inevitably brings workloads' competitions for system resources, such as the CPU and the memory resources. These competitions result in that the user experience (the request latency) of the online services cannot be guaranteed. More and more efforts try to assure the latency requirements of services as well as the system resource efficiency. Mixing the cloud workloads and quantifying resource competition is one of the prerequisites for solving the problem. We proposed a benchmark suite—DCMIX as the cloud mixed workloads, which covered multiple application fields and different latency requirements. Furthermore the mixture of workloads can be generated by specifying mixed execution sequence in the DCMIX. We also proposed the system entropy metric, which originated from some basic system level performance monitor metrics as the quantitative metric for the disturbance caused by system resource competition. Finally, compared with the Service-Standalone mode (only executing the online service workload), we found that 99th percentile latency of the service workload under the Mixed mode (workloads mix execution) increased 3.5 times, and the node resource utilization under that mode increased 10 times. This implied that mixed workloads can reflect the mixed deployment scene of cloud data center. Furthermore, the system entropy of mixed deployment mode was 4 times larger than that of the Service-Standalone mode, which implied that the system entropy can reflect the disturbance of the system resource competition. We also found that the isolation mechanism has some efforts for mixed workloads, especially the CPU-affinity mechanism.

Keywords: Cloud computing data centers · System entropy · Benchmark

C. Zheng and J. Zhan (Eds.): Bench 2018, LNCS 11459, pp. 105–117, 2019.
https://doi.org/10.1007/978-3-030-32813-9_10

1   Introduction

Today, more and more data centers are being used to provide cloud computing services, whatever the public cloud or the private cloud. To implement the economy of scale of cloud computing, consolidating more tenants' workloads is the basic idea [17]. Furthermore, the higher system resource utilization can bring more profits, so deploying diverse multi-tenant workloads on the same physical node is a popular way for the cloud data center. And typically, online services and offline analytics applications are co-located on shared resources [10]. However, the co-locating deployment inevitably brings workloads' competitions for system resources, such as CPU and memory resources within the same node. These competitions always result in high response latency of online service workload and further lead to poor user experience.

More and more previous work tries to assure the user experience as well as the system efficiency, such as Intel's Cache Allocation Technology [8], Linux Containers Technology [11], Labeled von Neumann Architecture [1], et al. Benchmarks measure the systems and architectures quantitatively, so the cloud data center benchmark is one of the prerequisites for solving the problem. There are two main challenges: first, the benchmark suite should reflect the application characteristic of cloud data center as well as the mixed execution pattern of cloud data center. Second, we need a metric to quantify the resource competition of mixed execution workloads.

In this paper, we propose DCMIX—a cloud data center benchmark suite covering multiple cloud application fields and the mixed workloads' execution mechanisms. DCMIX has 17 typical cloud data center workloads, which covered four typical application fields and the latencies of workloads range from microseconds to minutes. Furthermore, DCMIX can generate mixed execution sequence of workloads by the user customization, and it supports the mixture of serial execution and parallel execution. Then we propose system entropy as the joint entropy of system resource performance data, to reflect system resource competitions. We chose four system level metrics (CPU utilization, memory bandwidth, disk I/O bandwidth, and network I/O bandwidth) as the basic elements of the system entropy, and the system entropy is the joint entropy of them. The elements of the system entropy can easily get by monitoring the target node without third party application's participation, which is more suited for the public cloud scenes.

Finally, we conduct a series of experiments under five different modes on the X86 platform, which are Service-Standalone (only online services), Analytics-Standalone (only offline analytics applications), Mixed (workloads mix without any isolation setting), Mixed-Tied (workloads mix under the CPU-affinity setting), and Mixed-Docker (workloads mix under Linux containers). Compared with the Service-Standalone mode, we found that the latency of the service workload under the mixed mode increased 3.5 times, and the node resource utilization under that mode increased 10 times. Furthermore, the system entropy of the Mixed mode was 4 times larger than that of the Service-Standalone mode.

We also found that the isolation mechanisms have some efforts under the mixed mode, especially the CPU-affinity mechanism.

2 Related Work

Related work is summarized from two perspectives: cloud data center benchmarks and the system entropy.

For cloud data center benchmarks, we classify cloud data center benchmarks into two categories from the perspective of the co-locating deployment. The first one is generating multiple workloads individually, such as CALDA [12], Hibench [7], BigBench [5], BigDataBench 4.0 [4,16], TailBench [9], and Cloud-Suite [3]. These benchmarks don't consider the co-locating deployment, and they provide multiple typical cloud data center workloads. CALDA provides Cloud OLAP workloads; Hibench provides Hadoop/Spark data analytics workloads; TailBench provides diverse tail latency sensitive service workloads; CloudSuite and Bigdatabench provide multiple workloads of the data center; BigBench provides an end-to-end data center workload. The second one is mixed workloads. SWIM [2] and CloudMix [6] build a workload trace to describe the realistic workloads mixed by mining production trace, and then run synthetic operations according to the trace. However, how to generate real workloads on the basis of mixture is still an open question.

In the area of the system entropy, the information entropy, also called Shannon entropy, is often used to quantify the degree of uncertainty of which information is produced by a stochastic source of data. Google [13] applied entropy for the system monitor, which is used to assess the stability of the profiling and sampling. BDTune [14] applied the relative entropy, which is the relative value of performance metrics on different data center nodes, to troubleshoot anomalous nodes in the data center. How to quantify resource competition in the cloud data center is still an open question.

3 DCMIX

Figure 1 shows the framework of DCMIX, there are four main modules: Workloads, User interface, Mixed workloads generator, and Performance monitor. DCMIX contains two types of workloads: online services and data analytic workloads, and they are all deployed on the target system. User interface is the portal for user, and users can specify their workload mix requirements, including workloads and mixture patterns. Mixed workloads generator can generate online services' requests and submit data analytics jobs to the target system. Performance monitor can monitor the performance data of the target system, and the system entropy is calculated by these original monitor data.

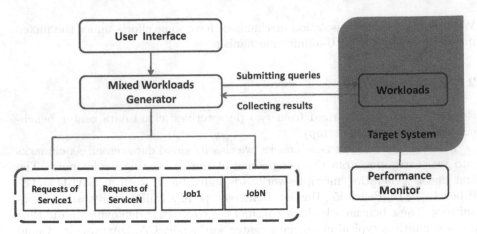

Fig. 1. The DCMIX framework

3.1 Workloads

DCMIX contains two types of workloads: online services and data analytic work-loads. As shown on Fig. 2, these workloads have different application fields and different user experience (latency). DCMIX's application fields are big data, artificial intelligence, high-performance computing, transaction processing databases, et al. The latencies of DCMIX workloads range from microseconds to minutes.

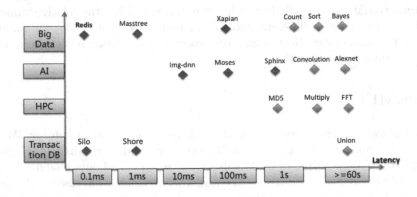

Fig. 2. The DCMIX workloads

The details of workloads are shown on Table 1. DCMIX Workloads are from two famous benchmark suites, which are Bigdatabench 4.0 [4,16] and TailBench [9].

Table 1. The DCMIX workloads

Workloads	Application type	Domain	Latency requirement
Count [16]	Offline analytics application	Big data	Larger than 10 s
Sort [16]	Offline analytics application	Big data	Larger than 10 s
Bayes [16]	Offline analytics application	Big data	Larger than 10 s
Convolution [16]	Offline analytics application	AI	Larger than 10 s
Alexnet [16]	Offline analytics application	AI	Larger than 10 s
MD5 [16]	Offline analytics application	HPC	Larger than 10 s
Multiply [16]	Offline analytics application	HPC	Larger than 10 s
FFT [16]	Offline analytics application	HPC	Larger than 10 s
Union [16]	Offline analytics application	Transaction DB	Larger than 10 s
Redis	Online service	Big data	Less than 0.1 ms
Xapian [9]	Online service	Big data	1–100 ms
Masstree [9]	Online service	Big data	1–10 ms
Img-dnn [9]	Online service	AI	1–20 ms
Moses [9]	Online service	AI	1–100 ms
Sphinx [9]	Online service	AI	1–10 s
Silo [9]	Online service	Transaction DB	Less than 0.1 ms
Shore [9]	Online service	Transaction DB	1–10 ms

3.2 Mixed Workload Generator

Mixed workloads generator can generate the mixed workloads through submitting queries (service requests queries and data analytics job submitting queries). Mixed workloads generator supports the mixture execution of serial execution and parallel execution. Serial execution means that the workload must start up after the previous workload complete. Parallel execution means that multiple workloads start up at the same time.

Moreover, in the workload generator configuration file, users can set request configurations for each workload. For online-services, we provided request intensity, number of requests, number of warmup requests, etc.; for offline-analytics, we provide path of the data set, threads number of jobs, etc. Table 2 lists the parameters in the workload generator configuration file.

4 System Entropy

System entropy is used to reflect system resource disturbances, i.e., the uncertainty associated with resources usage.

Although the concept of system entropy has been proposed [18], there is no formal definition and corresponding calculation method. In this section, we defined the concept of system entropy as the joint entropy S of system resource performance data, to reflect system resource competition. The definition of System Entropy is based on the Shannon entropy. Shannon entropy is often used to quantify the degree of uncertainty of which information is produced by a stochastic source of data. The measure of Shannon entropy associated with each

Table 2. Parameters in workload generator configuration

Parameter name	Description
WarmupReqs	For online services. The number of requests for warm-up
Reqs	For online services. The total number of requests (not include Warmup Reqs)
QPS	For online services. The average request rate, i.e., queries per second
ServerThreads	For online services. The number of server threads for processing requests
ClientThreads	For online services. The number of client threads for generating requests
ServerIP	For online services. The IP address of the server
ServerPort	For online services. The TCP/IP port used by the server
JobThreads	For offline analytics workloads. The number of threads for executing jobs
DataPath	For offline analytics workloads. The path of data set

possible data value is the negative logarithm of the probability mass function for the value [15].

We chose four architecture-independent system metrics, which are CPU utilization, memory bandwidth utilization, disk I/O utilization, and network I/O bandwidth utilization, as elements of the system entropy. And the system entropy is the sum of these four elements' entropies. In other words, we measure system uncertainty with variations of the four most common system resource utilization.

As shown in Formula 1, S is the variable of system entropy, S contains four elements. C is the CPU utilization, which is defined as the percentage of time that the CPU executing at the system or user level. M is the memory bandwidth utilization, which is the occupied memory bandwidth divided by the peak memory bandwidth. D is the disk I/O utilization, which is the occupied disk I/O bandwidth divided by the peak disk I/O bandwidth. N is the network I/O utilization, which is the occupied network I/O bandwidth divided by the peak network I/O bandwidth.

$$S = (C, M, D, N) \tag{1}$$

As shown in Formula 2, the entropy of S is the joint entropy of (C, M, D, N), and we assume that these elements are independent of each other, so the calculation of $H(S)$ is the sum of them.

$$H(S) = H(C) + H(M) + H(D) + H(N) \tag{2}$$

The principle of system entropy is according with the information entropy. According to the information entropy calculation formula given by Shannon, for any discrete random variable X, its information entropy is defined as Formula 3 [15].

$$H(X) = -\sum_{x \in X} p(x) * \log_2 p(x) \tag{3}$$

So, the entropy of each element can be obtained by Formula 3. And we take C as the example to describe the calculation of $p(x)$. As shown on Formula 4, $p(c)$ is the probability of C, the $Num(c)$ is the count of the value is c in the sample, and n is the total number of the sample.

$$p(c) = \frac{Num(c)}{n} \tag{4}$$

5   Experiment and Experimental Analysis

5.1   Experimental Configurations and Methodology

Experimental Configurations. We used two physical nodes for experiments, one is the target node (Server node) and the other is the workload generator node (Client node). The operating system of the Server node is Linux Ubuntu 16.04. The Server node is equipmented with Intel Xeon E5645 processor and 96GB memory. The detailed configurations are summarized in Table 3.

Table 3. The configuration of the server node

CPU	Intel(R) Xeon(R) E5645 2.40G
Memeory	96 GB DDR3 1333 MHz bandwidth: 8 GB/s
Network	Ethernet 1G bandwidth: 943 Mbits/s
Disk	SATA 1T bandwidth: 154.82 MB/s
OS	Ubuntu 16.04 and the kernel is 4.13.0-43-generic
GCC	4.3
Redis	4.2.5

We chose four workloads in the experiments, they are Redis (the online service workload), Sort (the offline analytics workload), Wordcount (the offline analytics workload), and MD5 (the offline analytics workload). Redis is a single thread in-memory database, which has been used in the cloud widely. Sort and Wordcount are multi-threaded big data workloads, which is implemented with OpenMP in our experiment. MD5 is a multi-threaded HPC workload, which is also implemented with OpenMP. Four workloads are deployed on the Server node. And we deployed the workload generator on the Client node. We generated the mixed workloads with the parallel execution mode, in which four workloads start up at the same time and run together. For the offline analytics workloads, we submitted jobs of Sort, Wordcount and MD5 with 8GB data scale. For the online service workload, the client request intensity of Redis is 50,000 requests per second, and follows the exponential distribution.

Experimental Methodology. We conduct the experiment under five different modes, which were Service-Standalone, Analytics-Standalone, Mixed, Mixed-Tied, and Mixed-Docker. For the Service-Standalone mode, we only run the Redis workload on the physical machine. For the Analytics-Standalone mode, we run all of offline workloads on the physical machine. For the Mixed mode, we co-located Redis and offline workloads on the physical machine without any isolation setting, but the total thread number is according with the total hardware thread number of the target platform. For the Mixed-Tied mode, we run Redis and offline workloads on separated cores through the CPU affinity setting. Different with the Mixed mode, we run Redis on one core, while run the other offline workloads on the other cores. For the Mixed-Docker mode, Redis and offline workloads were executed in two separate Docker containers (Redis run on one container, and offline workloads run on the other container).

Metrics. The evaluation metrics cover the spectrum of user-observed metrics, system level metrics, and micro-architectural metrics. As for user-observed metrics, we chose the average latency and the tail latency. In terms of system level metrics, we chose CPU utilization, memory bandwidth utilization, disk bandwidth utilization, and network I/O bandwidth utilization.

5.2   Experiment Results and Observations

The User-Observed Metric. Figure 3 shows the latency of Redis. From Fig. 3, we have the following observations:

First, the tail latency is severe, even in the Service-Standalone mode. In the Service-Standalone mode, we only run Redis (the single thread workload) on the multi-core node (Intel Xeon processor), the 99th latency (0.367 ms) is 2 times to the average latency (0.168 ms), and 99.9^{th} latency (0.419 ms) is 2.5 times to the average latency. This implied that the state-of-practice system architecture, i.e., CMP micro-architecture and time-sharing OS-architecture, would incur the high tail latency.

Second, mixed deployment without any isolation mechanism also incurs the high latency. In the Mixed mode, the average latency is 0.429 ms (2.6 times to the Service-Standalone mode) and 99.9^{th} latency is 16.962 ms (27 times to the Service-Standalone mode). Although, the thread number accords with the total hardware thread number of the target platform, the interfere of mixed deployment should incur the high latency of online services.

Third, the CPU affinity setting can relieve the competition. The average latency of Mixed-tied is 0.173 ms and 99.9^{th} latency is 1.371 ms. So in our condition, the CPU affinity setting can relieve the competition efficiently.

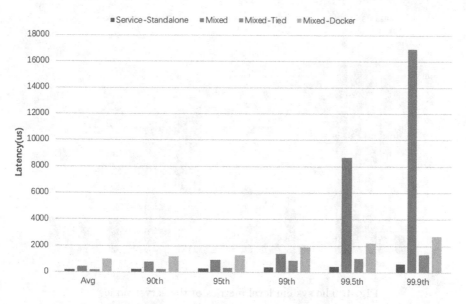

Fig. 3. The request latency of the redis

Fourth, the average latency of Mixed-Docker is 0.977 ms and 99.9^{th} latency is 2.75 ms. The container can relieve the tail latency, but make the average latency higher.

The System Level Metrics for the System. Figure 4 presents the resource utilization of server node. From Fig. 4, we find that mixed deployment can prompt the resource utilization. The CPU utilization of the Service-Standalone mode is only 4%, while the mixed deployment can achieve 46%–55%.

Figure 5 shows the system entropy of server node. From Fig. 5, we find that the system entropy of the Service-Standalone mode is only 5.9, while that of the Analytics-Standalone, the Mixed mode, the Mixed-Tied mode, and the Mixed-Docker mode are 20, 23, 22, 25 respectively. Furthermore, the system entropy of the Mixed-tied mode is the minimum among all of the mix modes.

The Architecture Level Metrics for the System. Figure 6 shows the micro-architecture metrics of server node. From Fig. 6, we find larger L1I cache misses and L2 cache misses under the Service-Standalone mode, smaller L1I cache misses and L2 cache misses under Analytics-Standalone mode, and that the micro-architecture metrics have minor variations among three mixed modes. In other words, the micro-architecture metrics can not reflect the disturbance caused by system resource competition.

Offline Analytics Application Execution Time. Figure 7 shows offline analytics application execution time under four different modes. From Fig. 7, we find

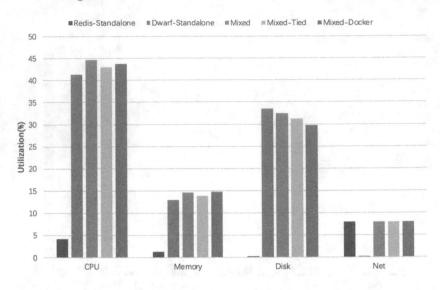

Fig. 4. The system level metrics of the server node

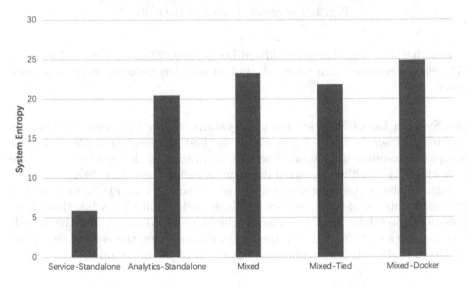

Fig. 5. The system entropy of the server node

that the execution time of Sort under the Analytics-Standalone mode is 495 s, and that under the Mixed mode, the Mixed-Tied mode, and the Mixed-Docker mode are 519 s, 534 s, 486 s respectively. Interference has less impact on offline analytics applications than that on the online services.

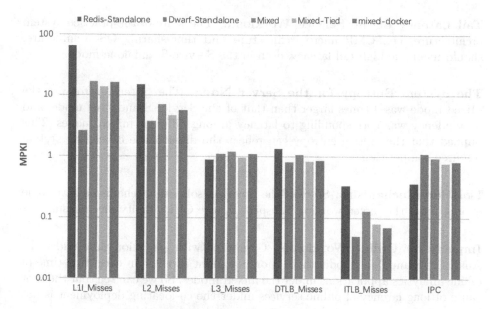

Fig. 6. The architecture metrics of the server node

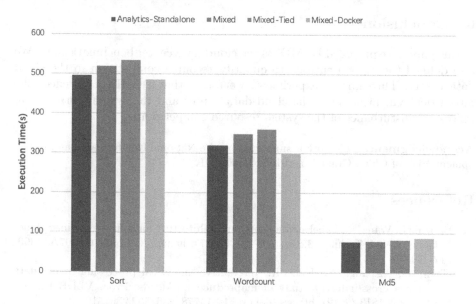

Fig. 7. Offline analytics application execution time

5.3   Summary

Mixed Workloads. Compared with the Service-Standalone mode, we found the latency of the service workload under the Mixed mode increased 3.5 times, and the node resource utilization under that increased 10 times. This implied that mixed workloads can reflect the mixed deployment scene.

Tail Latency of the Service Workload. The state-of-the-practice system architecture, i.e., CMP micro-architecture and time-sharing OS-architecture, should incur the high tail latency, even in the Service-Standalone mode.

The System Entropy for the Server Node. The system entropy of the Mixed mode was 4 times larger than that of the Service-Standalone mode, and its tendency was corresponding to latency among different mixed modes. This implied that the system entropy can reflect the disturbance caused by system resource competition.

Isolation Mechanisms. State-of-the-practice isolation mechanisms have some efforts under the mixed workloads, especially the CPU-affinity mechanism.

Impacts for Offline Workloads. Compared with execution time under the Analytics-Standalone mode, there is only a slight increase in execution time of offline analytics applications under the mixed modes. So we can see that the root cause of long latency of online services under the co-locating deployment is not insufficient resources, but the short-term disorder competitions.

6   Conclusion

In this paper, we proposed DCMIX as the cloud data center benchmark suite. We also defined the system entropy to quantify resource competition in the cloud data center. Through the experiment, we found that DCMIX can reflect the mixed deployment scene in the cloud data center and the system entropy can reflect the disturbance of the system resource competition.

Acknowledgment. This work is supported by the National Key Research and Development Plan of China Grant No. 2016YFB1000201.

References

1. Bao, Y.G., Wang, S.: Labeled von neumann architecture for software-defined cloud. J. Comput. Sci. Technol. **32**(2), 219–223 (2017). https://doi.org/10.1007/s11390-017-1716-0
2. Chen, Y., Alspaugh, S., Katz, R.: Interactive analytical processing in big data systems: a cross-industry study of mapreduce workloads. Proc. VLDB Endow. **5**(12), 1802–1813 (2012). https://doi.org/10.14778/2367502.2367519
3. Ferdman, M., et al.: Clearing the clouds: a study of emerging workloads on modern hardware, p. 18 (2011)
4. Gao, W., et al.: Bigdatabench: a scalable and unified big data and AI benchmark suite. Under review of IEEE Trans. Parallel Distrib. Syst. (2018)
5. Ghazal, A., et al.: Bigbench: towards an industry standard benchmark for big data analytics. In: Proceedings of the 2013 ACM SIGMOD International Conference on Management of Data, SIGMOD 2013, pp. 1197–1208. ACM, New York (2013). https://doi.org/10.1145/2463676.2463712

6. Han, R., Zong, Z., Zhang, F., Vazquez-Poletti, J.L., Jia, Z., Wang, L.: CloudMix: generating diverse and reducible workloads for cloud systems. In: 2017 IEEE 10th International Conference on Cloud Computing (CLOUD), pp. 496–503, June 2017. https://doi.org/10.1109/CLOUD.2017.123

7. Huang, S., Huang, J., Dai, J., Xie, T., Huang, B.: The hibench benchmark suite: characterization of the mapreduce-based data analysis. In: 2010 IEEE 26th International Conference on Data Engineering Workshops (ICDEW 2010), pp. 41–51, March 2010. https://doi.org/10.1109/ICDEW.2010.5452747

8. Intel Corporation: Improving Real-Time Performance by Utilizing Cache Allocation Technology, April 2015. http://www.intel.com/content/dam/www/public/us/en/documents/white-papers/cache-allocation-technology-white-paper.pdf

9. Kasture, H., Sanchez, D.: Tailbench: a benchmark suite and evaluation methodology for latency-critical applications. In: 2016 IEEE International Symposium on Workload Characterization (IISWC), pp. 1–10, September 2016. https://doi.org/10.1109/IISWC.2016.7581261

10. Liu, Q., Yu, Z.: The elasticity and plasticity in semi-containerized co-locating cloud workload: a view from alibaba trace. In: Proceedings of the ACM Symposium on Cloud Computing, SoCC 2018, pp. 347–360. ACM, New York (2018). https://doi.org/10.1145/3267809.3267830

11. Merkel, D.: Docker: lightweight Linux containers for consistent development and deployment. Linux J. **2014**(239), 2 (2014). http://dl.acm.org/citation.cfm?id=2600239.2600241

12. Pavlo, A., et al.: A comparison of approaches to large-scale data analysis. In: Proceedings of the 2009 ACM SIGMOD International Conference on Management of Data, SIGMOD 2909, pp. 165–178. ACM, New York (2009). https://doi.org/10.1145/1559845.1559865

13. Ren, G., Tune, E., Moseley, T., Shi, Y., Rus, S., Hundt, R.: Google-wide profiling: a continuous profiling infrastructure for data centers. IEEE Micro **30**(4), 65–79 (2010). https://doi.org/10.1109/MM.2010.68

14. Ren, R., Jia, Z., Wang, L., Zhan, J., Yi, T.: BDTUne: hierarchical correlation-based performance analysis and rule-based diagnosis for big data systems. In: 2016 IEEE International Conference on Big Data (Big Data), pp. 555–562, December 2016. https://doi.org/10.1109/BigData.2016.7840647

15. Shannon, C.E.: A mathematical theory of communication. Bell Syst. Tech. J. **27**(3), 379–423 (1948)

16. Wang, L., et al.: BigDataBench: a big data benchmark suite from internet services. In: 2014 IEEE 20th International Symposium on High Performance Computer Architecture (HPCA), pp. 488–499, February 2014. https://doi.org/10.1109/HPCA.2014.6835958

17. Zhang, Q., Cheng, L., Boutaba, R.: Cloud computing: state-of-the-art and research challenges. J. Internet Serv. Appl. **1**(1), 7–18 (2010). https://doi.org/10.1007/s13174-010-0007-6

18. Zhiwei, X., Chundian, L.: Low-entropy cloud computing systems. SCIENTIA SINICA Inform. **47**(9), 1149 (2017). https://doi.org/10.1360/N112017-00069. http://engine.scichina.com/publisher/ScienceChinaPress/journal/SCIENTIASINICAInformationis/47/9/10.1360/N112017-00069

Machine-Learning Based Spark and Hadoop Workload Classification Using Container Performance Patterns

Mikhail Genkin[✉], Frank Dehne, Pablo Navarro, and Siyu Zhou

School of Computer Science, Carleton University, Ottawa, Canada
michael.genkin@carleton.ca
https://carleton.ca/scs/

Abstract. Big data Hadoop and Spark applications are deployed on infrastructure managed by resource managers such as Apache YARN, Mesos, and Kubernetes, and run in constructs called containers. These applications often require extensive manual tuning to achieve acceptable levels of performance. While there have been several promising attempts to develop automatic tuning systems, none are currently robust enough to handle realistic workload conditions. Big data workload analysis research performed to date has focused mostly on system-level parameters, such as CPU and memory utilization, rather than higher-level container metrics. In this paper we present the first detailed experimental analysis of container performance metrics in Hadoop and Spark workloads. We demonstrate that big data workloads show unique patterns of container creation, completion, response-time and relative standard deviation of response-time. Based on these observations, we built a machine-learning-based workload classifier with a workload classification accuracy of 83% and a workload change detection accuracy of 74%. Our observed experimental results are an important step towards developing automatically tuned, fully autonomous cloud infrastructure for big data analytics.

Keywords: Big data cloud performance · On-line automatic tuning · YARN · Hadoop · Spark

1 Introduction

1.1 Background

Key big data technologies such as Hadoop map-reduce jobs, Spark applications, Hive, Hbase and others run on hardware clusters that are managed by open-source and commercial resource managers, such as YARN, Mesos, and Kubernetes. Resource managers arbitrate resources available to different applications, to form a key architectural layer in the cloud computing paradigm. Resource managers use constructs called *containers* to manage analytic and other applications running on the cluster. Containers manage, and gate, CPU memory and

© Springer Nature Switzerland AG 2019
C. Zheng and J. Zhan (Eds.): Bench 2018, LNCS 11459, pp. 118–130, 2019.
https://doi.org/10.1007/978-3-030-32813-9_11

disk resources assigned by the resource manager to the application. Containers make sure that a given application does not exceed it's allotted share of resources. Applications, and analytic frameworks, interact with the resource manager to schedule tasks to run in these containers. The way a container is implemented by the resource manager varies among resource managers. In some cases, such as in YARN, containers are explicitly defined data structures used by the resource manager for resource arbitration and internal book-keeping. In other cases, such as with Mesos, the resource manager uses an operating-system-level technology, such as Docker, to attach container semantics to it's internal resource arbitration mechanism. Regardless of how the container concept is implemented, the end result is essentially the same - application tasks run in containers, and thus examining container performance can provide insights into application performance.

1.2   Problem

Apache Hadoop and Spark each have dozens of configurable parameters that can significantly affect performance of analytic jobs. A poorly tuned configuration can result in order-of-magnitude slower performance than for an optimally-tuned one. Manual tuning involves experimenting with different combinations of tunable parameters. Considering that each experiment, at multi-Terabyte data scale, can take hours to days to run, this can turn into a very long and expensive procedure.

1.3   Limitations of Previous Approaches

To solve this problem, there have been a number of attempts to automatically tune big data applications [1,2,4–13]. These focused primarily on automatically tuning the Hadoop MapReduce framework. More recently there have been attempts to automatically tune Spark as well. In our previous work we developed KERMIT - the first on-line automatic tuning engine for YARN, capable of automatically tuning CPU and memory for both Apache Hadoop and Apache Spark [3]. KERMIT was able to demonstrate better tuning efficiency for standard Hadoop and Spark benchmarks.

Most studies demonstrated improvements only on small data sets that are not representative of data volumes in big data applications. Furthermore, performance improvements were only documented on very simple, single-user workloads based on a few sample applications. For real-life big data applications, systems such as Hadoop or Spark need to be dynamically tuned to handle large scale, big data workloads that arise from a multitude of applications and user requirements, and change over time. Such real-life scenarios are not addressed by any of the published automatic tuning approaches.

For on-line automatic tuning applications - "to tune or not to tune?" - is the key question that the tuning engine needs to be able to answer accurately in order to achieve optimal performance. Too much tuning causes an overhead that can sometime cancel out any performance benefit from optimizing tunable parameters. Not enough tuning results in jobs running slower due to sub-optimal tuning.

A number of researchers studied big data workload characteristics [4,6,9]. However, virtually all of these studies focused on lower-level operating system metrics such as CPU, memory and disk utilization, and even lower-level hardware counters such as L1, L2 and L3 cache hit rates. While these data provide important insights about the workload, it is difficult to relate them directly to Hadoop and Spark tunable parameters and develop a tuning strategy at the resource manager level. No published research to date has focused on container performance analysis. However, as discussed above, resource managers operate on and interact with *containers*. Optimizing performance of big data applications deployed on containerized cloud infrastructure requires optimizing the performance of the containers in which they run.

1.4 Our Contribution

We present the first experimental study of container performance patterns observed in Hadoop and Spark workloads. We focus on the following container performance metrics:

- container duration (response-time),
- container response-time relative standard deviation (RSD),
- container creation rate,
- container completion rate.

We demonstrate that for realistic big data workload sizes (e.g. 2 TB data sets) all important workload changes that are relevant for on-line automatic tuning are accompanied by:

- order of magnitude changes in container creation rate,
- statistically significant changes in RSD.

Our experiments demonstrate that the above metrics provide very clear statistical markers that can be used by automatic tuning systems to detect changes in workload characteristics and initialize local and global parameter searches. We also observed that many Hadoop MapReduce and Spark jobs have distinctive signatures that can be used by machine learning systems to identify jobs on the fly and apply effective tuning parameters.

Based on these observations, we built a machine-learning based workload classifier with a workload classification accuracy of 83% and a workload change detection accuracy of 74%. Our observed experimental results are an important step towards developing automatically tuned, fully autonomous cloud infrastructure for big data analytics.

1.5 Resource Managers and Containers

YARN, Mesos and Kubernetes are the most popular open-source resource managers used today. Resource managers arbitrate system resource such as CPU, memory and disk among different applications that run on a cluster. Resource managers use containers to assign and track resource allocations to different applications. In the context of this study the term container refers to a construct the resource manager uses to track resources allocated to an application. The container may be an abstract construct, or it may be backed by a technology such as Docker that enforces resource utilization at the operating system level and ensures isolation of one application from another. Most resource managers available today implement this container concept even though it is not called the container in all cases. YARN, Mesos and Kubernetes provide Docker integration.

2   Evaluation Methodology

Our evaluation methodology focused on simulating common Hadoop and Spark workloads and workload transitions using well-understood big data benchmarks. Container performance metrics were compiled by analyzing log data.

Before capturing container performance statistics for each workload transition experiment, runs were performed to establish the optimal sampling window length. The sampling window duration was chosen so that the majority of windows had a statistically valid number of containers recorded. For example, if all container creation and completion events were recorded during a single, very long, window then this would not make for a compelling analysis.

2.1   Container Performance Metrics

As part of our experiments, the following container performance metrics were collected and analyzed:

1. **Container Creation Rate.** This is the number of containers created during a given observation window.
2. **Container Completion Rate.** This is the number of containers that finish execution during a given observation window.
3. **Container Average Response-Time.** This is the average response-time calculated for all containers that complete execution during a given observation window.
4. **Container Response-Time Relative Standard Deviation (RSD).** This metric measures the degree of scatter among container response time measurements in a given observation window. It is defined as the standard deviation of container response-times, divided by the average container response-time for container response-times in a given observation window. Small RSD indicates tightly clustered data while large RSD indicates widely scattered data. Increase in the RSD value across a workload transition can indicate the introduction of a bottleneck due to a change in processing.

Our analysis focuses on calculating both the absolute values for container metrics at steady state, and the relative amount of change that occurs as the workload passes through each transition. The relative amount of change equals the average metric value observed in two observation windows after the transition, divided by the average metric value in the two windows immediately before the transition.

2.2   Workloads and Workload Transitions

Table 1 summarizes the different workloads and workload transitions analyzed in this study, with the benchmarks, data size, and procedure used in each case.

2.3   Parameter Settings

Unless stated otherwise, the Hadoop MapReduce and Spark configurations used default values. For YARN, the yarn.nodemanager.resource.cpu-vcores parameter in the yarn-site.xml file was set to the total number of CPUs shown by the operating system on each of the cluster nodes. The yarn.nodemanager.resource.memory-mb and yarn.scheduler.maximum-allocation-mb parameters were set to the total amount of memory on each data node. In mapred-site.xml, the parameter mapreduce.job.reduces was set to 36. The parameters mapreduce.output. fileoutputformat.compress and mapreduce.map.output.compress were set to true. The parameters mapreduce.output.fileoutputformat.compress.codec and mapreduce.map.output.compress.code were set to org.apache.hadoop.io.compress. Default in order to avoid running out of space in the HDFS during bigger runs. The parameter mapred.child.java.opts was modified to increase the maximum JVM heap size setting from the default to 850 MB. This was done to remove the possibility of a memory bottleneck impacting container performance. On the Spark side, the spark.executor.memory configuration parameter was set to 6G to ensure that most memory on our nodes was utilized.

2.4   Hardware and Software

All measurements were performed on a 8-node cluster comprising 1 management node and 7 compute/data nodes (all KVM virtual machines running on IBM S822L Power8 with Dual 10-core Power8 3.42 GHz; one bare metal server was used for every two VMs). Each node was equipped with a 100 GB SSD drive for operating system and Hadoop stack installation. All the nodes shared access to a 12 TB network shared drive connected through a 10Gb fiber switch. Each node was also equipped with 48 GB RAM and 10 virtual cores. All nodes were running the Ubuntu 16.04 ppc64le operating system. The test cluster topology is shown in Fig. 1. We used Hadoop 2.7.3 and Spark 2.1.1. In order to facilitate container metric collection, a jar file containing the YARN resource manager and our KERMIT library [3] was built and deployed to replace the standard YARN jar.

Table 1. Workloads, workload transitions, and benchmarks.

Transition	Description	Benchmarks, procedure and data size
Hd-sj-1	Transition from map to reduce processing in a single Hadoop map-reduce job	HiBench WordCount benchmark. 2 TB
Hd-sj-2	Transition from map to reduce processing in a single Hadoop map-reduce job	TeraSort benchmark. 2 TB
Hd-sj-3	Transition from reduce-shuffle to reduce processing in a single Hadoop map-reduce job	TeraSort. 2 TB
Hd-sufl-4	Transition from TeraGen to TeraSort processing in a Hadoop single-user job flow	TeraGen-TeraSort-TeraValidate sequence of jobs. 2 TB
Hd-sufl-5	Transition from TeraSort to TeraValidate processing in Hadoop single-user job flow	TeraGen-TeraSort-TeraValidate sequence of jobs. 2 TB
Hd-sj-6	Transition from one iteration to another within Hadoop K-Means machine learning job	HiBench K-Means. 2 TB
Hd-sufl-7	Transition from Hadoop WordCount reduce processing to TeraSort map processing in a single-user job flow	HiBench WordCount-TeraSort-K-Means job flow. 2 TB
Hd-sufl-8	Transition from TeraSort reduce processing to K-Means processing in a single-user job flow	HiBench WordCount-TeraSort-K-Means job flow. 2 TB
Hd-mufl-9	Multi-user transition from TeraSort shuffle to K-Means	2 users (1 running TeraSort, and 1 K-Means) 2 TB
Hd-mufl-10	Multi-user transition from K-Means iteration back to TeraSort reduce phase	2 users (1 running TeraSort, and 1 K-Means) 2 TB
Hd-mufl-11	Multi-user transition from TeraSort map phase to K-Means iteration	2 users (1 running TeraSort, and 1 K-Means) 2 TB
Hd-mufl-12	Multi-user transition from K-Means iteration to TeraSort map phase	2 users (1 running TeraSort, and 1 K-Means) 2 TB
Hd-mufl-13	Multi-user transition from TeraSort map phase to K-Means iteration	3 users (1 running TeraSort, and 2 K-Means) 2 TB
Hd-mufl-14	Multi-user transition from K-Means iteration to TeraSort reduce phase	3 users (1 running TeraSort, and 2 K-Means) 2 TB
Sp-sj-1	Transition from map() to reduceByKey() processing in a single Spark job	Spark ARL TeraSort. 2 TB
Sp-sufl-2	Transition from Spark K-Means processing to TPC-DS-inspired Q3	SMB-2 1 user, use case 2 (batch analytics) Spark job sequence. 2 GB per application
Sp-sufl-3	Transition from Spark TPC-DS-inspired Q3 to Q53	SMB-2 1 user, use case 2 (batch analytics) Spark job sequence. 2 GB per application
Sp-sufl-4	Transition from Spark TPC-DS-inspired Q53 to Q89	SMB-2 1 user, use case 2 (batch analytics) Spark job sequence. 2 GB per application
Sp-sufl-5	Transition from Spark TPC-DS-inspired Q89 to Q8	SMB-2 1 user, use case 2 (batch analytics) Spark job sequence. 2 GB per application
Sp-mufl-6	Transition from Spark single-user batch processing to multi-user (3 interactive users)	SMB-2 1 batch user + 3 interactive users, use case 3 (mixed analytics) Spark job sequence. 2 GB per application
Sp-mufl-7	Transition from Spark multi-user (3 interactive users) to single-user batch processing	SMB-2 1 batch user + 3 interactive users, use case 3 (mixed analytics) Spark job sequence. 2 GB per application
Sp-sufl-8	Initiation of Spark streaming	spark-perf benchmarking suite
Sp-sufl-9	Completion of Spark streaming	spark-perf benchmarking suite
Sp-sufl-10	Transition from Spark aggregateByKey to aggregateByKey(Int)	spark-perf benchmarking suite, data scale 3
Sp-sufl-11	Transition from Spark aggregateByKey to sortByKey()	spark-perf benchmarking suite, data scale 3
Sp-sufl-11	Transition from Spark count() to filter()	spark-perf benchmarking suite, data scale 3

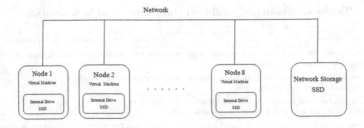

Fig. 1. Test-bed topology.

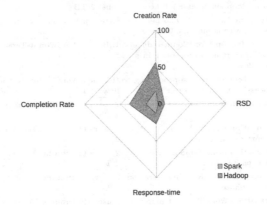

Fig. 2. Radar chart showing average Hadoop and Spark workload metric values.

3   Results

Below we present our workload analysis, workload classification and workload transition detection findings.

3.1   Steady State Workload Characteristics

Figure 2 shows a radar chart that compares container performance metric averages observed for Hadoop and Spark workloads. To construct this chart, a random sampling of observation windows for Hadoop and Spark observed during steady state conditions were selected for analysis. Container performance statistics, including maximum, minimum, average, and standard deviation were calculated for all metrics. Although averages are shown in Fig. 2, maximum values were also examined and found to show almost exactly the same trend as averages. For brevity, only averages are shown.

It was observed that for Hadoop workloads, average container metric values showed much greater range than for Spark workloads. Average container creation rate, container completion rate, container response-time and RSD were all observed to be about 3x greater for Hadoop than for Spark. There is an area on the radar chart where Hadoop and Spark workloads do overlap, but there is a much larger area where they do not overlap.

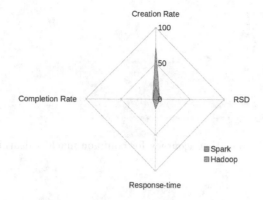

Fig. 3. Radar chart showing average Hadoop and Spark workload transition values.

3.2 Dynamic Workload Characteristics - Workload Transitions

Figure 3 shows a radar chart that compares container performance metric changes observed for Hadoop and Spark workloads. The change of a metric is defined as the average metric value observed after the workload transition divided by the average metric value observed before the workload transition. Figure 3 shows average changes observed for all transitions measured during this study. As for steady-state performance statistics, full statistics including maximum, minimum, average, and standard deviation were calculated and examined for all cases. Since maximum values were found to show almost exactly the same trend as averages, only averages are shown.

Hadoop workloads were observed to produce container creation rate changes and container response-time changes that were on average 3x greater than corresponding changes produced by Spark workloads. Changes in RSD and container completion rate were observed to show a similar trend. As with steady-state metrics, an area of overlap between Hadoop and Spark workloads can be observed in Fig. 3. However, we observe a larger area where workload transition metrics do not overlap.

4   Identifying and Classifying Workloads

A prototype classifier using several popular machine-learning algorithms was constructed. The prototype was developed in Scala, using Apache Spark Mlib to implement k-means, logistic regression, decision tree, gradient-boosted trees, and random forest algorithms. A machine learning data-set (in libsvm format) was compiled from workload transition data that were labeled as either Spark or Hadoop. The data set was randomly split into training and testing data sets using a 70-30 rule, and the accuracy of prediction for each algorithm was evaluated. The process of splitting, training and testing was repeated 100 times for each algorithm to study the variance produced by the random splits.

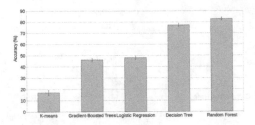

Fig. 4. Workload classification accuracy for common machine-learning algorithms.

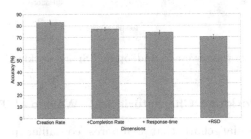

Fig. 5. Impact of using different container performance statistics on the classification accuracy of the Random Forrest algorithm.

The average classification accuracy (and standard deviation) for each algorithm is shown in Fig. 4. We observe that the Random Forest algorithm achieves the best workload classification accuracy of 83%.

To investigate how different container performance measures affect accuracy of prediction, several additional experiments were performed. The following data sets were prepared: (1) Container creation rate data only. (2) Container creation rate data plus container completion rate data. (3) Container creation rate data plus container completion rate data plus container response-time data. (4) Container creation rate data, plus container completion rate data, plus container response-time data, plus RSD data. The same random split procedure as described above was performed on each data set. The accuracy of classification was evaluated for the Random Forest algorithm. Results are shown in Fig. 5.

The findings are surprising. We observe that using container creation rate data alone resulted in the best classification accuracy. Adding data from other dimensions reduced rather than enhanced the classification accuracy.

5   Detecting Workload Transitions

Data collected for a typical Hadoop single-user job flow are shown in Fig. 6. This flow executes the following benchmark sequence back-to-back: WordCount-TeraSort-K-Means. Workload transitions are marked with vertical dashed lines and indicated in Fig. 6. The horizontal axis records the observation window number. The job flow is divided into a series of observation windows. Window number

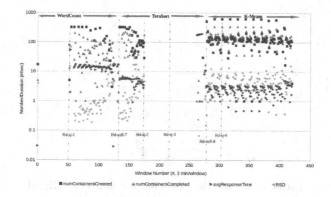

Fig. 6. Container performance metrics observed for Hadoop WordCount-TeraSort-K-Means job flow, using a 2 min observation window and 2 TB data size.

0 represents the very beginning for the entire job sequence. The duration of each window is fixed (set at the beginning of the job flow). The y-axis records the value of each container metric for a given observation window.

Figure 7 shows a multi-user Spark job flow. In this case a single-user thread was started. This thread executed the sequence of batch-type Spark jobs including a K-Means machine learning job and longer-running TPC-DS-inspired queries Q3, Q8, Q53 and Q89. After a delay of 600 s, 3 more user threads were started. Each of those user threads executed a sequence of 8 shorter TPC-DS-inspired queries running under a single Spark context. These queries were meant to simulate interactive drill-down operations initiated by a human analyst.

Container metric values measured during the course of a single observation window are shown as different symbols described in the figure legend. As we move right along the x-axis we can see drops and jumps in the patterns of symbols as we cross the workload transitions, represented by vertical dashed lines.

Observation window data collected for all data points were replayed as a real-time stream. A rolling average and standard deviation for each container metric were computed for 5 consecutive windows in the stream. During each computation, Welch's test was performed to evaluate whether a statistically meaningful difference existed between the means observed at current and previous steps. Welch's test was performed double-sided, using 95% confidence.

In those cases where a statistically meaningful difference was observed, our prototype code recorded the current observation window and noted a transition there. Transitions identified by the prototype were compared with transitions identified manually by examining YARN, MapReduce and Spark executor logs. Transition detection accuracy for each metric was calculated by dividing total transitions identified by the prototype by total transitions identified manually from logs and multiplying by 100. Results are shown in Fig. 8.

Surprisingly, workload change detection was observed to be the least accurate when using the container creation rate metric (18%), and the most accurate (74%) when using the RSD metric. Changes in nature of processing being per-

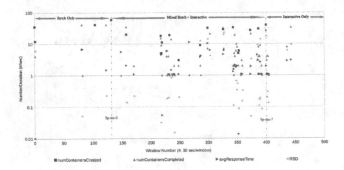

Fig. 7. Container performance metrics observed for multi-user Spark workload with batch and interactive query components, using a 30 sec observation window, 2 GB data.

formed by containers result in increased variance of the data. This is reflected in different RSD values before and after the transition even in those cases where changes in average container creation rate, container completion rate, and response-time are not statistically significant.

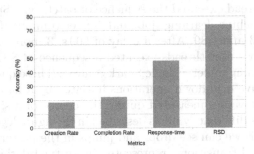

Fig. 8. Workload transition detection accuracy for different container performance metrics.

6 Relative Value and Importance of Container Performance Metrics

Based on our findings presented above, it is possible to propose a ranking of container performance metrics:

1. **Container Creation Rate.** This metric was observed to deliver the most accurate workload classification. It is possible to achieve very good classification results using this metric alone.
2. **Container Response-Time Relative Standard Deviation (RSD).** Although less effective than the first two metrics for both workload classification, RSD was observed to be very effective for detecting important workload transitions.

3. **Container Average Response-Time.** The average container response-time was observed to allow reasonably accurate identification of workload transitions.
4. **Container Completion Rate.** Container completion rate was observed to be less useful than the first three metrics for both workload classification and workload transition detection.

7 Conclusion

In this paper we presented a new way of capturing and analyzing workload characteristics of Spark and Hadoop workloads. We demonstrated that is possible to identify and classify big data analytic workloads with high degree of accuracy using their container performance characteristics. We also demonstrated that it is possible to use container performance metrics to accurately identify important workload transitions.

The most useful metrics were found to be the container creation rate and RSD. Using these metrics, it was possible to accurately distinguish Hadoop and Spark workloads, and identify important workload transitions. Based on these observations, we built a machine-learning based workload classifier and transition monitor with a workload classification accuracy of 83% and a workload change detection accuracy of 74%.

Our observed experimental results are an important step towards developing automatically tuned, fully autonomous cloud infrastructure for big data analytics. The next generation of on-line automatic tuning systems can leverage our findings to develop tuning approaches that are more fine-grained than tuning end-to-end performance of a job. Resource managers and analytic frameworks can begin to move away from exposing large numbers of tuneable parameters, and instead focus on implementing intelligent automatic tuners.

References

1. Awan, A.J., Brorsson, M., Vlassov, V., Ayguade, E.: Micro-architectural characterization of apache spark on batch and stream processing workloads. In: 2016 IEEE International Conferences on Big Data and Cloud Computing (BDCloud), Social Computing and Networking (SocialCom), Sustainable Computing and Communications (SustainCom) (BDCloud-SocialCom-SustainCom), pp. 59–66. IEEE (2016)
2. Ding, X., Liu, Y., Qian, D.: JellyFish: Online performance tuning with adaptive configuration and elastic container in Hadoop yarn. In: 2015 IEEE 21st International Conference on Parallel and Distributed Systems (ICPADS), pp. 831–836. IEEE (2015)
3. Genkin, M., Dehne, F., Pospelova, M., Chen, Y., Navarro, P.: Automatic, on-line tuning of yarn container memory and cpu parameters. In: 2016 IEEE 18th International Conference on High Performance Computing and Communications; IEEE 14th International Conference on Smart City; IEEE 2nd International Conference on Data Science and Systems, pp. 317–324. IEEE (2016)

4. Huang, S., Huang, J., Dai, J., Xie, T., Huang, B.: The HiBench benchmark suite: characterization of the mapreduce-based data analysis. In: 2010 IEEE 26th International Conference on Data Engineering Workshops (ICDEW), pp. 41–51. IEEE (2010)
5. Jia, Z., et al.: Auto-tuning spark big data workloads on POWER8: prediction-based dynamic SMT threading. In: Proceedings of the 2016 International Conference on Parallel Architectures and Compilation, pp. 387–400. ACM (2016)
6. Jia, Z., et al.: Characterizing and subsetting big data workloads. In: 2014 IEEE International Symposium on Workload Characterization (IISWC), pp. 191–201. IEEE (2014)
7. Mishra, A.K., Hellerstein, J.L., Cirne, W., Das, C.R.: Towards characterizing cloud backend workloads: insights from google compute clusters. ACM SIGMETRICS Perform. Eval. Rev. **37**(4), 34–41 (2010)
8. Moreno, I.S., Garraghan, P., Townend, P., Xu, J.: An approach for characterizing workloads in google cloud to derive realistic resource utilization models. In: 2013 IEEE 7th International Symposium on Service Oriented System Engineering (SOSE), pp. 49–60. IEEE (2013)
9. Mulia, W.D., Sehgal, N., Sohoni, S., Acken, J.M., Stanberry, C.L., Fritz, D.J.: Cloud workload characterization. IETE Tech. Rev. **30**(5), 382–397 (2013)
10. Wang, G., Xu, J., He, B.: A novel method for tuning configuration parameters of spark based on machine learning. In: 2016 IEEE 18th International Conference on High Performance Computing and Communications; IEEE 14th International Conference on Smart City; IEEE 2nd International Conference on Data Science and Systems (HPCC/SmartCity/DSS), pp. 586–593. IEEE (2016)
11. Wang, K., Tan, B., Shi, J., Yang, B.: Automatic task slots assignment in Hadoop MapReduce. In: Proceedings of the 1st Workshop on Architectures and Systems for Big Data, pp. 24–29. ACM (2011)
12. Wasi-Ur-Rahman, M., Islam, N.S., Lu, X., Shankar, D., Panda, D.K.: MR-advisor: a comprehensive tuning tool for advising HPC users to accelerate mapreduce applications on supercomputers. In: 2016 28th International Symposium on Computer Architecture and High Performance Computing (SBAC-PAD), pp. 198–205. IEEE (2016)
13. Zhang, R., Li, M., Hildebrand, D.: Finding the big data sweet spot: towards automatically recommending configurations for Hadoop clusters on docker containers. In: 2015 IEEE International Conference on Cloud Engineering (IC2E), pp. 365–368. IEEE (2015)

Testing Raft-Replicated Database Systems

Guohao Ding[1], Weining Qian[1(✉)], Peng Cai[1], Tianze Pang[2], and Qiong Zhao[2]

[1] East China Normal University, Shanghai, China
guohaoding@stu.ecnu.edu.cn, {wnqian,pcai}@dase.ecnu.edu.cn
[2] Bank of Communications, Shanghai, China
{pangtz,qiongzhao}@bankcomm.com

Abstract. The replication technique based on Raft protocol is essential in modern distributed and highly-available database systems. Although Raft is a protocol easy to understand and implement, testing a Raft-replicated database system is still a challenging task due to multiple sources of nondeterminism. Conventional testing techniques, such as unit, integration and stress testing, are ineffective in preventing serious but subtle bugs from reaching production. This paper first introduces evaluation metrics after the abstraction of general Raft-replicated database systems. These metrics are defined from several aspects including correctness, performance, and scalability. Then, we present test dimensions for the design of test cases, which contain various fault types, different workloads and system configurations. Finally, we describe test results of Raft-replicated open source database system.

Keywords: Raft · Distributed database · Test

1 Introduction

In recent years, the amount of data created by human activities goes far beyond the storage and processing power of a single computer. In order to process massive amounts of data, distributed systems, especially distributed database systems, are becoming more and more popular. It serves millions of users in many important applications. However, distributed database systems are notoriously hard to design, implement and test because they introduce more variables into a design than a single machine does, making the root cause of an application problem much harder to discover.

Developers of distributed systems use many testing techniques, such as unit testing, integration testing, stress testing, and fault injection. In spite of extensive use of these testing methods, many bugs that arise from subtle combinations of concurrency and failure events that are missed during testing and get exposed only in production. According to the interview [4], many technical leaders and senior managers in famous companies, such as Microsoft, Amazon and Google, have the consensus that one of the most critical problems today is how

© Springer Nature Switzerland AG 2019
C. Zheng and J. Zhan (Eds.): Bench 2018, LNCS 11459, pp. 131–144, 2019.
https://doi.org/10.1007/978-3-030-32813-9_12

to improve testing coverage so that bugs can be uncovered during testing and not in production.

Distributed consensus is a fundamental problem in distributed system. As we all know, Paxos [8,9] is an important algorithm for solving distributed consensus problems, proposed by Lamport in 1998, but over the years, few people can really understand Paxos algorithm. Therefore, in order to let more people understand the distributed consensus algorithm and also provide a better foundation for building practical systems, Ongaro and Ousterhout proposed Raft [12] protocol, which can be used as an alternative to the Paxos protocol. According to the official website of the Raft protocol, there are currently over 50 different implementations of Raft listed on their website. For a distributed system using the Raft protocol, the correctness of the Raft implementation is critical, and we must have a rigorous test. The amount of code used for testing should be higher than the implementation Raft itself, which can be used as a reference for open source implementation selection. The correctness of the Raft algorithm is theoretically proven (specific reference paper [12]). That is to say, it is correct as long as the algorithm is implemented correctly. But there is no uniform standard on how to test the correctness of such systems, what metrics are needed to be tested and how to design test cases.

In this paper, we define some evaluation metrics for testing distributed database system based on the Raft protocol and propose how to design test cases from different test dimensions. This further provides a reference for distributed system developers and testers to verify the correctness of the Raft-based distributed system.

To the best of our knowledge, we are the first to systematically propose test metrics and test dimensions of distributed database system based on Raft protocol, and design hundreds of test cases to test the Raft-replicated database systems in the actual production environment.

To summarize, our contributions are as follows:

- Abstract a general distributed database system model based on Raft protocol.
- Define the evaluation metrics for testing such system based on the Raft protocol and explain why these metrics are important.
- Describe the test dimensions and design hundreds of test cases to test Raft-replicated open source database system in the actual production environment.

The remaining of this paper is organized as follows. Section 2 introduces the background of replicated state machine problem and Raft. Section 3 gives a Raft-based system model abstraction. Section 4 defines the evaluation metrics for testing. Section 5 describes the different test dimensions. Section 6 evaluates the performance of the Raft we implemented in the system. Section 7 presents related work.

2   Background

This section first introduces the replicated state machine problem and then gives an overview of basic Raft [12] protocol.

2.1   Replicated State Machines

Consensus protocols generally appear in the context of a replicated state machine [14]. In a distributed environment, a group of machines (at least 3) execute the same sequence of instructions, so that each machine finally has the same state. When a machine fails, the system can continue to provide services as long as most of the machines can work normally and communicate with each other. However, how to ensure that the machines in this group have the same state, a direct way is to ensure that the same sequence of instructions is executed by machines in this group. In order to have each machine execute the same sequence of instructions, we write each command to log file. When the master server (we specify one of the servers as the master and the others as the slave servers) accepts the instructions from the client, it first records this command in its log, then sends the corresponding command to all other servers. When most of the servers receive the log and respond to the master, the master can submit the command (that is to say, the command is executed) after receiving the response from most of the slaves. The slave server executes these commands asynchronously to maintain the same state as the master. The consensus algorithm is to ensure that the same sequence of instructions is recored in the logs on each server under various abnormal conditions, such as machine fails, network failure, etc. Thus, the whole system looks like a server, so clients can get consistent results no matter which server is requested.

2.2   Raft Overview

Raft is a distributed consensus protocol that is mainly used to manage the consistency between replicated log. In order to make the consensus protocol easy to understand, the Raft protocol separates the key elements of consensus into three main parts: leader election, log replication, and safety.

Leader Election. A Raft cluster consists of a set of servers, the cluster can provide services as long as a majority of servers are working. Five servers are typical in a Raft cluster, which allows the system to tolerate two failures. The Raft protocol classifies server states into three types: *leader, follower, and candidate.*

- **Leader:** An active node which is currently leading the cluster, this node handles requests from clients to interact with the replicated state machine.
- **Follower:** A passive node which only responds to requests from the leader and candidates and will not initiate any communications.
- **Candidate:** An active node which is attempting to become a Leader. If the node finds that there is no available leader, it can transfer from follower state to candidate state.

Each server is only in one of the above three states at any given time. Under normal circumstances, there is only one leader and all other servers are followers in a Raft cluster, and candidates only appear in the process of election. In the

Raft protocol, the concept of the leader is strengthened, and all requests are required to go through the leader, then the leader copies logs to all other servers.

A new leader is elected when the existing leader fails or when you start your cluster. The Raft protocol divides the time into small consecutive periods, called terms. Each of them has own ID which is a natural number and increases monotonically. At the beginning of a term, participants determine a leader of this term. Then, the leader executes the log replication. The following three situations may occur in each leader election:

- One of the candidates receives votes from majority of servers and becomes the new leader.
- Candidates discover the new leader and convert its own state to follower.
- No leader is elected, then candidates restart a new leader election after waiting for a random time.

Log Replication. When a leader is elected in the Raft cluster, then it can receive requests from clients and all requests must pass through the leader. If the request is sent to the follower, the follower forwards the request to the leader. Each request contains a command to be executed by the replicated state machines. Leader first appends the command as a log entry to the local log and then replicates the log to all other servers by sending an RPC request. If the leader receives a response from majority servers, it regards the log can be submitted safety, that is to say, the command can be applied to the replicated state machine. If some of the servers are down or the network fails, the leader will continue to send RPC requests until the log entry is finally stored by all servers.

Safety. Through the previous leader election and log replication, Raft works fine in most cases, but in some cases it is impossible to guarantee safety. There is no guarantee that the state machines on each server will execute the same sequence of instructions in the same order. In order to achieve security, Raft adds the following constraints:

- The elected leader must contain all the log entries that have been committed.
- The leader commits log entries by counting replicas only for the current term.

3   System Model

We abstract a distributed database state machine system model as the basis for defining our goals, and we believe this model is general enough to capture the behaviors of many practical systems.

A distributed database system usually consists of different types of nodes and each node type is designed to perform a specific set of things. We believe this design separates concerns and simplifies the complexity of the overall system. Therefore, we abstract our distributed database system architecture model into

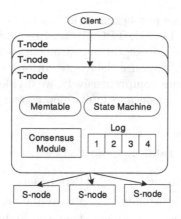

Fig. 1. System model

two basic types of nodes: Transaction-node (abbreviated as T-node) and Storage-node (abbreviated as S-node). As shown in Fig. 1, there are three T-nodes and three S-nodes. Each type of node supports scalability, and we usually deploy different types of nodes on different servers (but can also be deployed on the same server).

- **T-node:** This node is mainly responsible for the transaction processing of the distributed database system, similar to most distributed clusters, one of which is the leader T-node, which receives read and write requests from clients. All T-nodes consist of four parts: the replicated state machine, the consensus module, the memory table (Memtable), and the log. For read and write operations, the leader T-node first records the operation in the log, and then the consensus module sends the corresponding command log to all other T-nodes. If the leader T-node receives response from most of the other T-nodes, it can consider the modified log can be submitted safely. The T-node applies the commands in the log to the replicated state machine, and the replicated state machine updates the data in the memory table. The memory table here is actually a memory index structure which is persisted to disk either periodically or after some maximum limit is reached, and eventually the data on the disk will be merged into the Storage-nodes.
- **S-node:** This node is mainly used to store data of the table and provides read service. Data can be stored in chunks and these data are usually immutable. S-nodes follow a shared-nothing architecture and there is no single point of contention among the nodes. The nodes have no knowledge of one another and are operationally simple, and they only know how to load, drop, and serve immutable chunks.

4   Evaluation Metrics

Evaluation metrics are an essential part of any test benchmark definition and may be the most controversial when trying to reach agreements between different vendors. There are some test benchmarks from different perspectives to test database system, such as TPC-H, TPC-C, etc. However these test benchmarks are usually focused on a certain aspect of test metrics according to the workload type, such as throughput, response delay, etc. In order to test Raft-replicated distributed database systems comprehensively, we divided the tests into correctness test (namely basic function and fault-tolerant test) and performance test. As is shown in Table 1.

Table 1. Evaluation metrics

	Correctness	Performance
Test metrics	Availability	Recovery time, Throughput
	Data consistency	Lantency, Stability

4.1 Correctness

Correctness testing can also be understood as functional and fault-tolerant testing, which is mainly used to test whether the different parts of the system meet the functional requirements of the design. Correctness testing is the most basic test for both centralized and distributed software systems, but it is often overlooked. The correctness test is required to verify whether the system is operating normally in accordance with the expected design under normal and fault conditions. Here we divide the test metrics of correctness into two categories: availability and data consistency.

Availability. Availability refers to whether all nodes or some nodes in the system can continue to serve upper-layer services when a node or link failure occurs. For the sake of discussion, we only consider link failure (also known as network partition). Node failure can be regarded as a special network partition (the failure node is separated from the user in addition to being separated from the rest of the nodes).

When a network partition occurs, as long as there is a majority in a partition, then the whole system can still provides services. Service-level high availability does not require all nodes to be available after the failure, but it is required that some nodes are available, and the process of switching to an available node is fully automated, so the service is not interrupted or only for a short period of time.

Data Consistency. In a distributed system, in order to deal with possible failures, the system holds multiple replicas of each data and stores them on different nodes. When a node fails, the system can migrate the service to other nodes. In all replicas, there is usually one primary replica, the update operation will be performed on the primary replica firstly, and then synchronized to other backup replicas. The essence of Raft protocol is to guarantee the consistency between different data replicas, so the data consistency between replicas is an important test metrics.

4.2 Performance

The Raft performance metrics are similar to other consensus algorithms, where high availability is an important performance metric for distributed database based on Raft. One way to evaluate high availability is to test the system's non-service time in the event of a failure. For database, we often use throughput and response latency as an important metric. The stability can also directly affects the throughput of the system and the response time that users care about, so it is also an important part of the performance test.

Recovery Time. The recovery time refers to the time interval from the system can not provide external service to normal service when the system encounters a failure, and it is an important metric to evaluate the availability of the system. In a distributed system, we need to deal with various exceptions, such as node crash, network partition. When the system fails, the system may not be able to provide services for a period of time. In order to improve system availability, we need to minimize system non-service time. Because all requests are sent to the leader in Raft-replicated database systems, the system can not be able to provide services if the leader is down. Therefore, the leader election timeout is a key factor in determining the recovery time. In addition, some leader switching and initialization operations are required before the new elected leader can provide services, so we define the recovery time equal to the election timeout plus the time of the leader switching and the initialization.

Throughput. The throughput of the system refers to the number of requests that can be processed in a certain period of time, which is usually measured by the number of read operations per second (QPS, query per second) or the number of write operations (TPS, transaction per second).

Latency. The system's response latency is the elapsed time from the time a request is sent until the response is received. It is usually measured by the average latency or the request latency of 99.9% or more. The response latency and throughput of the system are often contradictory, and it is often difficult to achieve extremely low latency in systems that pursue high throughput. The throughput is limited in systems that pursue low latency. Therefore, there is a trade-off between these two metrics when we design a system.

Stability. System stability can also be called system reliability. The standard definition of reliability is "the ability of a system or component to perform its required functions under stated conditions for a specified period of time" [2]. There are many factors that could affect the ability of a system to function as expected, such as unpredictable hardware faults or even natural disasters. However, most software failures are caused by programming errors, which introduce unintentional behaviour during program execution. Ensuring the absence of bugs is a prerequisite for building systems that execute reliably.

At present, there is no definite test metric for database stability. In this paper, we define a stability metric model based on TPS fluctuations. In order to evaluate system stability, we simulate the user's workload and let the system run for a period of time. The changes of system's TPS are recorded during this period. Finally, we put the test results into a stability model to see if the system meets the requirement of stability.

TPS fluctuation trajectories can be summarized into two categories:

- TPS has significant fluctuations and instability. For example, the trajectory of TPS is like waterfall type which declines slowly and then rises slowly. The trajectories of these TPSs reflect performance bottlenecks in some point that require test or development engineers to look for performance bottlenecks.
- The TPS trajectory is relatively stable, but there are also some fluctuations. This type of fluctuation is not obvious, so it is difficult to determine whether there is a performance bottleneck directly.

It is necessary to judge the range of fluctuations to determine whether it is stable for the second category. In statistics, the mean and standard deviation are important factors in measuring whether the data is stable. The average value of TPS ($\overline{TPS}$ in (1)) refers to the number of transactions processed per second by the system for a specified period of time. The standard deviation of TPS ($\sigma(TPS)$ in (1)) is based on the concept of mathematical statistics, reflecting the fluctuation of the system under testing. The smaller the standard deviation, the smaller the fluctuation and the more stable the system.

The stability metric model is defined as follow:

$$\theta(TPS) = \sigma(TPS)/\overline{TPS} * 100\% \tag{1}$$

$\theta(TPS)$ is the fluctuation range of TPS, and the acceptable range of fluctuation is 5% plus or minus 3% according to our production environment (can also be configured according to different scenarios).

4.3   Scalability

Scalability means that distributed storage systems increase system storage capacity, compute capacity, and performance capabilities by adding the number of servers. As the business development, the performance requirements for underlying storage systems continue to increase, and the better way to improve system performance is to add more servers. The ideal distributed storage system can achieve "linear scalability" that the overall performance of the system is linear with the number of servers.

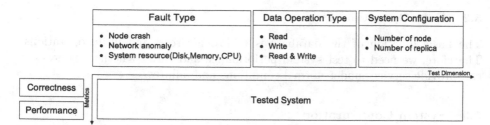

Fig. 2. Test design

5   Test Dimensions

In this section, we mainly introduce how to design test cases. It is difficult to exhaust all test cases for large-scale distributed database systems, so we need a systematic, simple and effective design method of test case. Systems based on the Raft protocol generally divide the system into several functional modules, such as leader election and log replication. We adopt a modular design approach. For each module, test cases are designed according to the following three different dimensions, i.e., fault type, data operation type (workload), and system configuration. As is shown in Fig. 2.

5.1   Fault Type

We need to deal with various failures in a distributed environment. The fault types are mainly divided into three categories, including node crash, network anomaly and insufficient system resources. In this test dimension, we need to test system under normal conditions firstly.

- **Node crash:** Many factors may cause node downtime, such as memory error, server power failure, etc. Node downtime may occur at any time. When node downtime occurs, the node can not work normally. For highly available distributed database which allows some nodes failures as long as a large number of nodes can work normally, the whole system can provides services. Therefore, We need to test the impact on different test metrics in the case of different number of nodes crash.
- **Network anomaly:** The cause of network anomaly may be message loss, out of order messages, or network packet errors. There is a special network exception called "network partition" where all nodes in the cluster are divided into multiple areas, the nodes in each area can communicate normally, but they can not communicate between the areas. We assume that the network is always unreliable, so it is necessary to test the impact of different test metrics according to whether the primary node is located in the majority partition when the network partition appears.
- **Insufficient system resources:** This type of failures are mainly hardware limitations, such as insufficient disk storage space or memory, CPU is under high load, etc.

5.2   Data Operation Type

The basic function of the database is to provide read and write operations. Therefore, we need to test system performance and verify whether the system can provide services under normal conditions and failures.

5.3   System Configuration

Distributed database system can be deployed to multiple servers through data distribution and replication. We can make the database scalable by increasing the number of copies or the number of nodes. Therefore, it is necessary to test the impact on metrics with different nodes and replicas.

6   Experiments

6.1   Experimental Setups

We implemented a variant of the Raft protocol on the open source distributed database OceanBase [1], which is developed by Alibaba. In our implementation, we mainly focus on two types of nodes: Rootserver and Updateserver. The Rootserver is used to manage all other servers and the Updateserver is an in-memory database engine of OceanBase, which is equivalent to a replication state machine. There are multiple Updateservers in a cluster deployment of OceanBase, one of which is called leader. All write requests are sent to the leader Updateserver, and the leader Updateserver synchronizes the logs to other slave Updateservers. If the leader Updateserver fails, a slave Updateserver will be elected to continue to provide services to ensure the system is highly available. Raft is mainly used to manage the Rootserver election and Updateserver log replication in a OceanBase cluster.

According to the above performance test metrics, we mainly test the performance of the system from four aspects: recovery time after the leader node is down, throughput, latency and stability. The experimental configuration is shown in Table 2.

Table 2. Server setup

Type	Description
OS	CentOS release 6.5 (Linux version 2.6.32)
CPU	2*Intel(R) Xeon(R) CPU E5-2620 0 @ 2.00 GHz (6 cores/CPU)
Memory	165G
Network	Broadcom Corporation NetXtreme BCM5719 Gigabit Ethernet

6.2   Recovery Time

From the perspective of fault recovery, one of the most important performance metrics of Raft-based system is fault recovery time, which is the time required for the system to recover from non-availability to normal operation when the system fails. The recovery time includes the expiration time of the previous leader's lease (default 9 s in our configuration) plus the time to elect a new leader. In different fault types, the recovery time may also be different. Here we test the average fault recovery time when the node is down, which is a common type of fault. The test results are shown in Fig. 3. With the increase of the number of servers, the recovery time increases slightly. After many tests, the average recovery time is about 10 s.

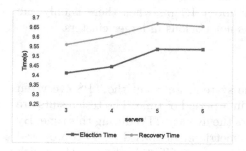
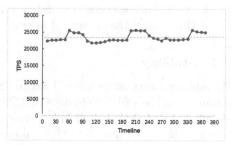

Fig. 3. Recovery time   Fig. 4. Stability

6.3   Throughput and Latency

The system throughput refers to the number of write requests successfully processed per second, and the latency refers to the time that a request is successfully processed. We use a multi-threaded client to continuously send write requests to the leader Updateserver to measure the throughput and latency of the system

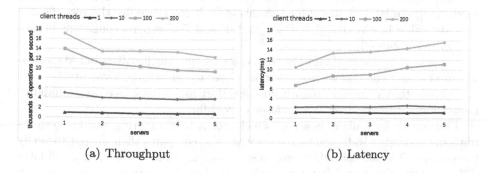

(a) Throughput   (b) Latency

Fig. 5. Performance

under different number of threads and Updateservers. The test results are shown in the Fig. 5. The abscissa represents the number of Updateservers.

Figure 5(a) shows the throughput of the system. As we can see from the result, one server has the highest throughput under different number of servers because it does not to replicate logs to other servers, about 17000 operations per second with 200 threads. When the number of client threads is the same, the throughput of the system decreases slightly with multiple servers, but it does not change significantly with different number of servers because the leader replicates its logs to all other slave servers in parallel and it respond to the client as long as it receive a majority response. In addition, the throughput obviously increases with the number of threads when the number of servers is the same.

Figure 5(b) shows the latency of the system. Similarly, the latency is the lowest when there is only one server because the leader does not need to copy the logs to other servers. The latency is about 1.1 ms when there is only one client thread and the change of latency is not obvious in larger clusters.

6.4   Stability

By adding a certain pressure load to the system, we count the TPS every ten minutes, and record the changes of TPS in a period of time. The test results are shown in Fig. 4. The dotted line represents the average TPS during this time. By putting the test results into the stability metric model based on TPS proposed in Sect. 4.2, we conclude that the fluctuation range of TPS is about 5.44% which is within the acceptable fluctuation range.

7   Related Work

Raft is a consensus algorithm that keeps replicated logs of transactions to a database or key-value store. It has received a lot of attention despite its recent release. However, each implementation is slightly different, and this introduces possibilities for protocol errors and inconsistent corner case performance.

Distributed system protocols are known to be difficult to design correctly. Thus, a systems design is often accompanied by a formal English proof of correctness, typically relegated to a technical report or thesis. Examples include Paxos [13], the BFT protocol for Byzantine fault tolerance [3], the reconfiguration algorithm in SMART [10], Raft [11,12], and Zookeeper's consistent broadcast protocol Zab [7].

Coracle [6] by Howard and Crocroft is a tool that verifies distributed consensus and claims to do it at settings that are closer to realistic deployments. Coracle also claims that consensus algorithms like Raft and Paxos face an availability issue when deployed in scenarios closer to real-life.

Flotsam [5] by Gilbert is a tool which works by comparing various systems implemented using Raft against one another and compares their output to verify the systems. The author of [15] proposes the development of a tool that validates different key-value based implementations of Raft. Validation is done based on testing various test cases for distributed systems.

8   Conclusion

Consensus protocol is the foundation of constructing distributed database system and many database systems are built based on Raft because it's easy to understand and implement. However, how to evaluate these different implementations has not been studied extensively and it is difficult to test in a distributed environment which has to deal with various exceptions.

In this paper, we addressed the issue of testing for Raft-replicated database systems from three aspects, including abstraction of system model, definition of test metrics and test dimensions. Finally, we give the test result on an open source distributed database system. In the future work, we hope to build an automated testing framework based on our test metrics and test dimensions, including automatic system deployment, automatic generation of test cases and automatic comparison of test results.

Acknowledgements. This research is supported in part by National Science Foundation of China under grant number 61432006, and National Key R&D Program of China (2018YFB1003303).

References

1. Oceanbase website (2019). https://github.com/alibaba/oceanbase/
2. ISO/IEC/IEEE international standard - systems and software engineering-vocabulary. In: ISO/IEC/IEEE, pp. 1–541 (2017)
3. Castro, M., Liskov, B.: Practical byzantine fault tolerance and proactive recovery. ACM (2002)
4. Deligiannis, P., et al.: Uncovering bugs in distributed storage systems during testing (not in production!). In: USENIX Conference on File and Storage Technologies, pp. 249–262 (2016)
5. Gilbert, C.: Flotsam: evaluating implementations of the raft consensus algorithm (2019, unpublished). http://www.scs.stanford.edu/14aucs244b/labs/projects/flotsam.pdf
6. Howard, H., Crowcroft, J.: Coracle: evaluating consensus at the internet edge. In: ACM SIGCOMM Computer Communication Review, vol. 45, pp. 85–86. ACM (2015)
7. Junqueira, F.P., Reed, B.C., Serafini, M.: Zab: high-performance broadcast for primary-backup systems. In: 2011 IEEE/IFIP 41st International Conference on Dependable Systems and Networks (DSN), pp. 245–256. IEEE (2011)
8. Lamport, L.: The part-time parliament. Acm Trans. Comput. Syst. **16**(2), 133–169 (1998)
9. Lamport, L., et al.: Paxos made simple. ACM Sigact News **32**(4), 18–25 (2001)
10. Lorch, J.R., Adya, A., Bolosky, W.J., Chaiken, R., Douceur, J.R., Howell, J.: The smart way to migrate replicated stateful services. ACM Sigops Oper. Syst. Rev. **40**(4), 103–115 (2006)
11. Ongaro, D.: Consensus: bridging theory and practice. Ph.D. thesis, Stanford University (2014)

12. Ongaro, D., Ousterhout, J.: In search of an understandable consensus algorithm. In: 2014 USENIX Annual Technical Conference (USENIX ATC 14), pp. 305–319. USENIX Association, Philadelphia, PA (2014). https://www.usenix.org/conference/atc14/technical-sessions/presentation/ongaro
13. De Prisco, R., Lampson, B., Lynch, N.: Revisiting the paxos algorithm. In: Mavronicolas, M., Tsigas, P. (eds.) WDAG 1997. LNCS, vol. 1320, pp. 111–125. Springer, Heidelberg (1997). https://doi.org/10.1007/BFb0030679
14. Schneider, F.B.: Implementing fault-tolerant services using the state machine approach: a tutorial. ACM Comput. Surv. (CSUR) 22(4), 299–319 (1990)
15. Vishwanath, D.: Validating key-value based implementations of the raft consensus algorithm for distributed systems (2018)

Big Data

Benchmarking for Transaction Processing Database Systems in Big Data Era

Chunxi Zhang, Yuming Li, Rong Zhang[✉], Weining Qian, and Aoying Zhou

School of Data Science and Engineering, East China Normal University,
Shanghai, China
{cxzhang,ym.li}@stu.ecnu.edu.cn, {rzhang,wnqian,ayzhou}@dase.ecnu.edu.cn

Abstract. Benchmarking is an essential suite supporting development
of database management systems. It runs a set of well defined data
and workloads on a specific hardware configuration to gather the results
to fill the measurements. It is used widely for evaluating new technology or comparing different systems so as to promote the progress of
database systems. To date, under the requirement of data management,
new databases are designed and issued for different application requirements. Most of the state-of-the-art benchmarks are also designed for
specific types of applications. Based on our experiences, however, we
argue that considering the characteristics of data or workloads in big
data era, benchmarking transaction processing databases (TP) must put
much effort for domain specific needs to reflet $4V$ properties (i.e. volume,
velocity, variety and veracity). With the critical transaction processing
requirements of new applications, we see an explosion of designing innovative scalable databases or new processing architecture on traditional
databases dealing with high intensive transaction workloads, which are
called SecKill and can saturate the traditional database systems by high
workloads, for example "11·11" of Tmall, "ticket booking" during China
Spring Festival and "Stock Exchange" applications.

In this paper, we first analyze SecKill applications and the implementation logics, and also summarize and abstract the business model in
details. Then, we propose a totally new benchmark called PeakBench
for simulating SecKill applications, including workload characteristics
definition, workload distribution simulating, and logics implementing.
Additionally, we define new evaluation metrics for performance comparison among DBMSs under different implementation architecture from the
micro- and macro- points of views. At last, we provide a package of tools
for simulating and evaluating purpose.

Keywords: DB-testing · Transaction processing · Intensive
workloads · Evaluation

1 Introuduction

Big data have been generated and used in different kinds of domains, such as
e-commerce, financial, and search engine, as well as scientific research areas.

© Springer Nature Switzerland AG 2019
C. Zheng and J. Zhan (Eds.): Bench 2018, LNCS 11459, pp. 147–158, 2019.
https://doi.org/10.1007/978-3-030-32813-9_13

It brings new chance for new applications, but also puts new requirements for novel technology. Then it gives birth to a bunch of new application-oriented data management systems, for data store, search or analysis.

Generally, benchmarking aims to generate application-oriented workloads, evaluate the performance by simulating the real intensity and produce the valuable results for guiding comparisons or designs [16]. Database (DB) management systems are general tools for data management in different domains, which have also been extended or redesigned for new critical applications. For example, Hbase [12] for fast read, VoltDB [17] for in-memorty transaction processing, Oceanbase [19] for distributed transaction processing and so on. One possibility to test the new databases is to use TPC-series benchmark [6], which are domain specific. The dataset and workloads can be scaled to desired sizes. Developers and vendors have used these benchmarks to compare and improve their products. Researchers can use them to test their new algorithms, technology or prototypes. Thus TPC benchmarks have played an important role in the growth of database industry and the progress of database research. However, there is a tremendous varieties of databases for applications, which may have total different performance requirements on a set of specific workloads. Since TPC benchmarks are domain specific, which can not cover new applications or give a concrete measurement for new applications.

At present data storage of massive data, large scale parallel query processing or high contention of parallel data accessing has become new challenges for databases. Especially commercial developments have promoted the new style of business model. One of the most representative ones is **Second Kill** (abbr. SecKill), which has a massive scale of transactions, especially Write, erupting within a short period, e.g., in a second. It has become a popular application in E-commerce for sale promotion or advertising, such as "black Friday" in USA, "11·11" or train ticket booking during Spring Festival in China. For this kind of real application, dealing with large dynamic changes in high workload, high concurrency, and high contention access is a new challenge for databases. In real applications, the traditional system architecture, that is, the request directly falls on the database, is likely to be implemented at a high cost, and may not meet the demand. The SecKill service is usually supported by a system architecture of read-write separation. Traditional classic database benchmarks such as the TPC series cannot fully satisfy the analysis and evaluation of the SecKill application. Within this context, we propose our insights into the requirement and challenges in developing new benchmarks for databases supporting transaction processes. And we give a brief introduction to our new benchmark tool PeakBench supporting intensive workload testing on TP databases.

According to these new features in the applications, it generates a new requirement for benchmarking work to simulate such intensive workloads. We compare the related benchmarks, *TPC-C* and *TPC-E* [6] are the most popular benchmarks for transaction processing systems (OLTP); *YCSB* [9] and *YCSB++* [14] benchmark R/W workloads on key-value stores, which is widely used to benchmark NoSQL Databases for the I/O performance; DebitCredit [15] is used to define a throughput measurement on Transaction Processing. All of its transactions involve a small number of tuples, which is too simple to be used nowadays. SmallBank [5] workload models a banking application where transactions perform simple read and update operations on customers accounts. TATP [18] benchmark simulates a caller location system used by telecommunication providers, in which transactions contain only 1–3 queries and 80% of them are read-only. This benchmark provides a useful workload scenario for measuring a DBMS's ability to run non-conflicting transactions concurrently.

Contention have never been taken seriously by all of those benchmarks, which have been said to be important in OLTP-Bench [11]. However, OLTP-Bench is a testbed instead of a benchmark. Workloads are usually generated statistically by predefining the percentages among different kinds of workloads, which represents a global workload distribution and cannot easily simulate distribution changes on each type of workloads along the time. Contention simulation has not been explicitly declared by most of the benchmarks even in TPC-C which simply controls contentions by changing the number of Warehouse or the number of concurrent posts. The other benchmarks control the contention by changing the size of data tables accessed by workloads, which is too rough to serve performance comparisons among databases. Most of benchmarks have provided workload skewness distributions on data items. However, skewness can be different among different types of workloads and change along the time, which has been overlooked until now. So current benchmarks have not been designed for most of the characteristics of this kind of applications with intensive workloads, and an apples-to-apples comparison cannot be promised.

This paper design and implement benchmark, evaluate the ability of different database systems for transaction processing and query processing in peak testing; and integrate different database systems to define different loads. As well as load distribution, measure the system architecture performance supporting peak traffic and give detailed performance analysis.

2   Requirements and Challenges

The benchmark of database refers to the specification for evaluating and comparing the performance of different database systems. Generally, benchmark includes definition and generation to three basic elements, which are data generation, workload generation and measurement definition, shown in Fig. 1, which is used to objectively and comprehensively evaluate the performance each database system. Each developer or company can update or select a system that meets their needs based on the evaluation report. The definition of the benchmark with the objectives of "FEAS":

Factuality: This includes the factuality of data generation and the workload simulation. On the one hand, how to get the data set. Some test data can be obtained from real application data sets, but most of the data is confidential, so the data needs to be generated based on characteristics to ensure the factuality. On the other hand, how to define the workload, it is crucial to abstract

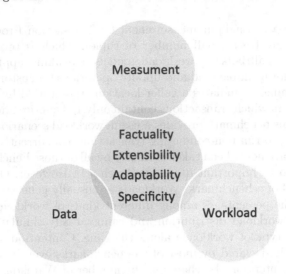

Fig. 1. Benchmark ingredient

the workload characteristics according to the actual application, determine the logical relationship between the workloads, and simulate the workload closer to the real application, e.g. big data and workload dynamics.

Extensibility: It had better be extensible for different scale of testing requirements, either for data/workload size or system size. And it shall be easy to adjust configurations for different workload generation and easy to add new database for testing, or deployments for different systems or on different platforms.

Adaptability: Includes configurable parameters for data generation and workload simulation, as well as flexibility for reserved interfaces. During the execution process, various types of data and workload characteristics are classified to determine various parameters, so that users can configure to generate data and workload according to requirements. With more configurable interfaces, users can customize the workload and easily add new test functions.

Specificity: The measurements must expose the main purpose of benchmark tasks, which must be specific and valuable, e.g. TPS and Latency of databases. And define new evaluation metric based on application characteristics requirements, making the meaning of the standards more fair, objective, and usable.

2.1 Data Generation

Automatic empirical data generation is the first fundamental requirement for benchmarking work. One of the most important issues here is to deal with the scaling problem. Researchers have proposed a number of database generation techniques [1,2,4], which are able to create databases with specific characteristics or based on a seed dataset. It may be easy to control the generation for data size, which is volume, such as Terabyte (TB) or Petabyte (PB). Velocity is controlled by increasing or decreasing generation threads. Variety has been defined statically, which denotes the range of data type or sources. Veracity is required to reflect the inherent and important characteristics of raw data, which has been verified by comparing the data distribution among attributes. Previous data generation methods obviously lose the dynamics from the view of data generation, including data distribution changes and data quantity changes along time.

Although some benchmarks use the real data as inputs to guarantee data veracity, it can not be adapted to other application scenarios, and the seed data is a static snapshot at some specific time, which can not represent the later evolution of data. But usually evolution of data leads to totally different performance on TP databases, which is the other kind of variety.

2.2 Workload Generation

Generally speaking, we can divide the benchmarks into two kinds: micro benchmark and macro benchmark. Micro benchmark is designed to test or evaluate the specific technology supporting the whole software/hardware systems. For example, for a new file system, we may test its advantages with I/O intensive workloads; for an indexing algorithm in DB, we may exhibit the performance by the specific select workloads. So micro benchmark is especially useful and necessary for technology innovators. For vendors or system developers, a testing result is meaningful only when applying an application-oriented benchmark [16], which is the Macro benchmark. It is challenging to develop benchmarks to reflect various workload cases. And identifying the typical workloads for applications and automatically generating these workloads are the prerequisite of system evaluation.

Though TPC series workloads are well extracted and defined from real applications, it is too general to be applied to specific applications and still lack of consideration in fine granularity execution simulation between workloads and data. First, current benchmarks provide the control for workload distribution on data items and the distributions among themselves, but it still neglects the dynamic distribution changes among workloads. Second, there is almost no work considering workload interactions along time. Different access pattern will affect TP performance greatly. Last but not the least, candidate size along the query tree is one of the most crucial elements deciding performance. None of current benchmarks has put effort to control the intermediate results.

2.3 Measurement Definition

In the benchmark, the performance of the database is measured by multiple sets of measurement, including request latency, throughput, resource utilization, concurrency, cost-effective, stability, maintainability, scalability, and so on. The latency is the time between when the user sends a request and when the returned result is received, usually measured by the average response time of number test. The throughput usually refers to QPS/TPS (query/transaction response requests per second), and the throughput is also limited by the number of concurrent connections of the database. When the number of connections does not reach the peak, the greater the number of connections, the higher the throughput. For different database systems, the optimal concurrent connection state is usually selected, and the throughput of the system is tested for comparison. Resource utilization generally refers to system cpu utilization and memory consumption. Concurrency testing of databases means that multiple users access the database at the same time to do the same operation. Highly concurrent tests can also measure the stability of the database system and discover design problems in the system. The cost-effective measurement formula is usually: cost-effective = performance-value/price-value, which can better balance the performance and price.

Measurement shall be valuable and specificity considering different applications. Current benchmarks usually take *Throughput* and *Latency* as the general measurements. Since different applications have different workloads, the general ones can not guide the design or implementation well. For example, for workloads having intensive burst, developers or vendors desire to exploit self adaptive capability, and it may not be easy to catch database disadvantage by the average *Throughput* or *Latency* metrics.

2.4   Others

For the easy use of benchmarks, it is preferred to prepare benchmark packages which are tools for data/workload generation and deploying. For implementation, we shall guarantee the parallel generation for both data and workloads, which is called extensibility on both volume and system scale. For package deployments, it is required to be easy to use, having friendly user interfaces.

During implementation, the most challenge part is to guarantee the workload interaction patterns distributedly, e.g. contention, among distributed workloads, which can not obstruct the data/workload generation paces.

3   PeakBench: Benchmarking Transaction Processing Database Systems on Intensive Workloads

In order to facilitate the generation of a TP benchmark satisfying the properties of "FEAS", we define and implement **PeakBench**, open sourced in Github [7]. PeakBench is implemented from four levels described in the following parts:

Generation Control for Extensibility: In order to make benchmarks scalable for different data/workload size requirements or on different system scale, our data/workload generators can run on threads, supporting distributed deployment.

Configuration for Factuality: PeakBench exposes enough parameters for users to specify their own data and workload demands. It allows to declare both the static and dynamic demands on data and workloads characteristics. For example, we can characterize data by its static properties, e.g. item quantity, record size, table arrangement, distributions; we can also define the dynamic properties, such as distribution changes of workloads along time. The most important thing is that we have a fine granularity control on workload execution for simulating contention, which has not been well studied until now.

Executor for Adaptability: Data generator and workload generator are designed based on requirements assigned in Configuration level, and we design new evaluation metrics to show system stability under dynamic environment, which is totally new. Our workload executor can distribute the workloads on distributed clients scalability. However simulation on distributed workload interaction is still a hard work.

Storage for Generality: Our tool can apply, run and test on different databases with general interfaces. Generated data and workloads can be stored in different DBs with different scales.

3.1 Business Description

Generally for an item booking and buying, we have the following steps: first, browse and check the interested items; second, put the expected items into the shopping cart or buy items directly; third, pay for the items or cancel the order actively or passively by a period of time. SecKill applications have especially rigorous requirements on DSC^2. The most different thing is the obvious distribution separation between Read (R) and Write (W) operations at SecKill start time point, and the severe contention on hot items: **ReadPhase:** Before SecKill start time point, all SecKill items can only be browsed (Read) since customers are searching or keeping monitoring the interested ones. It will be read-heavy.

CriticalityPhase: It reaches read peak closing SecKill time. Almost all customers start focusing on the status changing of items and continuously refreshing, when SecKill time approaches.

KillPhase: It turns almost all browsers (R) into buy (W) at the point of kill start. It will be write-heavy and contention-intensive, especially for hot items.

3.2 Implementation of Benchmark Tool

We have developed a benchmark tool Called **PeakBench tool** to generate/deploy workloads/data and execute the benchmarks. The most important and unique work in PeakBench tool is that it can support fine granularity definition of skewness and dynamics, we make transaction contention controllable, which is the most tough but essential work for evaluating TP databases.

The architecture is shown in Fig. 2, which includes 5 important functional modules.

3.3 Workloads

On RDB, we meet five kinds of browse queries and one periodical updating requirement. Users can browse on product categories Q_2, keywords Q_3, price Q_4 or shops Q_5 and then browse the details Q_1. Since we have the R/W separate architecture, Q_6 is used to promise the weak consistency by updating RDB according to WDB for the change in the number of KilProds *skpcount* in table *seckillplan* and the number of payed products *paycount* in *seckillpay*.

On WDB for KilProds, we have 5 kinds of operations (Q_7–Q_{11}), including submit, pay, cancel, browse orders and one cancel overdue orders actions. On WDB, it also includes transactions to non-KilProd, since it does not generate the high pressure for databases compared to KilProds, we overlook these workloads.

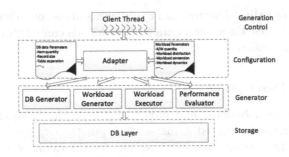

Fig. 2. Benchmarking components

4   Test of PeakBench

We define an E-commerce scenario, and show the main characteristics of Peak-Bench, and workload details can be found in Github [7].

Table 1. Default data size

Table	Size
Customer	$8 \cdot 10^4$
Supplier	$5 \cdot 10^2$
Item	10^5
Order	$4 \cdot 10^5$
OrderItem	$8 \cdot 10^5$
SecKill	10^2
scaleFactor	10
skScaleFactor	10

Table 2. The default settings for parameters

Parameter	Value
CR	50 %
CI	5
Connection thread for MySql&PG	80
Connection thread for VoltDb	60
Partition number for VoltDB	3
zipfian(s, N)	s = 2, N = 10
Submit order size (SuO)	10^6
α and β	0.5 & 0.5

Our experiments are conducted on a cluster with 8 nodes configured in RAID-5 on CentOS $v.6.5$. There two nodes which are equipped with 2 Intel Xeon

E5-2620 @ 2.13 GHz CPUs, 130 GB memory and 3 TB HDD disk; the other 6 nodes are equipped with 2 Intel Xeon E5-2620 @ 2.0 GHz CPUs, 64 GB memory and 2.1 TB HDD disk. The cluster is connected using 1 Gigabit Ethernet. We demonstrate the effectiveness of PeakBench by running it on three popularly used open sourced database systems MySQL ($v.$ 14.14), Postgresql ($v.$ 9.5) and a distributed database VoltDB ($v.$ 7.8.2) [17]. In order to make the results comparable, we test and configure the parameter on each DB for its best performance, which include the cache size and the number of processing threads and the partition number. In our implementation, we set the connection threads to 80 which are tested to get almost the best performance on Mysql and PG in our cluster. For VoltDB, configured with 3 partitions and 60 connection threads, our workload will reach the best performance. Default parameter setting is shown in Table 2. The default size of our benchmark is listed in Table 1. We have two scale factors, which are *scaleFactor* for the first 5 tables to expand the basic tables and *skScaleFactor* for the last two ones to expand the kill items.

All metrics used in PeachBench are defined as followings: **Transaction per Second (TPS):** The number of transactions processed per second.

Latency: The average process time for each query.

Sys_Stability: With sharp dynamics on loads, we evaluate the ability to recover to the stable status by:

$$Sys\_Stability = \alpha \star \delta t \star \beta \star \delta L / \bar{L}, \alpha + \beta = 1.$$

where t, L and $\bar{L}$ represent the range of time arriving stable status, latency and average latency, and α and β define the importance for t and L with default values 0.5. Smaller value will be better.

Since for DB, only its client latency can be affected by the size of workloads instead of DB latency, so we use client latency for L in *Sys_Stability*.

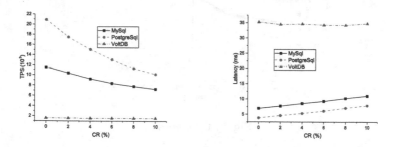

Fig. 3. Contention simulation in PeakBench

Contention Simulation. It defines CR (contention ratio) to represent the percentage of transaction contentions in each time unit. In Fig. 3, we show the result generated by PeakBench. It is easy to see that PeakBench can control contention simulation precisely, where performance is affected obviously by increasing CR.

Dynamics. We can simulate workloads changes along time. In Fig. 6, we generate workloads by changing the ratio between Read and Write dynamically, in which we simulate sharp changes among workloads.

Stability. In Fig. 5 we show the stable ability between MySql and PostgreSql by using the workloads generated in Fig. 6. It can be see that PostgreSql is more stable than MySql with the workloads.

Scalability. In Fig. 4, we can generate massive workloads by expanding the client nodes. It generates workloads almost linearly.

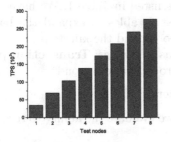

Fig. 4. Scalable generator

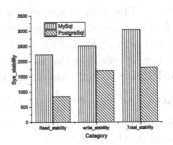

Fig. 5. Stability

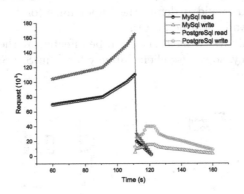

Fig. 6. Dynamics

5   Related Work

Benchmarking and performance evaluation attract considerable attention in the late of 1980s and early 1990s [3, 13]. Generally, it aims to generate application-oriented workloads, evaluates the performance by simulating the real intensity and produces the valuable results for guiding comparisons or designs [16].

Until now for traditional transaction processing (OLTP), TPC series, e.g., TPC-C or TPC-E [6] are still in fashion. TPC-C simulates a warehouse-centric order processing application. Transaction contentions is simulated by adjusting the number of warehouses which is not controllable or effective. TPC-E portrays the activities of a stock brokerage firm, which has more complex schema and workloads than TPC-C. However, it does not mention about the parallel access control, and can't simulate high contention workloads. Workloads in CHbenCHmark [8] are a mixture of TPC-C and TPC-H [10] designed for databases supporting both OLTP and OLAP workloads. It does not specify more about contention or dynamics simulation.

There are also some other well defined TP benchmarks for traditional TP system testing. SmallBank [5] models a banking application where transactions perform simple read and write on customer *accounts*. Despite the contentions mentioned in SmallBank, it was not effectively controlled and simulated. TATP [18] simulates a caller location system to test in-memory databases. It then considers little about the performance for concurrence control. DebitCredit [15] simulates a typical bank account change on a bank database, which tests system throughput without considering workload distributions or contentions among reads and updates.

In industry, recently Yahoo! develops its cloud serving benchmark, YCSB [9], to evaluate NoSQL data stores. It emphasizes client scalability (concurrency) and one kind of write-heavy workloads, but still lacks dynamics simulation on different workloads. YCSB++ [14] is an extension of YCSB, which emphasizes more on the evaluation of table storage characteristics, and still can not be adapted for simulating workload intensive applications. OLTP-Bench [11] is a comprehensive test platform integrating tens of benchmarks, with the purpose to provide enough workloads or datasets for evaluation.

Though we have so many different kinds of benchmarks, benchmarking for intensive workloads, e.g. SecKill, is still absent, which is able to describe high concurrency, sharp dynamics intensive skewness or high contention. Some benchmarks have already provide concurrency control to evaluation DB scalability. Until now no benchmarks have provided the support to dynamics which has been declared important in OLTP-Bench [11]. Contention control has never been exposed explicitly by any existing benchmarking work, which is the most important aspect affecting DB performance.

6   Conclusion

With the rapid occurrence of new applications and development of new database systems, traditional benchmarks are too old to catch up with emerging applications. In this paper, we summarize the lessons learned during system developments and analyze the requirements and challenges in design new benchmarking work. We also introduce our benchmark tool PeakBench, which aims to fill the gap between benchmarking and business requirements. However distributed workload generation with interaction control among workloads is still a difficult problem, which is left as our future work.

Acknowledgment. We are partially supported by the Key Program of National Natural Science Foundation of China (No. 2018YFB1003402) and National Science Foundation of China (No. 61432006).

References

1. Arasu, A., Kaushik, R., Li, J.: Data generation using declarative constraints. In: Proceedings of the 2011 ACM SIGMOD International Conference on Management of Data, pp. 685–696. ACM (2011)
2. Binnig, C., Kossmann, D., Lo, E., Özsu, M.T.: QAGen: generating query-aware test databases. In Proceedings of the 2007 ACM SIGMOD International Conference on Management of Data, pp. 341–352. ACM (2007)
3. Bitton, D., DeWitt, D.J., Turbyfill, C.: Benchmarking database systems: a systematic approach. Computer Sciences Department, University of Wisconsin-Madison (1983)
4. Bruno, N., Chaudhuri, S.: Flexible database generators. In: Proceedings of the 31st International Conference on Very Large Data Bases, pp. 1097–1107. VLDB Endowment (2005)
5. Cahill, M.J., Röhm, U., Fekete, A.D.: Serializable isolation for snapshot databases. ACM Trans. Database Syst. (TODS) **34**(4), 20 (2009)
6. Chen, S., et al.: TPC-E vs. TPC-C: characterizing the new TPC-E benchmark via an I/O comparison study. ACM SIGMOD Rec. **39**(3), 5–10 (2011)
7. Zhang, Y.L.R., Zhang, R.: https://github.com/daseecnu/db-testing
8. Cole, R., et al.: The mixed workload CH-benchmark. In: Proceedings of the Fourth International Workshop on Testing Database Systems, p. 8. ACM (2011)
9. Cooper, B.F., Silberstein, A., Tam, E., Ramakrishnan, R., Sears, R.: Benchmarking cloud serving systems with YCSB. In: Proceedings of the 1st ACM Symposium on Cloud Computing, pp. 143–154. ACM (2010)
10. Trans-Pacific Partnership Council: TPC-H benchmark specification, vol. 21, pp. 592-603 (2008). http://www.tcp.org/hspec.html
11. Difallah, D.E., Pavlo, A., Curino, C., Cudre-Mauroux, P.: OLTP-bench: an extensible testbed for benchmarking relational databases. Proc. VLDB Endow. **7**(4), 277–288 (2013)
12. George, L.: HBase: The Definitive Guide: Random Access to Your Planet-size Data. O'Reilly Media, Inc., Newton (2011)
13. Gray, J.: Benchmark Handbook: For Database and Transaction Processing Systems. Morgan Kaufmann Publishers, Inc., Burlington (1992)
14. Patil, S., et al.: YCSB++: benchmarking and performance debugging advanced features in scalable table stores. In: Proceedings of the 2nd ACM Symposium on Cloud Computing, p. 9. ACM (2011)
15. Stonebraker, M.: A measure of transaction processing power. Datamation **31**(7), 112–118 (1985)
16. Tay, Y.C.: Data generation for application-specific benchmarking. VLDB **4**, 1470–1473 (2011)
17. LLC VoltDB: VoltDB technical overview. Whitepaper (2010)
18. Wolski, A.: TATP benchmark description (version 1.0) (2009)
19. Yang, Z.: The architecture of oceanbase relational database system. J. East China Norm. Univ. (Nat. Sci.) **9**(5), 141–148 (2014)

UMDISW: A Universal Multi-Domain Intelligent Scientific Workflow Framework for the Whole Life Cycle of Scientific Data

Qi Sun, Yue Liu$^{(\boxtimes)}$, Wenjie Tian, Yike Guo, and Bocheng Li

School of Computer Engineering and Science, Shanghai University,
Shanghai 200444, China
sunqichn@163.com, yliu@staff.shu.edu.cn, tianwenjie1997@163.com,
y.guo@imperial.ac.uk, 1124129934@qq.com

Abstract. Existing scientific data management systems rarely manage scientific data from a whole-life-cycle perspective, and the value-creating steps defined throughout the cycle constitute essentially a scientific workflow. The scientific workflow system developed by many organizations can well meet their own domain-oriented needs, but from the perspective of the entire scientific data, there is a lack of a common framework for multiple domains. At the same time, some systems require scientists to understand the underlying content of the system, which virtually increases the workload and research costs of scientists. In this context, this paper proposes a universal multi-domain intelligent scientific data processing workflow framework (UMDISW), which builds a general model that can be used in multiple domains by defining directed graphs and descriptors, and makes the underlying layer transparent to scientists to just focus on high-level experimental design. On this basis, the paper also uses scientific data as a driving force, incorporating a mechanism of intelligently recommending algorithms into the workflow to reduce the workload of scientific experiments and provide decision support for exploring new scientific discoveries.

Keywords: Scientific workflow · Intelligent · Scientific data · Universal framework

1 Introduction

Scientific research has entered the era of big data. Instruments and equipment with ever-increasing data collection capabilities and ever-evolving computing facilities and simulation methods are important sources of scientific big data, causing explosive growth in data size, which is happening in different scientific domains [1–3]. At the same time, because scientific data faces greater "broadness" and "depth" than commercial data, the processing patterns and methods of scientific data are also diversified. It can be said that the management and processing of scientific data now face enormous challenges.

© Springer Nature Switzerland AG 2019
C. Zheng and J. Zhan (Eds.): Bench 2018, LNCS 11459, pp. 159–171, 2019.
https://doi.org/10.1007/978-3-030-32813-9_14

In this case, many organizations have carried out a series of work on the structure and system of scientific data management from different perspectives, and developed many scientific data management systems or analytical frameworks. Such as SkyServer for managing SDSS data [4], Paradise for storing geographic information [5], Google's virtual digital earth system Google Earth for visualization [6], Apache's big data high-performance computing framework Hama [7], etc. These systems perform well at some point in management, analysis, or visualization, but lack a complete solution from the perspective of the whole life cycle of scientific data. Scientific data creates value, and the whole lifecycle of scientific data defines the various steps in creating value, including importing, storing, processing, visualizing, analyzing, re-storing, and so on, as well as the conditions associated with each step. These steps essentially constitute a workflow, or data flow, information flow.

The concept of workflow has been widely used in many fields, such as business processes, industrial manufacturing, scientific research, medicine, etc. [8]. For scientific workflows, the most common representation is to create a high-level graph composed of directed graphs, related nodes and edges that define the sequence and interaction between the various steps associated with the scientific workflow, and this graphy defines the sequence and interaction between the various steps. In addition, because of the diversity and complexity of scientific research, only one directed graph is not sufficient to represent the processing flow of multiple scientific domains, so additional descriptors are needed to specifically identify and control the nodes of a series of steps. The information exchange standard proposed by the Open Provenance Model (OPM) core specification [9] for data traceability and the concepts and terminology defined in the S88 standard [10] for production recipe process can be applied to the scientific workflow. The scientific workflows that will be presented later in this paper also refer to the relevant content of these two standards.

It turns out that it is feasible to use workflow to represent the processing of scientific data, many organizations continue to develop their own field-oriented scientific workflow system based on their needs. From the combination of scientific workflows, it is divided into text-based combinations such as BPEL4WS [11], DAGMan, SCUFL; graphics-based combinations such as Triana [12], VisTrails, Kepler [13]; semantic-based combinations such as K-WF, Pegasus, Taverna [14]. These scientific workflow systems have brought great convenience to the processing of scientific data to a certain extent, but there are also some problems:

- It is more difficult to meet the needs of many types of users. Domain experts are more focused on domain-related research than on the scheduling of underlying resources related to specific calculations.
- Most of the existing scientific workflows are only for a single domain, lacking a universal framework.
- Lack of a more efficient method of scheduling. Users usually need to choose different methods to compare to select the better one, so that the workload of scientific experiments is increased.

In summary, based on the previous research [15], this paper proposes a Universal Multi-Domain Intelligent Scientific data processing Workflow (UMDISW), which solves the problems of current scientific workflow from the perspectives of model, structure and application. The second section of this paper describes the state and status of the proposed workflow in previous research. In the third section, the model of the UMDISW is analyzed. And in the fourth section, we describes the structure of the UMDISW. What's more, the fifth section introduces the application scenario of the UMDISW, highlighting the characteristics of intelligence, and the sixth section is to introduce the workflow implementation in combination with the previous research. Finally, we have a conclusion in the seventh section.

2 The Status of UMDISW in System Architecture

In previous research, we proposed a scientific big data management system architecture for multiple domains and roles, The architecture is divided into four areas: Basic Service Function Area (BSFA), Storage and Access Area (SAA), Query Function Area (QFA), and Analysis Function Area (AFA). Each area has its own corresponding function. For example, the AFA is responsible for processing scientific data in different domains using machine learning or domain methods. On this basis, we integrated UMDISW proposed in this article in the AFA, and the AFA is updated to have three component: the Asset Loader (AL), the Pipeline Manager (PM), and the Pipeline Tool (PT). These three components show the composition of the UMDISW in the architecture, where the AL is used to get the data and algorithms needed by the experiments; the PM is responsible for the design, build, and integration of the workflow; the PT is responsible for providing the operating environment and execution engine. Each component has its own port and interface to interact with outside. The model, structure and implementation of the UMDISW in the AFA will be detailed later.

3 The Model of UMDISW

The UMDISW proposed in this paper consists of the following modules: workflow and task, data flow and information flow, data node and algorithm node. The functions of each of the modules will be described in the next few subsections.

3.1 Workflow and Task

The processing of scientific data can be divided into modules that depict the processing details, and a workflow is the sum of all these modules. On this basis, the workflow is essentially a container that defines the scope of data processing under the user's decision. Typically, scientific data processing will have one or more tasks, and the workflow should also consist of at least one task.

A task represents a collection of steps performed on or by an allocated resource. In science, these resources often refer to scientific devices, instrumentation, scientific software, scientific data and algorithms, and are distinct in different scientific domains. When a resource is shared by multiple tasks, the allocation of resources to perform a given task depends on its availability, suitability, and priority of the task to be completed. The start and execution of the task will be postponed until the resources are allocated to it.

3.2 Data Flow and Information Flow

Depending on the structure of the workflow, its execution will involve the transfer of entities (data, information, etc.) because they are generated or used during the execution of the workflow, and this transfer forms the data and information flows.

The data flow usually refers to the process or location of the data in the workflow, so it's necessary to define the nodes to represent the start and end of the data flow; define the input and output locations of subtasks to represent the current progress of the data; define connect lines to represent the movement of data between two subtasks, which is also a factor driving the workflow; define work areas to distinguish between different workflows. In order to describe the model of UMDISW in a graphical way in the following discussion, the data flow is represented by solid lines, which start from the start node (represented by a solid circle), or from the output of the subtask module (represented by rectangle), or from the data node (represented by rounded rectangle), and terminate at the end node (represented by triangle) or subtask module input. What's more, different workflows are divided into different areas (represented by lanes).

The information flow in the workflow also requires the above definition to represent the start and end, movement, and the classification of information. At the same time, the definition of data nodes and algorithm nodes is needed to display the development and changes of information during the execution of the workflow, such as data generation and update of algorithm parameters, and these changes based on the definitions form the workflow's information flow. Similarly, for graphical description, the information flow is designated as a dashed dotted arrow that begins at the subtask module and ends at the information module (represented by dashed rectangle).

3.3 Data Node and Algorithm Node

Defining data nodes and algorithm nodes for two purposes: first, they contain data inputs and algorithm inputs for a module in the workflow, or metadata information that is used to standardize the module's output; second, they contain addresses that point to the actual stored data and algorithms in the databases. An algorithm node and several data nodes combine to form a module of the workflow, that is, a subtask in the task.

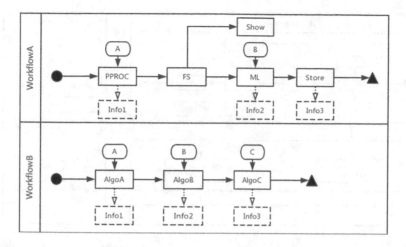

Fig. 1. Workflow sample diagram

Algorithm Node. According to the above description, the number of algorithm nodes in a workflow should be equal to the length of the workflow (remove the start and end nodes). In addition to the metadata information of the corresponding algorithm and the actual stored reference address, the algorithm node needs to indicate what format of input and output are needed in this step to improve the efficiency of the user to build the workflow. The algorithm corresponding to the algorithm node here may be a file or an algorithm program that has been integrated in the system.

Data Node. Data nodes are divided into data input nodes and data output nodes. The data input node can be combined with the algorithm node to become a subtask or a module of the workflow, and it may be a data file, a database table or a value; the data output node is an online result set or image (available for download), but it is not displayed in the workflow, and will only be displayed in the user interface when clicking on an algorithm node.

3.4 Example

Figure 1 shows two sample workflows that use machine learning methods to illustrate the workflow symbols mentioned earlier. There are two workflows, WorkflowA and WorkflowB, separated by lanes.

WorkflowA is a branched workflow that includes five subtasks: PPROC, FS, Show, ML, Store. Each subtask uses the corresponding algorithm for calculation and processing. WorkflowA starts from the subtask PPROC, which needs to input the data set pointed by the data node A. After a period of processing, the processing result is pushed to the subtask FS, and the corresponding information module Info1 is generated.

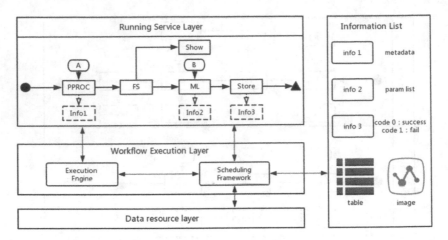

Fig. 2. Hierarchical structure of UMDISW

When the subtask FS gets the output of the previous step, it takes itself as its own input and starts executing. It should be noted that when the FS is executed, the output will be passed to the two subtasks, Show and ML, the former displays the results of the previous step to the page, and the latter combines the result of the previous step with the newly entered data B as its own input, and the result of the operation is passed to the next Store, and the corresponding information module Info2 is generated.

After executing the ML, the Store subtask will receive the result of the ML, which will save it to the database and generate the information module Info3, and end the WorkflowA.

The solid line in Fig. 1 reflects the flow of data during the execution of the workflow, which shows the process of data changes; the combination of the information modules corresponding to the dotted lines is the embodiment of the information flow in the workflow, which shows the gain process of the information.

WorkflowB is a linear workflow, and its execution process is similar to WorkflowA, except that each subtask has data input and information output, and there is no branch.

Although this sample workflow is only for machine learning processing, the nodes, modules, and regions shown in the figure provide the necessary functions to model the workflow of various scientific domains and non-machine learning methods. In addition, the graphical representation of the workflow provides a very compact view of the features and controls used to implement the workflow. In principle, since any organized process can be projected as a workflow, the proposed workflow model can facilitate the development of a common framework for managing related processes in different domains. Such a framework can promote understanding and application of cross-domain knowledge processing.

4   The Structure and Execution of UMDISW

In order to eliminate the inconsistency between scientific data and methods in different domains, the UMDISW proposed in this paper is transparent to the bottom and inside, and can be divided into three layers to meet the needs of different domains.

As shown in Fig. 2, UMDISW consists of three layers: Running Service Layer (RSL), Workflow Execution Layer (WEL), and Data Resource Layer (DRL). Each layer interacts with each other to complete the execution of the workflow and save the information.

4.1   Running Service Layer

The Running Service Layer is the only open part of the UMDISW, located at the top of the entire structure, providing a series of methods to interact with the user. Its core function is to instantiate user-created workflow models and display workflow information.

The RSL is web-based, thus allowing users to dynamically design workflows on the browser and to support visual editing operations such as adding, copying, dragging, and double-clicking on graphical elements representing components. When the page is loaded, an area is first drawn in the page according to the initialization incoming data as the working area of the workflow, and the related components are instantiated. At this time, the user needs to click the component to complete the binding operation of the data and the algorithm. When the above operation is completed, the components and connect lines in the entire area will be locked, and the workflow will be instantiated by the RSL and passed to the WEL.

In addition, as a layer of display information, the RSL also supports the relevant data information transmitted on the underlying layer and rendered on the page.

4.2   Workflow Execution Layer

Workflow execution typically involves one pass of all modules modeled in the workflow or the whole life cycle of scientific data. For such a loop, the workflow starts from the initial state and is converted by all or part of the finite state for each module. Workflow execution may be affected by a number of specific factors, such as the value of various parameters, the final application, decision logic, the execution engine, and the user's input at a particular point in the workflow. WEL is to implement the built-in or implicit logic in the workflow, and to perform a cycle of the workflow. The WEL consists of two core modules: Execution Engine and Scheduling Framework.

The Execution Engine's responsibility is to obtain the workflow objects instantiated in the RSL and combine them with the data and algorithms passed by the Scheduling Framework to form an executable workflow. When the combination is completed, the user selects whether to start executing the workflow.

If start, the Execution Engine starts executing the workflow until to the end or an abnormality occurs in the middle. Therefore, workflow execution is based on user-triggered events. When the execution ends, the execution engine passes the results to the Scheduling Framework for further processing.

According to the previous description, one duty of the Scheduling Framework is to pass data and algorithms to the Execution Engine to form an executable workflow. In addition, the Scheduling Framework is responsible for further processing the execution results, including passing it up to the RSL for visualization, and passing it down to the DRL for storage. However, no matter what processing is performed, the Scheduling Framework can form an information flow corresponding to the workflow as shown in the right half of Fig. 2 according to the original information and the result information, including the state of the data, the update of the parameters, and the results of each subtask.

4.3 Data Resource Layer

Facing heterogeneous multi-source scientific data, the DRL implements the maintenance of multi-domain scientific data storage and algorithms. Due to the different types of scientific data in different domains, this layer provides a variety types of databases, including relational databases, non-relational databases, and graph databases, and provides a unified access interface for data to achieve transparent operations, including data input and output interface, algorithm call interface, model save interface, etc. The information required by the other two layers are stored in the DRL.

5 The Application Scenario of UMDISW

Depending on the application scenario, the UMDISW can be transformed into different forms depending on the selection, including fully automated workflow, semi-custom workflow, and fully custom workflow. The difference between these three forms is that the amount of user interaction is different when building the workflow.

5.1 Fully Automated Workflow

In many scientific fields, a set of specifications may have been formed for some processes, and experts agree that the process is reasonable and will not change the process when doing experiments. Based on this situation, the UMDISW can form a template workflow based on domain specifications. The template workflow defines the corresponding tasks and subtasks according to the requirements of the experts, and the location of the data nodes and algorithm nodes also have corresponding requirements, and the data flow and information flow in the template workflow need to meet the domain specifications.

For the template workflow, the user only needs to select the workflow template in advance, and then the fully automated workflow as shown in the Fig. 3

will appear on the RSL. Figure 3 shows the gravitational wave data processing workflow. Each subtask, data node, algorithm node and information flow in the workflow are pre-defined. The user only needs to specify the data address corresponding to the data node, and then click to start running. The template workflow automatically obtains the data of the specified address from the DRL, and then passes the template instance and data to the WEL to complete the workflow execution, and finally return the result to the RSL to complete the display of the information flow.

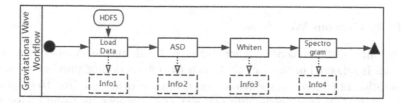

Fig. 3. Fully automated workflow

One use of this fully automated workflow is to examine the generalization capabilities of the same set of algorithms or processes for different data. Because the subtasks of the template workflow are fixed, the effect of the workflow in this case can be compared when accepting different data.

5.2 Semi-custom Workflow

In addition to the above-mentioned domain specification process, scientists may also customize a scientific data analysis process. The workflow in this application scenario is called a semi-custom workflow. The workflow requires the user to define the number of steps of the workflow, data nodes and algorithm nodes, and then RSL will generate the specified workflow based on these parameters. However, it should be noted that the algorithms and data corresponding to the subtasks of the created workflow are empty, and the user needs to select the required algorithms and data. The selection steps are the same as mentioned above. The information flow is also displayed by the WEL.

One function of this semi-custom workflow is to compare the results of the same data in the case of different algorithms. As shown in Fig. 4, these two semi-custom workflows built for users have the same structure, including the number of steps and input data, the only difference is that the subtasks, the subtask in Superalloy Experiment 1 is to analyze data A using the SVM algorithm, while the subtask in Superalloy Experiment 2 is to analyze data A using the random forest algorithm, returning the results to Info1 and Info2 respectively, to compare the effects of using different algorithms when processing the same data.

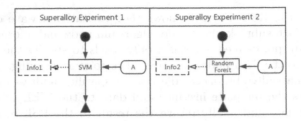

Fig. 4. Semi-custom workflow

5.3   Fully Custom Workflow

Fully custom workflows have a higher degree of freedom than semi-custom workflows. This is reflected in the fact that such workflows do not provide users with the generation of related components, and users can drag and drop to display on the RSL with their own needs, and connect the components using connectors. Of course, each node of the workflow at this time is still empty, so the user needs to select the corresponding data and algorithm. It is worth noting that after the user uses such a workflow and selects the data corresponding to the data node, the Scheduling Framework in the WEL intelligently recommends the appropriate machine learning algorithm according to the data selected by the user. So this kind of workflow is designed to provide users with an intelligent algorithm selection tool compared to the above two workflows, reducing the workload of users when conducting scientific experiments.

The recommended logic for machine learning algorithms is shown in Fig. 5. The data is first preprocessed into a conforming format, and then the data is parsed to see if feature reduction processing is required. If necessary, workflow will recommend the feature dimension reduction method of unsupervised learning class, such as FA, PCA, LDA and other topic model algorithms, or select Lasso, Ridge which are depending on the number of samples. If feature dimensionality reduction is not required, it will check if the dataset have decision attributes. If not, it will recommend clustering methods of unsupervised learning class, and recommend clustering algorithms such as k-means, hierarchical clustering, and FCM as needed. If there is a decision attribute, it will check whether the decision data belongs to a discrete class or a continuous class. If it belongs to the continuous class, workflow will recommend the regression method of supervised learning class, and recommend SVR, RF, Adaboost and other algorithms depending on the sample attributes. If the decision attribute is a discrete class, it will be recommended according to the sample type, if sample is image data, CNN is recommended, if it is time series data, RNN is recommended, and so on.

Of course, these recommended algorithms are just to give users a reference to help users make decisions. However, in practical applications, it can be found that this intelligent and fully custom workflow with recommendation mechanism does reduce the experimental steps, experiment time and workload for users who

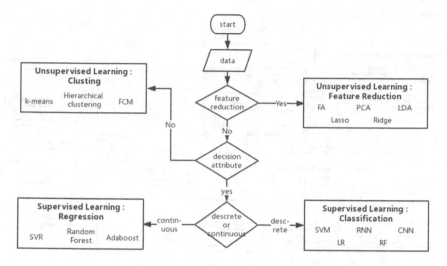

Fig. 5. The mechanism of intelligently recommending algorithms

do scientific experiments. Most importantly, it also plays a great role in exploring new scientific discoveries.

6   The Implementation of UMDISW

Since the proposal of UMDISW is based on previous research on the architecture of multi-domain scientific big data management system, the implementation of UMDISW is also dependent on the implementation and deployment of the architecture.

After integrating the content of the UMDISW into the architecture, the deployment of the entire architecture is updated as shown in Fig. 6. And as mentioned earlier, our proposed UMDISW is located in the AFA area.

As shown in Fig. 6, AFA consists of two subsystems: Spark as a workflow tool and gooFlow as a workflow manager. GooFlow is a UI component used to design flowcharts on the web page. It is based on Jquery development, and the great user experience makes the interface very easy to use. As a new generation of distributed processing framework, Spark's memory-based computing can speed up the execution of workflows, and it has an excellent machine learning library MLlib, which can be used as a tool for data analysis. The asset loader in the component diagram is replaced by an adapter "QFA-AFA Adapter". GooFlow also integrates the Spark tool with another adapter, the "Spark-gooFlow Adapter".

As can be seen from the deployment diagram, AFA connects to Bootstrap through the adapter "QFA-AFA Adapter" and the interface "asset provider". Through adapters and interfaces, gooFlow can get the data and algorithms stored in SAA that scientists want to experiment with. For the visualization of the workflow, gooFlow can be presented directly to the "Chinese visCloud" or Bootstrap via the interface "pipeline provider" and the adapter "Visualization

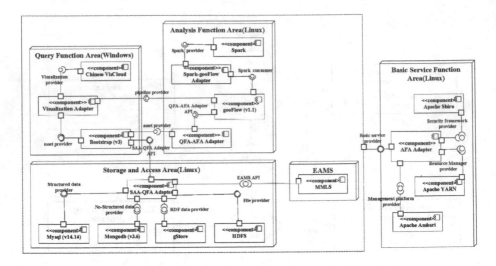

Fig. 6. The deployment of architecture and the implementation of UMDISW

Adapter". At the same time, the UMDISW also obtains the basic services and resource management functions in the BSFA through the interface "Basic service provider" and adapters.

7   Conclusion

Managing scientific data from a whole life cycle perspective is very helpful in mining the value of it. This paper proposes a General Multi-Domain Intelligent Scientific Workflow to help scientists create scientific value by dividing the whole life cycle steps.

The highlight of this article is: (1) using graphics and descriptors to model scientific workflows, eliminating the differences in heterogeneous scientific data, and building a universal framework to support consistency in multi-domain data processing; (2) transparency of the underlying architecture enables scientists to focus on high-level experimental design, reducing the time cost of learning and using the workflow; (3) incorporating a data-driven mechanism to intelligently recommend algorithms, reducing the amount of labor required for scientists to experiment and providing decision support for exploring new scientific discoveries.

Acknowledgments. This work is supported by the National Key Research and Development Plan of China (Grant No. 2016YFB1000600 and 2016YFB1000601).

References

1. Andreeva, J., Campana, S., Fanzago, F., Herrala, J.: High-energy physics on the grid: the ATLAS and CMS experience. J. Grid Comput. **6**(1), 3–13 (2008)

2. Chen, J., Wang, W., Zi-Yang, L.I., An, L.I.: Landsat 5 satellite overview. Remote Sens. Inf. **43**(3), 85–89 (2007)
3. Bengtsson-Palme, J., et al.: Strategies to improve usability and preserve accuracy in biological sequence databases. Proteomics **16**(18), 2454–2460 (2016)
4. Ivanova, M., Nes, N., Goncalves, R., Kersten, M.: MonetDB/SQL meets SkyServer: the challenges of a scientific database. In: International Conference on Scientific and Statistical Database Management, p. 13 (2007)
5. C. T. P. Team: Paradise: a database system for GIS applications. In: ACM SIGMOD International Conference on Management of Data, p. 485 (1995)
6. Patterson, T.C.: Google earth as a (not just) geography education tool. J. Geogr. **106**(4), 145–152 (2007)
7. Suchanek, F.M., Weikum, G.: Knowledge bases in the age of big data analytics. Proc. VLDB Endow. **7**(13), 1713–1714 (2014)
8. Schwartz, D.G., Te'Eni, D.: Encyclopedia of knowledge management. Online Inf. Rev. **5**(3), 315–316 (2006)
9. Moreau, L., et al.: The open provenance model core specification (v1.1). Future Gener. Comput. Syst. **27**(6), 743–756 (2011)
10. Batch control part 1: models and terminology (1995)
11. Reichert, M., Rinderle, S., Dadam, P.: On the modeling of correct service flows with BPEL4WS. In: EMISA 2004, Informations system in E-Business und E-Government, Beiträge des Workshops der GI-Fachgruppe EMISA, 6–8 October 2004, Luxemburg, pp. 117–128 (2004)
12. Taylor, I., Shields, M., Wang, I., Harrison, A.: Visual grid workflow in Triana. J. Grid Comput. **3**(3–4), 153–169 (2005)
13. Altintas, I., Berkley, C., Jaeger, E., Jones, M., Ludascher, B., Mock, S.: Kepler: an extensible system for design and execution of scientific workflows. In: SSDBM, pp. 423–424 (2004)
14. Turi, D., Missier, P., Goble, C., De Roure, D., Oinn, T.: Taverna workflows: syntax and semantics. In: IEEE International Conference on e-Science and Grid Computing, pp. 441–448 (2008)
15. Sun, Q., Liu, Y., Tian, W., Guo, Y., Lu, J.: Multi-domain and sub-role oriented software architecture for managing scientific big data. In: Ren, R., Zheng, C., Zhan, J. (eds.) SDBA 2018. CCIS, vol. 911, pp. 111–122. Springer, Singapore (2019). https://doi.org/10.1007/978-981-13-5910-1_10

MiDBench: Multimodel Industrial Big Data Benchmark

Yijian Cheng[1,2], Mengqian Cheng[1,2], Hao Ge[1,2], Yuhe Guo[1,2], Yuanzhe Hao[1,2], Xiaoguang Sun[1,2], Xiongpai Qin[1,2(✉)], Wei Lu[1,2], Yueguo Chen[1,2], and Xiaoyong Du[1,2]

[1] Key Laboratory of Data Engineering and Knowledge Engineering (MOE), Beijing, China
[2] School of Infomation, Renmin University of China, Beijing, China
{yijiancheng,chengmq,gh_daniel,guoyuhe,haoyuanzhe,xg.sun,qxp1990,
lu-wei,chenyueguo,duyong}@ruc.edu.cn

Abstract. Driven by the increasing industrial data over decades, big data systems have evolved rapidly. The diversity and complexity of industrial applications raise great challenge for companies to choose appropriate big data systems. Therefore, big data system benchmark becomes a research hotspot. Most of the state-of-the-art benchmarks focus on specific domains or data formats.

This paper presents our efforts on multimodel industrial big data benchmark, called MiDBench. MiDBench focuses on big data systems in crane assembly, wind turbines monitoring and simulation results management scenarios, which correspond to bills of materials (a.b.a BoM), time series and unstructured data format respectively. Currently, we have chose and developed eleven typical workloads of these three types application domains in our benchmark suite and we generate synthetic data by scaling the sample data. For the sake of fairness, we chose widely acceptable throughput and response time as metrics. Through the above we have established a set of benchmark applicable to high-end manufacturing with high credibility. Overall, experiment results show that Neo4j (representing graph database) performs better than Oracle (representing relation database) for processing BoM data. IotDB is better than InfluxDB in time series data for query and stress test. MongoDB performs better than ElasticSearch in simulation results management domain.

Keywords: Industrial · BoM · Time series · Unstructured

1 Introduction

The spurt of data in high-end manufacturing has brought a great number of big data systems. Big data systems can manage data and extract value from them. Therefore, many big data systems emerged. In addition to traditional relational databases such as MySQL [5] and Oracle [7] to manage structured data, there

---

The original version of this chapter was revised: the url link was corrected in reference 3. The correction to this chapter is available at https://doi.org/10.1007/978-3-030-32813-9_21

© Springer Nature Switzerland AG 2019, corrected publication 2021
C. Zheng and J. Zhan (Eds.): Bench 2018, LNCS 11459, pp. 172–185, 2019.
https://doi.org/10.1007/978-3-030-32813-9_15

are also many non-relational types, such as Neo4j [6] for graph data, InfluxDB [2] and IotDB [3] for time series data, MongoDB [4] and Elasticsearch [1] for unstructured data and so on. Such a large number of big data systems raise great challenge in choosing big data systems for companies.

It is of profound significance to establish a unified assessment benchmark for high-end manufacturing big data processing systems. Most of the state-of-the-art big data system benchmarks target specific data types or application scenarios. [9,10,12] pay attention to structured data, [16] targets graph data, [30] targets XML data and [8] targets time series data. Internet Services oriented BigDataBench [29] covers both structured and unstructured data. They may not be suitable in high-end manufacturing scenarios.

Here we present our benchmark IndustrialBigDataBench for high-end manufacturing. After investigating some kinds of scenarios, we chose three typical application domains which cover crane assembly, wind turbines monitoring and simulation results management scenarios to build our benchmark. The three most important factors to establish an effective benchmark are data generators, workloads, and metrics. Reasonable design of these three factors can make the benchmark more credible. The basic requirements of the generator is that it should generate datasets of various data sizes while keeping the characteristics of sample data. Therefore, we investigated BoM data for crane production, time series data for wind turbines monitoring and unstructured (such as json, xml and text) data for simulation result in high-end manufacturing and then model and scale these sample data.

The diversity and complexity of the requirements in high-end manufacturing make it difficult to investigate typical workloads. Finally, we chose and developed eleven typical workloads of these three types application domains through in-depth and detailed investigation.

For the sake of fairness, we need to choose a credible metrics. This mainly depends on the application scenarios. Different scenarios may focus on one or more of throughput, response time, and CPU or memory consumption. We select throughput and response time to judge the performance of different big data systems.

We used our benchmark to test different systems, and obtained the performance results of these big data processing systems in high-end manufacturing. Results show that Neo4j is better than Oracle in terms of import and query, which proves that Neo4j is more suitable for managing BoM data. In terms of time series data, InfluxDB performs almost equally with IotDB for data appending and data appending while querying, but IotDB performs better than InfluxDB for querying and querying while appending in both throughput and response time. MongoDB is better than Elasticsearch in dealing with unstructured data.

The rest of this paper is organized as follows. In Sect. 2, we discuss big data benchmarking requirements. Section 3 presents related work. Section 4 sumarizes our benchmarking methodology. Section 5 presents how we synthesize big data. Section 6 characterize experiments. Finally, we draw the conclusion in Sect. 7.

2   Big Data Benchmarking Requirements

This section discuss data generator, workloads and metrics, three important points for benchmarking [18].

Data generator is an important part of a benchmark. A good generator is capable of highly fitting sample data and generating data similar to sample data in terms of distribution, density and hierarchical relationship. Data generators can simulate real data better by using algorithms, probability distribution functions and so on.

Workload is used to measure the performance of big data processing systems. The results are obtained by executing the workload, and the differences between big data processing systems are judged according to the comparison of results. Therefore, the selection of query load becomes a guarantee of benchmark reliability.

Big data benchmarks must include diversity of data and workloads, which is the prerequisite for evaluating big data systems and architectures. The main function of benchmark is to test the big data system and judge the system performance by analyzing the results. But the prerequisite is that we have to establish a set of indicators. Different systems have different emphasis, such as time cost, throughput, CPU and memory consumption. However, the final selection of metrics depends on the real scenario requirement, which is an important basis for measurement selection.

3   Related Work

Benchmarks have been developing continuously, from the early relational database benchmark [9,10,12] to big data benchmark [19–22] in the past few decades.

TPC-H [13] and TPC-DS [11] are two typical representatives of big data benchmarks for relational database. TPC-H simulates the behaviors of purchasing and ordering in the actual scenario, and selects 24 complex queries and update statements.

TPC-DS is designed for decision support applications. Its schema uses the shared multi-snowflake schema. The dataset consists of 24 tables, and the workloads contain 99 randomly replaceable SQL queries. It chooses the number of queries executed per hour and the cost-effectiveness of the number of queries executed per hour as metrics. SetQuery [27] is also a typical benchmark extracted from multiple typical application scenarios. Its dataset consists of only one table, and workloads consist of six queries that contain an aggregate function.

Of course, some of the benchmarks are for non-closed databases [14,15,25,26]. XBench [30] is a family of XML benchmarks which recognizes that the XML data are quite varied and no one database schema and workload can properly capture this variety. XMach-1 [17] is a multi-user benchmark that is based on a Web application and considers text documents and catalog data. Compared to XMach-1, XMark [28] provides a more comprehensive set of queries, but it has no support for XML schema. These three are unstructured database benchmarks.

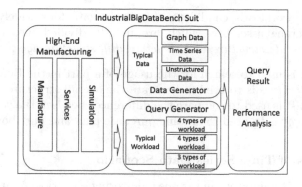

Fig. 1. The Architecture of IndustrialBigDataBench

XOO7 [23] is designed to test the efficiency of object-oriented DBMS. LinkBench [16] is based on traces from production databases that store "social graph" data at Facebook, a major social network. Time Series Benchmark Suite (TSBS) [8] was designed for benchmarking several time series databases, including TimescaleDB, MongoDB, InfluxDB, and Cassandra. BigDataBench [29] is a comprehensive benchmark which consists of BDGS [24] and BigOP [31], not only covers broad application scenarios, but also includes diverse and representative datasets. It can deal with structured data, unstructured data and semi-structured data.

4 Our Benchmarking Methodology

This section presents our methodology on IndustrialBigDataBench.

Our benchmark is designed according to the requirements mentioned in Sect. 2 and the architecture is shown in Fig. 1.

A good benchmark can help to choose a more suitable system for people. It needs to select the typical datasets and workloads from the diversity of the application scenarios. Therefore, we choose three scenarios of high-end manufacturing and conducted detailed analysis.

4.1 BoM Data Scenario Analysis

BoM is a widely used data format in high-end manufacture, which can be used to analyze the interdependence between parts, compare structural differences between products, track product changes, develop a procurement plan and so on.

We obtain the BoM data of assembling a crane from a company. The BoM data contains a total of 7 layers, each of which has a complex structure and a wide variety of components. Then, we analyze the distribution of the BoM data's vertexes and edges. Finally we generate synthetic datasets by scaling the sample data.

To consider workloads candidates, we investigate four widely used types of queries in crane assembly, which are mainly divided into the following *where_used*, *generate_structure*, and *structure_diff*, *structure_aggr*.

(1) *where_used* is used to search for the usage of a part in the BoM.
(2) *generate_structure* is to used to generate the overall structure of a product.
(3) *structure_diff* is used to compare the differences between the two structures.
(4) *structure_aggr* is to used to obtains purchase plan and part borrowing lists.

4.2 Analysis of Time Series Data Scenario

Time series data is ubiquitous in various monitoring scenarios. A large number of time series data will be produced in wind turbines monitoring every day. Making good use of these data can help us to find and solve problems such as device failure timely.

We use real monitor data provided by a company to train the wind model, simulate the power generation according to the cut-in and cut-out of the fan, and the energy conversion mechanism.

The following four are the most frequent workloads after investigating the companies' daily operations, including *data loading, data appending, query testing and stress testing*.

(1) *data loading* generates sensor data for one month, then tests the import performance of the target database.
(2) *data appending* continuously increases the number of devices to append data to the target database.
(3) *query testing* including simple window range queries and aggregated queries by time, which serves the purposes of monitoring and problem diagnosis.
(4) *stress testing* including two modes, i.e. increase the number of query with background data appending, and increase the number of devices to append data with background querying.

4.3 Unstructured Data Scenario Analysis

Simulation is an indispensable part in high-end manufacture, which will generate kinds of unstructured data consists of JSON, XML and text format. We generate the simulation files according to the type, size and quantity of the real simulation files.

How we can timely obtain massive simulation files, efficiently manage them and perform exception data detection are the main tasks in the current simulation. Through the refinement of the management scenarios of massive simulation files in the manufacturing industry, we designed the following workloads.

(1) *data transmission* including data generation and file uploading.
(2) *simple query* including detection on the currently uploaded file, annotating the exception file, analyzing and calculating the statistical value of the abnormal file.

Table 1. BoM DataSets

DataSet name	(Item,Edge)	Size
DataSet1	(40w,1300w)	700M
DataSet2	(70w,2900w)	1.5G
DataSet3	(100w,4900w)	2.5G
DataSet4	(150w,9700w)	5G

Table 2. Time Series DataSets

Rule	Proportion	Number of sensors	Number of data points	Size
Sine	0.036	6	222171429	9.08G
Constant	0.352	53	1962514286	80.17G
Random	0.512	77	2851200000	116.47G
Saw-Tooth	0.054	8	296228571	12.10G
Square-Wave	0.054	8	296228571	12.10G

(3) *complex query* including version management test, abnormal file detection test, hot-file query test and other load tests with features. It can be used to meet users' evaluation requirements in different levels.

5   Synthetic Data Generation

Generating scalable dataset is an important factors to be considered for a benchmark. Our IndustrialBigDataBench can generate three types of scalable datasets such as BoM data, time series data and unstructured data based on the raw data we investigated from diverse scenarios.

For the generation of BoM data, the data generator carries out statistical analysis of sample data and collect it, then analyzes the data distribution of the collected data. After that, we generate synthetic data by scaling the sample data with the characteristics. The BoM datasets we generated arc shown in Table 1 ("w" in Table 1 refers to "ten thousand").

For the generation of time series data, we use the real data provided by a company to train the wind model, simulate the power generation and generate relevant data according to the cut-in and cut-out of the fan and the energy conversion mechanism. For other sensors such as temperature and humidity which are seasonal, we use ARIMA model to train and generate data from the real data. The time series datasets generated are shown in Table 2.

For unstructured data, we have realized the rapid generation of massive small files according to the characteristics of high-end manufacture. We can generate a large number of files of different sizes and corresponding metadata files in a short period of time. The unstructured datasets generated are shown in Table 3.

Table 3. Unstructured DataSets

Parameters		File distribution			Exception file	Num. of file
Number of Device	50	1.8 MB	1.1 MB	0.4 MB		
Original dataset	Wind speed	10%	20%	70%	10%	1500
	Power Gen. efficiency	10%	20%	70%	10%	1500
	Power transmission	10%	20%	70%	10%	1500
Increment dataset	Wind Speed	10%	20%	70%	10%	1000
	Power Gen. efficiency	10%	20%	70%	10%	1000
	Power transmission	10%	20%	70%	10%	1000

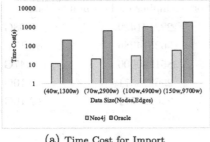

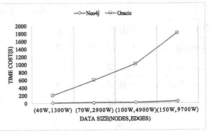

(a) Time Cost for Import   (b) Time Cost for Import

Fig. 2. Performance comparison for **Import** between Neo4j and Oracle

6 Workload Characterization Experiments

In this section, we present our experiments on different big data systems using IndustrialBigDataBench and demonstrate the performance comparison of different big data systems in high-end manufacturing scenarios. Our experiments are conducted on a server with Xeon E5-2620 processor, 32 GB memory, 2 TB HDD and the CPU frequency is 2.00 GHz.

6.1 Performance Tests on BoM Database Systems

We test the import and query performance of Neo4j and Oracle to judge the their abilities to process BoM data. The import performance of the two under different datasets are shown in Fig. 2. We can learn that Neo4j always maintains less time consumption. Oracle takes more time than Neo4j and time cost increases as the amount of data increasing.

We also execute the following four types of workloads, query the usage of the nodes (where_used), generate all structures from a node (generate_structure), compare the differences between two structures (structure_diff), structure aggregation and statistics (structure_aggr), and make performance evaluation through time consumption. The result are shown in Fig. 3.

We found that only the first query could run successfully(response time less than two hours) on Oracle, and the others could not finish on any other datasets. Furthermore, the first three queries will take much longer to execute on Oracle

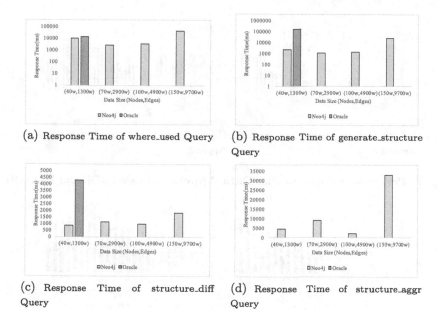

(a) Response Time of where_used Query

(b) Response Time of generate_structure Query

(c) Response Time of structure_diff Query

(d) Response Time of structure_aggr Query

Fig. 3. Performance comparison for **Query** between Neo4j and Oracle

than on Neo4j. The results prove the deficiency of relational database in dealing with graph data.

6.2 Performance Tests on Time Series Database Systems

The workloads of the timing series database, include data loading, data appending, query testing and stress testing.

In terms of data import, we first generate historical data of sensor for wind power plants during one month and save it in a file. Then load the data into memory and import it. We find that both InfluxDB and IotDB achieve 100% successful data import, but IotDB is better than InfluxDB in compression ratio and maximum import performance.

In terms of data appending, the write pressure increases as the number of requested clients increase. The results are shown in Fig. 4. We can learn that as the number of client threads increases, the throughput of the two continues to increase. When the number of clients reaches 300–500, the throughput of IotDB increases slowly while InfluxDB is still increasing.

The query test results are shown in Fig. 5. We can learn that the throughputs of the two increase as the number of client threads increases. In the case of 200 clients, the throughput of InfluxDB has reached saturation and the response time is more longer. So IotDB is better than InfluxDB in both throughput and response time.

We conduct stress testing which is divided into two modes on the target databases. The results are show in Fig. 6. The throughput of appending perfor-

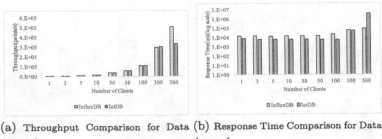

(a) Throughput Comparison for Data (b) Response Time Comparison for Data
Append   Append

Fig. 4. Performance comparison for **Data Append** between IotDB and InfluxDB

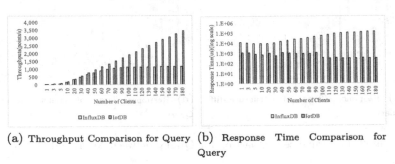

(a) Throughput Comparison for Query (b) Response Time Comparison for
Query

Fig. 5. Performance comparison for **Query** between IotDB and InfluxDB

mance with background querying is shown in Fig. 6(a). As the number of client threads increases, the throughput of both databases continues to increase, but InfluxDB has the best throughput. In terms of response time with background querying shown in Fig. 6(b), for IotDB, when the number of clients reaches close to 500, the response time of the appending operation increases. InfluxDB, with a small number of clients, has a comparable throughput to IotDB, but the response time is weaker than IotDB. When the number of clients continues to increase, IotDB performs better in terms of throughput and response time.

For the querying test with background appending, as the number of client threads increases, the throughput of the two databases as shown in Fig. 6(c) continues to increase. When the number of clients reaches 180, InfluxDB throughput has reached saturation, while IotDB does not. At the same time, the response time of InfluxDB far exceeds IotDB. We conclude that IotDB performs better than InfluxDB.

6.3 Performance Tests on Unstructured Database Systems

Through analysis of the management scenarios of massive simulation files in the manufacturing industry, we summarize the following requirements, which are divided into three categories, including data transmission test, simple query test

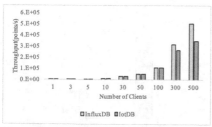

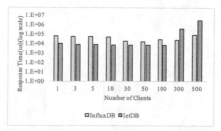

(a) Throughput of Appending While Querying

(b) Response Time of Appending While Querying

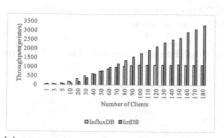

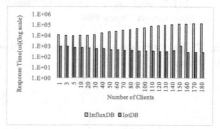

(c) Throughput of Querying While Appending

(d) Response Time of Querying While Appending

Fig. 6. Performance comparison for **Stress Testing** between InfluxDB and IotDB

and complex query test. Besides that version management test, abnormal file detection test, and hot-file query test meet users' evaluation requirements.

Data transmission test includes the import and export operation of binary and metadata files, measured by throughput. The results are shown in Fig. 7. We find that MongoDB's throughput is higher than Elasticsearch, and in general, the export speed of binary and metadata files is faster than the import speed.

The query load test includes seven types of test. The results of query test on MongoDB and Elasticsearch are shown in Fig. 8 (Q1–Q7 represent seven types of queries respectively). We can learn that the throughput of MongoDB is higher than Elasticsearch, especially in query for discrete-valued and query for range-valued, the advantage of throughput is more obvious.

Sorting load test includes the sorting of numeric values, the sorting of strings, and the sorting of time. The results of sorting load test on MongoDB and Elasticsearch are shown in Fig. 9 (Q1–Q3 respectively represent three types of sorting query). We learn that the throughput of Elasticsearch is slightly higher than MongoDB for the sorting of numeric values. For the sorting of strings and the sorting of time, the throughput of MongoDB is more than twice higher than Elasticsearch.

Statistical value calculation includes average calculation, minimum calculation and maximum calculation.

The results of the statistical value calculation are shown in Fig. 10 (Q1–Q3 respectively represent three types of statistical values calculation load). From

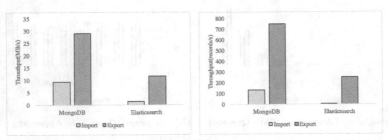

(a) Throughput Comparison for Import and Export Binary File

(b) Throughput Comparison for Import and Export Metadata

Fig. 7. Performance comparison for **Import and Export** between MongoDB and Elasticsearch

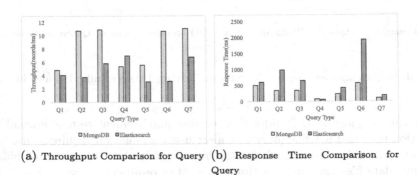

(a) Throughput Comparison for Query

(b) Response Time Comparison for Query

Fig. 8. Performance comparison for **Query** between MongoDB and Elasticsearch

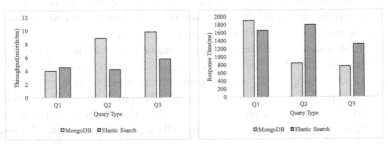

(a) Throughput Comparison for Sorting

(b) Response Time Comparison for Sorting

Fig. 9. Performance comparison for **Sorting** between MongoDB and Elasticsearch

the result, we can learn that MongoDB can support the load of statistical values calculation, while Elasticsearch does not support that.

For the average calculation, the throughput is 0.37 piece/ms, which is very low. For the minimum calculation and maximum calculation, the throughput of MongoDB is up to 20 piece/ms, which is high.

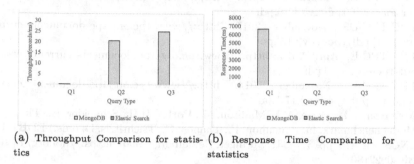

(a) Throughput Comparison for statistics

(b) Response Time Comparison for statistics

Fig. 10. Performance comparison for **Statistics** between MongoDB and Elasticsearch

Unfortunately, for version management, exception file detection and hot-file workloads, neither MongoDB nor Elasticsearch supports them.

7   Conclusion

In this paper, we propose a benchmark based on high-end manufacturing domain. We build our generator by analyzing the sample data of real system and we make a trade-off between choosing different types of workloads from typical scenarios. Also, we make our metrics referring to the real need of different application scenarios. We use the real datasets as the seed and generate synthetic data by scaling the seed data while keeping the characteristics of raw data. And we use our workloads to test different big data systems and finally make a credible performance evaluation of each big data system. Finally, we give our performance comparisons for each big data system.

Acknowledgment. The work is partially supported by the Ministry of Science and Technology of China, National Key Research and Development Program (No. 2016YFB1000702), and the NSF China under grant No. 61432006. You can visit our MiDBench at https://github.com/dbiir/MiDBench.

References

1. Elasticsearch. https://www.elastic.co/
2. InfluxDB. https://www.influxdata.com/
3. IoTDB. https://iotdb.apache.org/

4. MongoDB. https://www.mongodb.com/
5. MySQL. https://www.mysql.com
6. Neo4j. https://neo4j.com/
7. Oracle. https://www.oracle.com
8. Time series benchmark suite (TSBS). https://github.com/timescale/tsbs
9. TPC.TPC-A, June 1994. http://www.tpc.org/tpca/spec/tpca_current.pdf
10. TPC.TPC-C, February 2010. http://www.tpc.org/tpc_documents_current_versions/pdf/tpc-c_v5.11.0.pdf
11. TPC.TPC-DS, November 2015. http://www.tpc.org/tpc_documents_current_versions/pdf/tpc-ds_v2.1.0.pdf
12. TPC.TPC-E, April 2015. http://www.tpc.org/tpc_documents_current_versions/pdf/tpc-e_v1.14.0.pdf
13. TPC.TPC-H, November 2014. http://www.tpc.org/tpc_documents_current_versions/pdf/tpc-h_v2.17.1.pdf
14. Anderson, T.L., Berre, A.J., Mallison, M., Porter, H.H., Schneider, B.: The Hyper-Model benchmark. In: Bancilhon, F., Thanos, C., Tsichritzis, D. (eds.) EDBT 1990. LNCS, vol. 416, pp. 317–331. Springer, Heidelberg (1990). https://doi.org/10.1007/BFb0022180
15. Arasu, A., et al.: Linear road: a stream data management benchmark. In: Proceedings of the Thirtieth International Conference on Very Large Data Bases, VLDB 2004, vol. 30, pp. 480–491. VLDB Endowment (2004). http://dl.acm.org/citation.cfm?id=1316689.1316732
16. Armstrong, T.G., Ponnekanti, V., Borthakur, D., Callaghan, M.: LinkBench: a database benchmark based on the Facebook social graph. In: Proceedings of the 2013 ACM SIGMOD International Conference on Management of Data, SIGMOD 2013, pp. 1185–1196. ACM, New York (2013). https://doi.org/10.1145/2463676.2465296
17. Böhme, T., Rahm, E.: Multi-user evaluation of XML data management systems with XMach-1. In: Bressan, S., Lee, M.L., Chaudhri, A.B., Yu, J.X., Lacroix, Z. (eds.) Efficiency and Effectiveness of XML Tools and Techniques and Data Integration over the Web. LNCS, vol. 2590, pp. 148–159. Springer, Heidelberg (2003). https://doi.org/10.1007/3-540-36556-7_12
18. Jin, C.-Q., Qian, W.-N., Zhou, M.-Q., Zhou, A.-Y.: Benchmarking data management systems: from traditional database to emergent big data. Chin. J. Comput. (2014). http://cjc.ict.ac.cn/online/bfpub/jcq-2014430143239.pdf
19. Ferdman, M., et al.: Clearing the clouds: a study of emerging scale-out workloads on modern hardware, pp. 37–48 (2012). https://www.industry-academia.org/download/ASPLOS12_Clearing_the_Clouds.pdf
20. Ghazal, A., et al.: BigBench: towards an industry standard benchmark for big data analytics. In: Proceedings of the 2013 ACM SIGMOD International Conference on Management of Data, SIGMOD 2013, pp. 1197–1208. ACM, New York (2013). https://doi.org/10.1145/2463676.2463712
21. Huang, S., Huang, J., Dai, J., Xie, T., Huang, B.: The HiBench benchmark suite: characterization of the MapReduce-based data analysis. In: 2010 IEEE 26th International Conference on Data Engineering Workshops (ICDEW 2010), pp. 41–51, March 2010. https://doi.org/10.1109/ICDEW.2010.5452747
22. Jia, Z., Wang, L., Zhan, J., Zhang, L., Luo, C.: Characterizing data analysis workloads in data centers. In: 2013 IEEE International Symposium on Workload Characterization (IISWC), pp. 66–76, September 2013. https://doi.org/10.1109/IISWC.2013.6704671

23. Li, Y.G., et al.: XOO7: applying OO7 benchmark to xml query processing tool. In: Proceedings of the Tenth International Conference on Information and Knowledge Management, CIKM 2001, pp. 167–174. ACM, New York (2001). https://doi.org/ 10.1145/502585.502614

24. Ming, Z., et al.: BDGS: a scalable big data generator suite in big data bench-marking. In: Rabl, T., Jacobsen, H.-A., Raghunath, N., Poess, M., Bhandarkar, M., Baru, C. (eds.) WBDB 2013. LNCS, vol. 8585, pp. 138–154. Springer, Cham (2014). https://doi.org/10.1007/978-3-319-10596-3_11

25. Myllymaki, J., Kaufman, J.: DynaMark: a benchmark for dynamic spatial indexing. In: Chen, M.-S., Chrysanthis, P.K., Sloman, M., Zaslavsky, A. (eds.) MDM 2003. LNCS, vol. 2574, pp. 92–105. Springer, Heidelberg (2003). https://doi.org/10.1007/ 3-540-36389-0_7

26. Nicola, M., Kogan, I., Schiefer, B.: An XML transaction processing benchmark. In: Proceedings of the 2007 ACM SIGMOD International Conference on Management of Data, SIGMOD 2007, pp. 937–948. ACM, New York (2007). https://doi.org/10. 1145/1247480.1247590

27. O'Neil, P.E.: The set query benchmark. In: The Benchmark Handbook (1991)

28. Schmidt, A., Waas, F., Kersten, M., Carey, M.J., Manolescu, I., Busse, R.: XMark: a benchmark for XML data management. In: Proceedings of the 28th International Conference on Very Large Data Bases, VLDB 2002, pp. 974–985. VLDB Endow-ment (2002). http://dl.acm.org/citation.cfm?id=1287369.1287455

29. Wang, L., et al.: BigDataBench: a big data benchmark suite from internet services. CoRR abs/1401.1406 (2014). http://arxiv.org/abs/1401.1406

30. Yao, B.B., Özsu, M.T., Khandelwal, N.: XBench benchmark and performance test-ing of XML DBMSs. In: Proceedings of the 20th International Conference on Data Engineering, ICDE 2004, pp. 621–632. IEEE Computer Society, Washington, DC (2004). http://dl.acm.org/citation.cfm?id=977401.978145

31. Zhu, Y., et al.: BigOP: generating comprehensive big data workloads as a bench-marking framework. In: Bhowmick, S.S., Dyreson, C.E., Jensen, C.S., Lee, M.L., Muliantara, A., Thalheim, B. (eds.) DASFAA 2014. LNCS, vol. 8422, pp. 483–492. Springer, Cham (2014). https://doi.org/10.1007/978-3-319-05813-9_32

Modelling and Prediction

Power Characterization of Memory Intensive Applications: Analysis and Implications

Yeliang Qiu[1,2], Congfeng Jiang[1,2]([✉]), Tiantian Fan[1,2], Yumei Wang[1,2], Liangbin Zhang[3], Jian Wan[4], and Weisong Shi[5]

[1] Key Laboratory of Complex Systems Modeling and Simulation, Ministry of Education, Hangzhou Dianzi University, Hangzhou 310037, China
[2] School of Computer Science and Technology, Hangzhou Dianzi University, Hangzhou 310037, China
cjiang@hdu.edu.cn
[3] College of Big Data and Software Engineering, Zhejiang Wanli University, Ningbo, China
[4] School of Information and Electronic Engineering, Zhejiang University of Science and Technology, Hangzhou 310023, China
[5] Department of Computer Science, Wayne State University, Detroit, MI 48202, USA

Abstract. DRAM is a significant source of server power consumption especially when the server runs memory intensive applications. Current power aware scheduling assumes that DRAM is as energy proportional as other components. However, the non-energy proportionality of DRAM significantly affects the power and energy consumption of the whole server system when running memory intensive applications. Thus good knowledge of server power characterization under memory intensive workloads can help better workload placement with power reduction. In this paper, we investigate the power characteristics of memory intensive applications on real rack servers of different generations. Through comprehensive analysis we find that (1) Server power consumption changes with workload intensity and concurrent execution threads. However, fully utilized memory systems are not the most energy efficient. (2) Powered memory modules of installed memory capacity, i.e. the memory capacity per processor core has significant impact on the application's performance and server power consumption even if the memory system is not fully utilized. (3) Memory utilization is not always a good indicator for server power consumption when it is running memory intensive applications. Our experiments show that hardware configuration, workload types, as well as concurrently running threads have significant impact on a server's energy efficiency when running memory intensive applications. Our findings presented in this paper provide useful insights and guidance to system designers, as well as data center operators for energy efficiency aware job scheduling and power reductions.

Keywords: Energy efficiency · Memory system · Memory intensive computing · Energy proportionality

© Springer Nature Switzerland AG 2019
C. Zheng and J. Zhan (Eds.): Bench 2018, LNCS 11459, pp. 189–201, 2019.
https://doi.org/10.1007/978-3-030-32813-9_16

1 Motivation

Many emerging workloads are constrained by the high cost of data access. Currently, in-memory data processing is one of the alternatives to tackle this problem. In a big data paradigm, one of the most critical challenges is highly efficient data storage and analysis [1,8,24,31,32]. Although today's single server equipped with 12TB memory has become available in the market, in many cases the data to be processed has already exceeded the server's memory capacity [7], such as sparse matrix vector multiplications [28]. Moreover, application-level scalability is also subject to memory capacity and communication latency constraints. To solve this problem, a commonly used solution is data parallelization by portioning the dataset into smaller subsets to fit in the memory capacity as well as parallelism speedup. More specifically, the data are streamed into and out of the processor in parallel like Spark for fast analysis [8,20,22,31]. New memory hierarchies like 3-D memory stacking have been introduced for improvements in bandwidth, energy efficiency, and scalability [4,6,9,26,29]. In large scale memory system, how to minimize data movement and energy consumption are also dependent on these new memory technologies. In-memory computing or processing-in-memory is also proposed to reduce the energy consumption of server systems by performing computation in the memory modules [1].Thus, good knowledge of server energy proportionality under a memory intensive workload can help better workload placement and augment energy savings for hybrid resource scheduling in data centers [12,14,23]. In virtualized environment, server's power consumption is also changing with varying workload types, workload intensities [13] and communication performance [11]. For example, when system scale increases, the memory per core also changes and can also affect the application performance as well as the overall cost.

In response to the increase of energy consumption in data centers, industrial standard organizations have developed benchmarks to evaluate a server's energy efficiency. SPECpower_ssj2008 [27] (SPECpower is used for short in the remainder of the paper) is developed and widely adopted to characterize a system's energy efficiency at varying utilization levels. Mainstream server vendors submit their SPECpower testing results to SPEC and the results are made available online after reviewing and auditing.

However, the SPECpower benchmark is a server side Java benchmark and does not stress the memory systems much. We list the statistics of memory per core (MPC, the ratio of installed memory capacity over installed processor cores) of the 479 servers with published SPECpower results before year 2017 in Table 1. It is observed that most of the servers have memory per core less than 4 GB/core. Even among the 33 servers with hardware availability year from 2015 to 2016, the minimal, average, median, and maximal memory per core is 0.89, 3.08, 1.78, and 16 GB/core. Among all the published 479 SPECpower results, there are only 12 servers with memory per core greater than or equal to 8 GB/core, and only two servers have the highest memory per core as 16 GB/core.

Table 1. Memory per core statistics of published servers with SPECpower_ssj result

Memory per core (GB/core)	0.06	0.25	0.5	0.67	0.89	1	1.2	1.33	1.45	1.5	1.6	1.78	2
Count		1	1	2	15	2	153	3	32	6	68	4	13	123
Memory per core (GB/core)	2.25	2.5	2.67	2.91	3	3.2	3.56	4	6	8	10.67	16	
Count	1	1	5	5	3	1	1	26	1	6	4	2	

In this paper, in order to investigate the energy efficiency of large memory servers running memory intensive applications, we use the STREAM benchmark to stress three rack servers at different workload intensities. Our experiments show that hardware configuration has significant impact on a server's energy efficiency of memory intensive applications. Our findings presented in this paper provide useful insights and guidance to system designers, as well as data center operators for energy efficiency aware job scheduling and energy savings.

The remainder of this paper is organized as follows. In Sect. 2, we first describe the server energy efficiency and energy proportionality from the published SPECpower benchmark and introduce the energy efficiency metric for servers with large memory installations. In Sect. 3, we provide experimental results, observations, and insights of the energy efficiency of servers with large memory. We summarize related work in Sect. 4 and conclude the paper and make remarks on future work in Sect. 5.

2 Evolution of Server Energy Efficiency

2.1 Metrics of Energy Efficiency and Energy Proportionality

The detailed workload characterization of SPECpower can be found in [5]. We give a sample result of a server with memory per core of 16 GB/core from the SPECpower_ssj2008 published results in the year 2016 in Table 2. For consistence and convenience, we list some notations and terms used based on the SPECpower benchmark results throughout this paper:

(1) Utilization. In this paper we define the server hardware utilization as the target load column in SPECpower result assuming that the benchmark excises all hardware components concertedly. In SPECpower result, there are ten utilization levels from 10% to 100%. Please note that here the utilization is NOT the CPU utilization.
(2) Peak utilization. We refer to 100% utilization as peak utilization.
(3) Energy efficiency (EE). The energy efficiency is defined as the performance to power ratio. In Table 2, the energy efficiency values are in the last column entitled "performance to power ratio". Specifically, we use energy efficiency at some specific utilization without unit. We also use EE in short for energy efficiency in the remainder of this paper. For example, in Table 2, we refer to 6619 as energy efficiency at 70% utilization. But for memory systems, we

use bandwidth per watt (BpW) to measure the memory energy efficiency (MEE):

$$MEE = BpW = \frac{PerceivedBandwid(MB/s)}{SystemPower(watts)} \tag{1}$$

(4) Server overall energy efficiency. Server overall energy efficiency is the overall performance to power ratio of a server, i.e. the ratio of sum of ssj_ops over sum of power for 10 utilization levels (from 10% to 100%) and active idle:

$$Server\ overall\ energy\ efficiency = \sum ssj\_ops / \sum power \tag{2}$$

The server overall energy efficiency is also used as the server's SPECpower score. For example, in Table 2 the server overall energy efficiency (overall score) is 5316, i.e. the last row of the result table.

(5) Peak energy efficiency. Peak energy efficiency is defined as the highest (peak) energy efficiency of a server among all utilization levels. For example, in Table 2, the server peak energy efficiency is 6619 (at 70% utilization).

(6) Energy Proportionality (EP). A server at idle or low utilization state consumes a small to large amount of power compared to power at 100% utilization and this calls for the energy proportional computing. For an ideally energy proportional server, its power consumption is proportional to its utilization. For example, the ideal server consumes 50% power at 50% utilization compared to power at 100% utilization. In this paper, we use the energy proportionality (EP) metric proposed in [25].

Table 2. An example of SPECpower_ssj2008 testing result in 2016

Performance			Power	Performance to power ratio
Target load	Actual load	ssj_ops	Average active power (W)	
100%	99.80%	24,662,648	3,868	6,377
90%	90.10%	22,252,836	3,481	6,393
80%	80.00%	19,758,684	3,032	6,517
70%	70.00%	17,284,975	2,611	6,619
60%	60.00%	14,824,481	2,340	6,336
50%	50.00%	12,350,615	2,143	5,764
40%	40.00%	9,877,126	1,971	5,011
30%	30.00%	7,410,001	1,823	4,064
20%	20.00%	4,949,964	1,674	2,956
10%	10.00%	2,475,968	1,531	1,618
Active idle		0	1,080	0
$\sum$ssj_ops/$\sum$power				5,316

Take the server in Table 2 as an example; we can draw its utilization-power curve in Fig. 1. Note that the power in Fig. 1 is normalized to its peak power. The solid line is the energy proportionality curve of the server in Table 2 and the dotted line is of an ideal energy proportional server. The dash line in Fig. 1 is our tested non-tuned server with memory per core of 16 GB/core running SPECpower benchmark. With the power-utilization curve in Fig. 1, we can compute the energy proportionality of a real server as the following [25]:

$$EP = 1 - \frac{Area_{real} - Area_{ideal}}{Area_{ideal}} \tag{3}$$

Thus, the power-utilization curve in Fig. 1 is also called the energy proportionality curve. From Eq. 3 we can see that EP is a value equal or larger than zero but less than 2.0. For an ideally energy proportional server, its EP value is 1.0. For the server in Table 2, we summarize the areas of ten trapezoids and then get its EP value 0.807 according to Eq. 3.

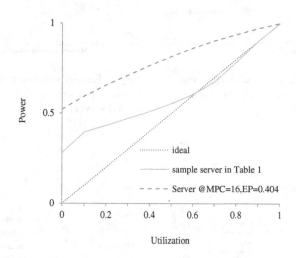

Fig. 1. Energy proportionality curve of the server in Table 2 and an ideally energy proportional server (power normalized to power at 100% utilization).

2.2   Experiment Setup

In order to derive the energy efficiency of servers running a memory intensive application, we run STREAM and SPECpower on three different 2U rack servers. All servers run the same x64 version CentOS 7 with Linux kernel 3.10. All the power data are measured by a WattsUP.Net power meter. The base configuration of these servers is listed in Table 3.

3 Experiment Results and Observations

3.1 Results of SPECpower Workload

We first run the SPECpower workload on each platform. In our experiments on 3 tested servers, the servers have lower energy efficiency at lower CPU frequency. Moreover, the energy efficiency does not stay constant when frequency decreases because the completed jobs decrease more significantly.

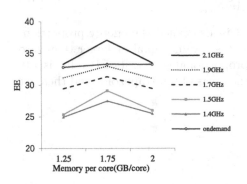

Fig. 2. Energy efficiency with different memory per core and CPU Frequency on #1 server.

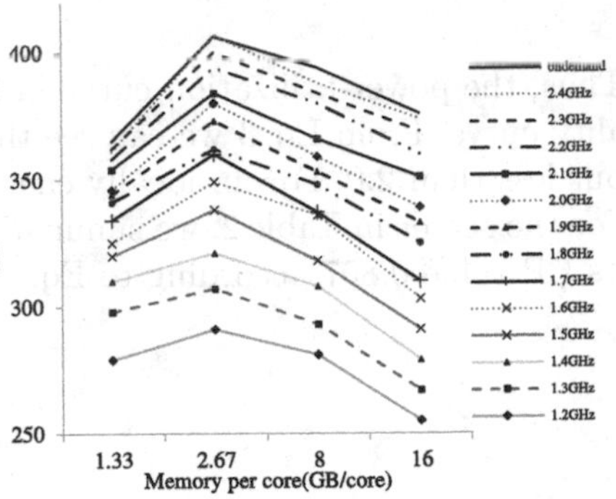

Fig. 3. Energy efficiency with different memory per core and CPU Frequency on #3 server.

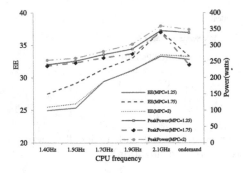
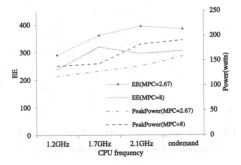

Fig. 4. Energy efficiency and peak power on server #1 with different memory per core and frequencies.

Fig. 5. Energy efficiency and peak power on server #2 with different memory per core and frequencies.

Figures 2 and 3 show that the on-demand governor has the highest energy efficiency and is very close to the energy efficiency with the highest frequency. We give the energy efficiency and peak power consumption on servers in Figs. 4, 5 and 6.

We observe that the server consumes more power at higher CPU frequency at the same memory per core configuration. When memory per core configuration

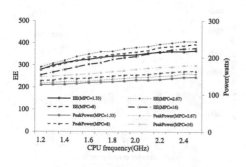

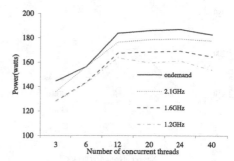

Fig. 6. Energy efficiency and peak power on server #3 with different memory per core and frequencies.

Fig. 7. Power consumption of server #2 with array size = 4 GB

Table 3. Base configuration of tested 2U servers

No	Name	Hardware availability year	CPU model	Total cores	CPU TDP (watts)	Memory (GB)	DISK
#1	Sugon A620r-G	2012	2*AMD Opteron 6272	32	115	64 (8G*8) DDR3 1600 MHz	4*SAS 300 GB 10K rpm (RAID10)
#2	ThinkServer RD640	2014	2*Intel Xeon E5 2620 #2	12	80	160 (16G*10) DDR4 2133 MHz	1*SSD 480 GB
#3	ThinkServer RD450	2015	2*Intel Xeon E5 2620 #3	12	85	192 (16G*12) DDR4 2133 MHz	1*SSD 480 GB

increases at fixed CPU frequency, the peak power consumption also increases. In addition, the on-demand consumes almost the same power with the highest CPU frequency.

3.2 Results of STREAM Workload

In order to stress the memory system, we run different numbers of concurrent STREAM threads with varying array size from 4 GB to 16 GB. Due to space limitation, we only provide the results of 4 GB. We present the power consumption of the tested servers in Figs. 7 and 8. From Fig. 8 we observe that usually memory systems are thought to be completely non-energy proportional (constant power consumption) during working. However, our experiments show that with the increment of concurrent threads and therefore memory utilization, the power consumption of the server also increases. We present the perceived bandwidth of single thread of the tested servers in Figs. 9 and 10. From Figs. 8, 9, 10 and 11, we observe that (take server #3 as an example):

(1) The power consumption and CPU utilization (except on-demand) is the highest for concurrent threads of 36 for CPU frequencies of 1.2 GHz,

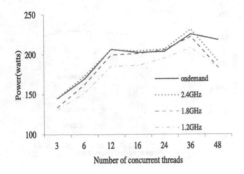

Fig. 8. Power Consumption of server #3 with array size = 4 GB.

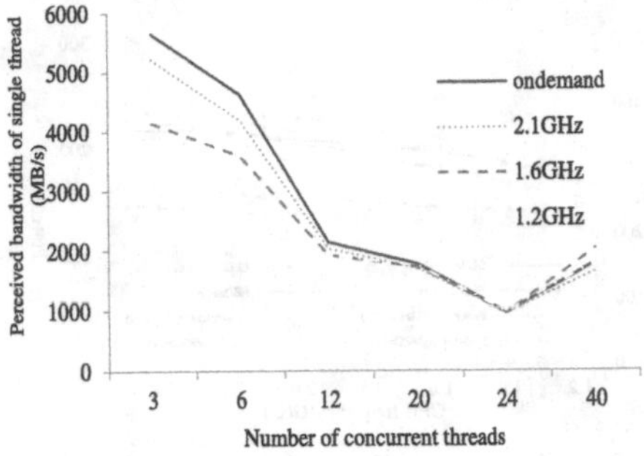

Fig. 9. Average Perceived bandwidth of single thread with array size = 4 GB (MB/s) on server #2.

1.8 GHz, 2.4 GHz, and on-demand governor. Intuitively, power consumption increases with the CPU frequencies.

(2) Memory utilization is the highest for 48 threads because all of the 48 threads consume most all of the memory. Furthermore, memory utilization increases with the number of concurrent running threads of STREAM.

(3) The perceived bandwidth of triad computation in single STREAM thread decreases when threads increase and it comes to the lowest at 36 threads and then bounces a little at 48 threads. This is mainly caused due to the contention and starvation of execution threads when we run 48 threads concurrently.

(4) While the perceived bandwidth increases when CPU frequency increases, the bandwidth beneficial from CPU frequency decreases when CPU frequency increases. Moreover, the difference of bandwidth induced by CPU frequency is the least at 24 threads. This is because the server has 12 physical cores and 24 execution threads in total.

(5) The memory energy efficiency decreases when the number of concurrent threads increases. As well, the difference of memory energy efficiency beneficial from CPU frequency with fewer threads is greater than that with more threads that are concurrent. This means that in a highly contented condition, frequency scaling cannot provide much memory energy efficiency improvements.

Similarly, we can obtain the results with array sizes of 8 GB, 12 GB, and 16 GB. For array size = 8 GB, we observe that

(1) The power consumption and CPU utilization at 24 threads are the highest for CPU frequency=1.2 GHz, 1.8 GHz, 2.4 GHz, and on-demand.

(2) The CPU utilization increases monotonically with the number of STREAM threads and the CPU utilization gets the highest at 24 threads.

(3) The memory utilization gets the highest at 16 threads and stays almost the highest at 24 threads.

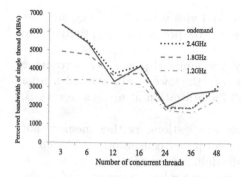

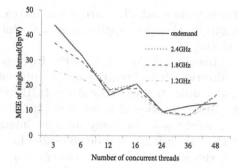

Fig. 10. Average perceived bandwidth of single thread with array size = 4 GB (MB/s) on server #3.

Fig. 11. Average memory energy efficiency of single thread with array size = 4 GB (MB/s) on server #3.

(4) The power consumption increases with CPU frequencies. The server has the highest power consumption or thread numbers of 3/6/12 with on-demand governor. For thread numbers of 16 and 24, the server has almost the same (less than 1% difference) power consumption for both on-demand governor and 2.4 GHz.

For array size = 12 GB, we observe that

(1) The server has the highest power consumption with CPU frequency = 2.4 GHz at fixed thread number (except 12 threads of on-demand governor).
(2) The server has the highest power consumption and memory utilization with 12 STREAM threads at fixed CPU frequency. Here the number of STREAM threads is equal to the number of physical cores in the servers.

For array size = 16 GB, we observe that

(1) The memory utilization and CPU utilization increase with the number of STREAM threads and both get the highest with 12 STREAM threads.
(2) The server has the highest power consumption with on-demand governor at fixed thread number (except 12 threads of CPU frequency at 2.4 GHz).

3.3   Insights on Energy Efficiency of Memory Intensive Applications

From the above observations, we derive some insights for memory intensive applications in data centers in terms of power and energy consumption.

Insight #1: For a fixed utilization, the server has higher power consumption per percentage utilization with high operating CPU frequency. The server has the lowest power consumption per percentage utilization with on-demand governor. This suggests that for memory intensive applications, the on-demand governor is the better choice than other frequency scaling.

Insight #2: The server power consumption per percentage utilization decreases when array size increases because the number of concurrent STREAM threads decrease when array size increases, and vice versa. This suggests that multiple threaded applications may increase the power consumption of the server.

Insight #3: At a fixed CPU frequency, the minimal power per percentage utilization shifts from the highest utilization to the lowest utilization, i.e. from 100% utilization at array size = 4 GB to 66.7% utilization at array size = 8 GB, to 50% utilization at array size = 16 GB.

Insight #4: For many memory intensive applications, neither memory nor CPU utilization is a good indicator for system power consumption. Therefore, we should not implement power aware scheduling only according to a single parameter like memory and CPU utilization even for large memory nodes running memory intensive applications.

4   Related Work

Nowadays, thanks to advancement in hardware technologies, growing main memory capacity has fueled the development of in-memory big data management and processing [32]. Since in-memory processing moves data into memory and eliminates disk I/O bottleneck, it is now possible to support interactive data analytics. However, in-memory systems are much more sensitive to other sources of overhead that do not matter in traditional I/O-bounded disk-based systems, including modern CPU and memory hierarchy utilization, time/space efficiency, parallelism, and concurrency control [10,21].

In many cases, the performance of computer systems is often limited by memory bandwidth. Moreover, due to pin and power constraints of packages, further increasing the bandwidth is challenging. To increase performance under these constraints, near-DRAM acceleration (NDA) architectures, near-DRAM Computing (NDC), Processing-In-Memory (PIM), Near Data Processing (NDP), or memory driven computing, have been proposed [2,16].

In multi-core platforms, memory is shared among all processor cores. However, the computational gains offered by multi-cores are often offset by performance degradation due to shared resources, such as main memory [3,17,19]. In some cases, such memory interference delay can be large and highly variable. Dirigent [34] is proposed to trade off the performance of latency-critical jobs that finish sooner than required with higher system throughput. Min et al. also tackled fine time granularity QoS problems for GPUs in heterogeneous platforms [18]. However, the progress heuristics used for the GPU were not general and the mechanism proposed is limited to managing main memory bandwidth contention between the CPU and GPU.

In big data analytics, Computation-in-Memory (CIM)-based architectures are proposed to address the problems of limited bandwidth, energy inefficiency, and limited scalability by enabling in-memory computations using non-volatile memristor technology [30]. In [33] the authors propose FusionFS, a distributed file system and distributed storage layer local to the compute nodes, which is responsible for most of the I/O operations and saves an extreme amount of data movement between compute and storage resources. FusionFS is better than popular file systems such as GPFS, PVFS, and HDFS. epiC [15] is a big data processing framework to tackle the Big Data's data variety challenge. epiC introduces a general actor-like concurrent programming model, independent of the data processing models, for specifying parallel computations.

In summary, a processor's frequency scaling and power optimization is well investigated, but memory related power performance optimization is still missing. Moreover, power consumption of large memory dominates when in-memory computing becomes the mainstream paradigm for big data analytics. This motivates us to investigate the power characteristics of servers running memory intensive applications.

5 Conclusions

Understanding energy efficiency of large memory systems running a memory intensive application can help data center designers and system operators in many folds, including system capacity planning, power shifting, job placement, and scheduling. In this paper, we conducted extensive experiments and measurements to investigate the power and energy characteristics of three 2U servers running various memory intensive benchmarks. Experiment results show that server power consumption changes with workload intensity and concurrent running threads. Moreover, different powered memory modules of installed memory capacity, i.e. the memory capacity per processor core has significant impact on the application's performance and server power consumption even if the memory system is not fully utilized. This provides useful implications for reconfigurable system design and real time power aware adaption. Last but not least, our experiments also show that memory utilization is not always a good indicator for server power consumption even when it is running memory intensive applications.

Our experiments show that both hardware configuration and concurrent running threads have significant impact on a server's energy efficiency of memory intensive applications. Our findings presented in this paper provide useful insights and guidance to system designers, as well as data center operators for energy efficiency aware job scheduling and energy savings. As future work, we plan to characterize the energy efficiency of large memory systems running more diverse memory intensive applications like in-memory databases, Hadoop, and Spark jobs.

Acknowledgements. This work is supported by Natural Science Foundation of China (No. 61472109, No. 61572163 and No. 61472112) and Key Research and Development Program of Zhejiang Province (No. 2018C01098, 2019C01059 and 2019C03134). This work is also supported in part by National Science Foundation (NSF) grant CNS-1205338 and CNS-1561216, and by the Introduction of Innovative R&D team program of Guangdong Province (No. 201001D0104726115). This work is supported by Alibaba Group through Alibaba Innovative Research (AIR) Program. This work is partially supported by Visiting Scholarship of Teachers' Professional Development Program (No. FX2018050).

References

1. Ahn, J., Hong, S., Yoo, S., Mutlu, O., Choi, K.: A scalable processing-in-memory accelerator for parallel graph processing. ACM SIGARCH Comput. Architect. News **43**(3), 105–117 (2016)
2. Asghari-Moghaddam, H., Son, Y.H., Ahn, J.H., Kim, N.S.: Chameleon: versatile and practical near-dram acceleration architecture for large memory systems. In: The 49th Annual IEEE/ACM International Symposium on Microarchitecture, p. 50. IEEE Press (2016)
3. Dasari, D., Nelis, V., Akesson, B.: A framework for memory contention analysis in multi-core platforms. Real-Time Syst. **52**(3), 272–322 (2016)
4. Goswami, N., Cao, B., Li, T.: Power-performance co-optimization of throughput core architecture using resistive memory. In: 2013 IEEE 19th International Symposium on High Performance Computer Architecture (HPCA2013), pp. 342–353. IEEE (2013)
5. Gray, L.D., Kumar, A., Li, H.H.: Workload characterization of the SPECpower_ssj2008 benchmark. In: Kounev, S., Gorton, I., Sachs, K. (eds.) SIPEW 2008. LNCS, vol. 5119, pp. 262–282. Springer, Heidelberg (2008). https://doi.org/10.1007/978-3-540-69814-2_17
6. Hajkazemi, M.H., Chorney, M., Jabbarvand Behrouz, R., Khavari Tavana, M., Homayoun, H.: Adaptive bandwidth management for performance-temperature trade-offs in heterogeneous HMC+ DDRx memory. In: Proceedings of the 25th edition on Great Lakes Symposium on VLSI, pp. 391–396. ACM (2015)
7. Hamdioui, S., et al.: Memristor based computation-in-memory architecture for data-intensive applications. In: Proceedings of the 2015 Design, Automation & Test in Europe Conference & Exhibition, pp. 1718–1725. EDA Consortium (2015)
8. Hirzel, M., Soulé, R., Schneider, S., Gedik, B., Grimm, R.: A catalog of stream processing optimizations. ACM Comput. Surv. (CSUR) **46**(4), 46 (2014)
9. Imani, M., Mercati, P., Rosing, T.: ReMAM: low energy resistive multi-stage associative memory for energy efficient computing. In: 2016 17th International Symposium on Quality Electronic Design (ISQED), pp. 101–106. IEEE (2016)
10. Islam, M., Scrbak, M., Kavi, K.M., Ignatowski, M., Jayasena, N.: Improving node-level mapreduce performance using processing-in-memory technologies. In: Lopes, L., et al. (eds.) Euro-Par 2014. LNCS, vol. 8806, pp. 425–437. Springer, Cham (2014). https://doi.org/10.1007/978-3-319-14313-2_36
11. Jiang, C., et al.: Interdomain I/O optimization in virtualized sensor networks. Sensors **18**(12), 4395 (2018)
12. Jiang, C., Han, G., Lin, J., Jia, G., Shi, W., Wan, J.: Characteristics of co-allocated online services and batch jobs in internet data centers: a case study from Alibaba cloud. IEEE Access **7**, 22495–22508 (2019)
13. Jiang, C., et al.: Energy efficiency comparison of hypervisors. Sustain. Comput.: Inform. Syst. **22**, 311–321 (2019)
14. Jiang, C., Wang, Y., Ou, D., Luo, B., Shi, W.: Energy proportional servers: where are we in 2016? In: 2017 IEEE 37th International Conference on Distributed Computing Systems (ICDCS), pp. 1649–1660. IEEE (2017)
15. Jiang, D., Wu, S., Chen, G., Ooi, B.C., Tan, K.L., Xu, J.: epiC: an extensible and scalable system for processing big data. Proc. VLDB Endow. **7**(7), 541–552 (2014)
16. Keeton, K.: Memory-driven computing. In: FAST (2017)

17. Kim, Y., Han, D., Mutlu, O., Harchol-Balter, M.: ATLAS: a scalable and high-performance scheduling algorithm for multiple memory controllers. In: 2010 IEEE 16th International Symposium on High Performance Computer Architecture (HPCA), pp. 1–12. IEEE (2010)
18. Min, K.J., Erez, M., Sudanthi, C., Paver, N.: A QoS-aware memory controller for dynamically balancing GPU and CPU bandwidth use in an MPSoC. In: Design Automation Conference, pp. 850–855 (2012)
19. Muralidhara, S.P., Subramanian, L., Mutlu, O., Kandemir, M., Moscibroda, T.: Reducing memory interference in multicore systems via application-aware memory channel partitioning. In: IEEE/ACM International Symposium on Microarchitecture, pp. 374–385 (2011)
20. Nair, R., et al.: Active memory cube: a processing-in-memory architecture for exascale systems. IBM J. Res. Dev. 59(2/3), 17:1–17:14 (2015)
21. Pattnaik, A., et al.: Scheduling techniques for GPU architectures with processing-in-memory capabilities. In: Proceedings of the 2016 International Conference on Parallel Architectures and Compilation, pp. 31–44. ACM (2016)
22. Pugsley, S.H., et al.: Comparing implementations of near-data computing with in-memory mapreduce workloads. IEEE Micro 34(4), 44–52 (2014)
23. Qiu, Y., Jiang, C., Wang, Y., Ou, D., Li, Y., Wan, J.: Energy aware virtual machine scheduling in data centers. Energies 12(4), 646 (2019)
24. Reed, D.A., Dongarra, J.: Exascale computing and big data. Commun. ACM 58(7), 56–68 (2015)
25. Ryckbosch, F., Polfliet, S., Eeckhout, L.: Trends in server energy proportionality. Computer 44(9), 69–72 (2011)
26. Sharad, M., Fan, D., Roy, K.: Ultra low power associative computing with spin neurons and resistive crossbar memory. In: Proceedings of the 50th Annual Design Automation Conference, p. 107. ACM (2013)
27. SPECpower: https://www.spec.org/power_ssj2008/
28. Tanabe, N., et al.: A memory accelerator with gather functions for bandwidth-bound irregular applications. In: Proceedings of the 1st Workshop on Irregular Applications: Architectures and Algorithms, pp. 35–42. ACM (2011)
29. Wang, Y., Yu, H.: An ultralow-power memory-based big-data computing platform by nonvolatile domain-wall nanowire devices. In: Proceedings of the 2013 International Symposium on Low Power Electronics and Design, pp. 329–334. IEEE Press (2013)
30. Yu, J., Nane, R., Haron, A., Hamdioui, S., Corporaal, H., Bertels, K.: Skeleton-based design and simulation flow for computation-in-memory architectures. In: IEEE/ACM International Symposium on Nanoscale Architectures, pp. 165–170 (2016)
31. Zaharia, M., Chowdhury, M., Franklin, M.J., Shenker, S., Stoica, I.: Spark: cluster computing with working sets. HotCloud 10(10–10), 95 (2010)
32. Zhang, H., Chen, G., Ooi, B.C., Tan, K.L., Zhang, M.: In-memory big data management and processing: a survey. IEEE Trans. Knowl. Data Eng. 27(7), 1920–1948 (2015)
33. Zhao, D., Zhang, Z., Zhou, X., Li, T.: FusionFS: toward supporting data-intensive scientific applications on extreme-scale high-performance computing systems. In: IEEE International Conference on Big Data, pp. 61–70 (2014)
34. Zhu, H., Erez, M.: Dirigent: enforcing QoS for latency-critical tasks on shared multicore systems. ACM SIGOPS Oper. Syst. Rev. 50(2), 33–47 (2016)

Multi-USVs Coordinated Detection in Marine Environment with Deep Reinforcement Learning

Ruiying Li, Rui Wang(✉), Xiaohui Hu, Kai Li, and Haichang Li

The Science and Technology on Integrated Information System Laboratory,
Institute of Software, Chinese Academy of Sciences, Beijing, China
{ruiying,wangrui,xiaohui,likai,haichang}@iscas.ac.cn

Abstract. In recent years, with the rapid development of deep reinforcement learning, numerous researches have begun taking more and more attention in military and civilian fields. Compared with ship monitoring and other technical means, USVs have more significant advantages in marine environment and is gradually becoming a concern of academic and marine management departments. However, single agent reinforcement learning cannot fit well in the multi-USVs cases because of the non-stationary environment and complex multi-agent interactions. In order to learn cooperation models among USVs, we propose a multi-USVs coordinated detection method based on DDPG and LSTM is used for storage about the sequence of states and actions. Besides, in order to adapt to the algorithm, we model the marine environment where every USV is considered as an agent. Experiments are constructed in simulation conditions and the results verify the effectiveness of the proposed method.

Keywords: Deep reinforcement learning · Multiple USVs · Coordinated detection

1 Introduction

Instead of the lack of data in the past, the era of Big Data has arrived [1,2]. Even though Big Data applications present our opportunities to discover new knowledge and create novel methods, there is a new question: we are drowning in data, but starving for knowledge. The most fundamental challenge for Big Data is to explore the large volumes of data and extract useful information or knowledge for future actions [3]. Fortunately, with the massive data, Artificial Intelligence (AI) emerges. Until now, AI has achieved practical products in many field, such as virtual personal assistants, smart cars, online customer service, referral services, security monitoring, and so on.

Deep Reinforcement Learning (DRL) has become the core interest in the field of AI, which leverages the perceived ability of deep learning and the decision

© Springer Nature Switzerland AG 2019
C. Zheng and J. Zhan (Eds.): Bench 2018, LNCS 11459, pp. 202–214, 2019.
https://doi.org/10.1007/978-3-030-32813-9_17

making ability of reinforcement learning. Deep learning is reborn of the artificial neural network and has become popular around the world with its transcendental effects in practical applications. Artificial neural networks have been able to achieve approximations of arbitrary complexity continuous functions [30]. Deep learning use super more hidden layers to enhance the ability, which requires exponentially hidden numbers to achieve comparable expression for shallow networks. The representation of deep learning is actually a combination of a large number of functions and can be trained by the means of backpropagation. Reinforcement learning is often considered as a branch of machine learning. In fact, reinforcement learning itself has a complete developmental context, and Bellman eventually brings together and formalizes the abstractions into MDP problems. Afterwards, with the expand of scientists, it has become a relatively complete system, often called approximate dynamic programming [31].

Unmanned Surface Vehicles (USVs) have been widely used in various military or civilian applications. Compared with ship monitoring and other technical means, the use of drones has significant advantages in achieving various types of emergencies at the marine environment, such as low cost, high efficiency and flexibility. It is gradually becoming a concern of academic and marine management departments at home and abroad. Unlike the land and airborne unmanned system, weak perception is the major challenges for marine unmanned system. There are mainly two reasons: first, until now, the detection methods of underwater sensor technology are still very scant; second, due to the limitation of volume and energy, the load carried by the marine unmanned system is restricted largely. These all greatly limits the sensing ability of the systems. Therefore, individual USV has very terminate capability in marine environment. It is particularly critical for multiple USVs to learn communication protocols and work in a collaborative way. The research on allowing the multi-USVs to interact information implicitly and understand the current situation as a whole effectively is meaningful. Through the intelligent coordination of multi-USVs, the system will have the ability to assess and predict the overall situation, then make intelligent decisions that comprehensively consider various requirements such as communication function, marine environment and cluster cooperation, and finally enhance the monitoring and sensing ability of the system with the strategy optimization.

In recent years, with the rapid development of deep reinforcement learning, numerous institutions, universities, corporations and militaries have begun taking more and more attention in the related field. In this paper, we introduce a multi-USVs coordinated detection method based on DDPG, as Fig. 1 shows, which allows USVs learn approximate models of other USVs online and simultaneously use them in their own policy learning procedure. Based on the DDPG algorithm, the strategy network for decision making and the value network for evaluation are implemented, and the sequence of states and actions is input into the LSTM network for memory storage. The key question is to map the optimal route of each USV to the suspected sea area where the target is located so as to effectively guide the system to find the target with a larger scale. Finally, marine environment modeling is constructed based on deep reinforcement learning. We make experiments in simulation conditions and the results verify the effectiveness of the proposed method.

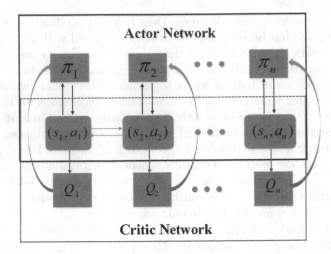

Fig. 1. The framework. Based on DDPG, multiple agents interact with each other to adjust to the non-stationary environment, and the sequence of states and actions is stored up with LSTM.

2   Background

2.1   USV Overview

In past three decades, the researches on USVs are mostly developed and leaded by the institutions, universities and militaries all over the world. The first USV was developed at MIT Sea Grant, named ARTEMIS [22], which was used to collect simple bathmetry data. One of the shortcomings of ARTEMIS was its small size, which limited its ability to work continuously. The interests in USVs for detection and reconnaissance missions emerged in the late 1990s [23].

USV was originally named as autonomous search and hydrographic vehicle (ASH), and later called Owl/Owl MK I, which was developed by the Office of Naval research (ONR). The Owls were widely used for mine field reconnaissance, shallow water monitoring and maritime interception. Navtec Inc. continued the development of the Owl MK II to Owl MK VI for the next decade. During these time, they construct a fully autonomous navigation system by using sensor fusion. The MK II with side scan sonar and video camera was the first American Navy USV to be deployed for a real world mission, which has been used in shipping lanes off Kuwait to detect live mines. Other countries have also paid much more attention to develop USVs with different features and missions. For example, Japan and Yamaha conducted two USVs, UMV-H and UMV-O [24]. UMV-H can be equipped with underwater cameras and sonar. But UMV-H is not totally unmanned, it can be also used in manned mode. The UMV-O is used just for monitoring of bio-geo-chemical, physical parameter of the oceans and atmosphere. There are also numerous USVs used for academic interests. For example, an Italian catamaran USV named SESAMO, with improved stability and greater wave resistance, was used in Antarctica for conducting oceano-graphic research [26]. In China, a lot of work also have been researched and done in USVs. Taiwan developed an USV named ZhengHe [25] in 2010, which can integrate scientific equipment such as WI-FI communication and a satellite-based global positioning (GPS). The system are appropriate for various types of inshore research and surveys, such as marine topography, sediment disposition analysis, inshore engineering measurements and the monitoring of hydrology.

Recent works about USVs have become a recognized technology for the use of surveillance, detection and other missions, but most existing USVs just have limited autonomy, endurance and intelligence. The USVs mentioned above mostly worked individually, they just had weak communication system and lacked the greater ability to cooperate together. Our method based on the technology of deep reinforcement learning can make the USVs more intelligent and cooperative for the mission of coordinated detection in marine environment. The multi-USVs system not only let every unique USV have a greater levels of autonomy to make a better decision independently, but also the cooperation enable the USVs have robust capabilities and situational awareness that is necessary for them to under-take the complex mission of detection. Our work focus mainly on the intelligence and cooperation of the USVs instead of the boat-design, costs and materials, and it is therefore related to a lot of recent work about deep learning [27] and rein-forcement learning [13,19,28,29].

2.2   Reinforcement Learning

Reinforcement learning (RL) [4] aims to solve sequential decision making prob-lem, which emphasizes how to act based on the environment and maximize the expected benefits. A typical setting where reinforcement learning operates is shown in Fig. 2. At each timestep t, agent receives the current state s_t from environment, obtains a reward r_t associated with the last state transition at the same time, then takes the next action a_{t+1} and releases it back to the environ-ment. The goal of RL is to learn a policy $\pi(a|s)$, i.e. a mapping from state s to action a, which can maximize the expected discount cumulative future reward: $E[R] = E[\sum_{t=0}^{T} \gamma^t r_t]$.

In fact, there is a long history in terms of interaction and collaboration among multi-agent settings [5,6]. In spite of the limitations to toy examples in the beginning, reinforcement learning, as a means, has widely been applied to multi-agent systems in order to learn optimal collaboration policies. Multi-agent reinforcement learning (MARL) is concerned with a set of autonomous agents that share a common environment [7]. Learning in MARL is fundamentally dif-ficult, because agents not only interact with the environment, but also with each other. This means that the environment is unstable: the changes in the policy of one agent usually will affect that of the others, and vice versa [8]. How to learn effective communication protocol, which can not result in changes of the environment, is of crucial importance to the success of multi-agent RL. Panait et al. [9] have shown that in cooperative games, agent who learns the effect of

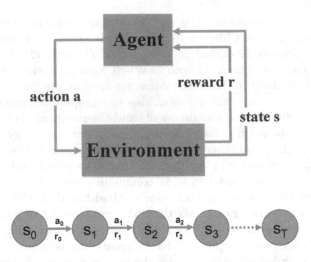

Fig. 2. Reinforcement learning scenario. Agent receives the current state from environment and reward, and then releases the next action back to the environment.

joint actions has better performance than those who do not in the same scenarios. Zhang *et al.* [16] propose that in order to limit the coordination set, agents dynamically decompose the coordination network in a distributed way and dramatically reduce communication without significantly affecting overall learning performance. Foerster *et al.* [17] adopt two steps: Reinforced Inter-Agent Learning uses deep Q-learning, and Differentiable Inter-Agent Learning exploits the error derivatives through communication channels among agents. [20] introduces a training regimen utilizing an ensemble of policies for each agent that leads to more robust multi-agent policies.

In the specific application of multi-USVs coordinated detection, we mainly use multi-agent collaboration algorithm based on DDPG [13], which draws on the successful experience of DQN [19]: experience reply and fixed Q-target network. DQN is a method based on Critic only and it is difficult to deal with large action space, especially continuous action. Because the network is impossible to search for the largest Q value among so many outputs. Conversely, DDPG is based on the Actor-Critic method. It uses a network to fit the strategy function in the action output, and then directly outputs the action, which can cope with the output of the continuous action and the large action space. DDPG consists of two networks: an Policy Network (Actor) and a Value Network (Critic). The policy network outputs action and is updated by the gradient calculation formula; the value network judges the action and is updated according to the target value.

3 Approach

In this section, we present an idea about the multi-USVs coordinated detection based on DDPG. The frame diagram is shown in Fig. 1. The USV is regarded as an agent and thus the research is transformed into a multi-agent collaborative detection problem, which requires special modeling for the marine environment and USVs.

3.1   Single-USV RL

Generally, RL based on single agent can be basically divided into policy-based methods and value-based ones. The former learns a policy with an indirect way by learning a value function or an action-value function; the latter is to directly model and then learn the policy, so it is also called policy optimization. According to whether based on value and policy or not, it can be divided into three groups [10,11]: Critic-only methods, Actor-only methods and Actor-Critic methods.

1. Critic-only method is based entirely on value, such as Q-learning [15] and DQN, which uses low variance temporal difference learning to estimate the Q-value: $Q(s,a;\omega) = E[R; s,a]$. The policy can be derived using greedy action selection, $i.e.$, $\pi(a|s) = a^* = argmax_a Q(s,a;\omega)$. They are usually used for discrete action as finding a^* is computationally intensive in continuous action space. Disadvantages of the method is that small changes in the value function can cause huge influence in the strategy, which lead to training not to converge. Especially after the introduction of function approximation, bias makes the convergence of training more difficult, even though the generalization ability of the algorithm is improved.

2. Actor-only method is based entirely on policy, for example, REINFORCE [12], which directly learns the parameterized policy $\pi(a|s,\theta)$. They can generate continuous action but suffer from high variance in the estimation of policy gradient. The gradient estimation variance is relatively high, which means it easily converges to a non-optimal solution. Also, since the estimation of each gradient does not depend on previous estimates, the known information can not be utilized fully.

3. Actor-Critic method integrates value-based and policy-based together, which jointly learns $\pi(a|s,\theta)$ and $Q(s,a;\omega)$: actor $\pi(a|s,\theta)$ gives high rewarding trajectory, which updates critic $Q(s,a;\omega)$ towards the right direction; critic $Q(s,a;\omega)$ picks out the good action for actor $\pi(a|s,\theta)$ to reinforce. This mutual reinforcement behavior preserves the advantages of both actor-only and critic-only, which helps avoid bad local minima and converges faster. Especially the embrace with deep learning, produces a chemical reaction and appears a batch of advanced algorithms, such as A3C [14] and other improvements and variants based on them.

DDPG is an approach that based on Actor-Critic method: the strategy function and the value function is simulated with deep convolutional neural network, namely the policy network and the Q network. The policy network integrates deep learning neural networks into Deterministic Policy Gradient:

$a_t = \mu(s_t|\theta^\mu)$, where μ represents the optimal behavior strategy. The Q network uses a deep learning model to simulate the approximation of the action-value function: $Q^\mu(s_t, a_t) = E[r(s_t, a_t) + \gamma Q^\mu(s_{t+1}, \mu(s_{t+1})]$, whose definition is a recursive expression and is solved with Bellman equation.

The training mode of DDPG is off-policy: behavior policy and target policy is not the same. Behavior strategy is only used to interact with the environment and generate data, that is, to make decisions during the training process; and then target strategy continuously learns from the data generated by the behavior strategy and optimizes itself. In the DDPG training process, random noise is introduced into the decision mechanism of the action, which help to learn potential better strategies while leveraging existing strategies, scilicet, behaviour policy. It changes the deterministic process to a random process, then the action is sampled from the random process and released to the environment for execution, as Fig. 3 shows. The final target strategy is optimized with the dataset generated by the behavior strategy.

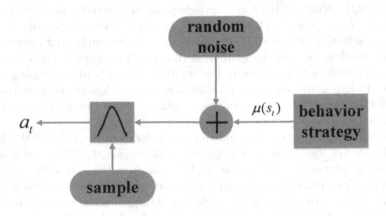

Fig. 3. Behaviour policy. The action is generated based on a given environment during the training process, so as to obtain the data set for training the optimal strategy.

3.2 Multi-USVs Coordinated Detection

Single-agent reinforcement learning approaches are poorly suited to multi-USVs environments. Each agent's policy is changing and results in the environment unstationary, which exhibit huge variance when coordination among multiple USVs. Also, traditional intelligent USVs system perceives interaction and delivers information mainly based on the behavior of biological clusters, which allows the system to work together at low cost and complete complex tasks in sinister environment. At present, the distribution of unmanned system is generally ensuring the maximum profit-loss ratio and task balance, which reflects synergistic operational advantages of the system. However, these algorithms are not very mature and are not suitable for independent planning of large scale complex tasks. The method of multi-USVs coordinated detection is based on DDPG, which allows USVs learn approximate models of other USVs online and simultaneously use them in their own policy learning procedure.

The Q value function and state value function are defined as that in the general reinforcement learning settings. For agent i, the state value $v_i(s)$ is defined as the expected discounted-cumulative rewards R_i for state s, where $R_i = E[\sum_{t=0}^{T} \gamma^t r_i^t | s]$ and γ is the discount for the reward. The Q value function is defined as $Q_i(s, a) = E[\sum_{t=0}^{T} \gamma^t r_i^t | s, a]$. The expectation is taken over the environment and the policy. Since the deterministic policy is used, the Q value function is equal to the state value function.

$$v_i(s) = Q_i(s, \mu(s)) = E[\sum_{t=0}^{T} \gamma^t r_i^t | s, \mu(s)] \tag{1}$$

where $\mu(s) = [\mu_1(s_1), \mu_2(s_2), \ldots, \mu_n(s_n)]$.

For multi-agent collaborative detection problem, we try to maximize the mean state value over all the agents in the environment, $i.e.\ Q = \frac{1}{n} \sum_{i=1}^{n} Q_i(s, a)$.

At every time t, the loss function of the agent i is:

$$min(R_i^t - Q_i(s_t, a_t))^2 \tag{2}$$

R_i^t represents the estimated reward, $i.e.\ R_i^t = r_i^t + \gamma Q_i(s_{t+1}, a_{t+1})$, where $Q_i(s_{t+1}, a_{t+1})$ is the target Q value function with its parameters periodically updated using the recent parameters of Q function.

The policy parameters is optimized by the policy gradient algorithm, and the objective function is defined with the mean Q value function of all the agents. The gradients for agent i with the policy parameter θ can be written as:

$$\nabla_a Q_i(s_t, a_t | \theta^Q)|_{a=\mu(s_t|\theta^\mu)} \nabla_{\theta^\mu} \mu(s_t | \theta^\mu) \tag{3}$$

In general, the sequence of states and actions are interrelated, and the current output of a sequence is also related to the previous output. We resort Recurrent Neural Networks (RNN) to connect previous information to the current state, which memorizes the previous information and applies it to the calculation of the current output, that is, the nodes between the hidden layers are also connected, and the input of the hidden layer includes not only the output of the input layer but also the output of the hidden layer at the previous moment. Here, we mainly adopt the LSTM network [21] to use the past pair (s, a) to help infer the next action.

In order to adapt multi-agent reinforcement learning to the marine environment, we carry out the environment modeling. The sea area and environment, intelligent unmanned system, decision making rules and other task related comprehensive jointly construct suitable marine monitoring space, where the interactive environment based on deep reinforcement learning is built, as shows in Fig. 4.

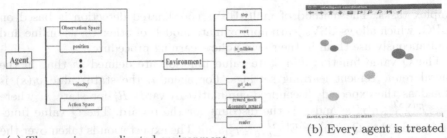

(a) The marine coordinated environment.

(b) Every agent is treated as a motion node

Fig. 4. Coordinated environment. The marine coordinated environment is constructed with defining the characteristic attributes, reward and punishment rules, the state space and action space of agents, where the red, blue and green are coordinated USVs and the black is detected target. (Color figure online)

4   Results and Discussion

In this section, based on the built marine coordinated environment, we verify the effectiveness of our proposed method in simulation conditions for Multi-USVs coordinated detection. The working range is limited to an area of 1.2 km * 1.2 km and the collaborative goal is to detect the target as much as more.

At the initial moment, the USVs are dispersed in their desired positions according to the needs of the detection, as shown in Fig. 5. In the process of detecting the suspected target, the USVs cooperate to maneuver and surround the intrusion target in the shortest time and the objective is to ensure the maximum range of target detected. The experimental results in different directions are shown in Fig. 7. The goal of coordinated detection is to make the system adapt to the changing marine environment and various emergencies and have continuous detection capability in weak sensing and weak communication condition.

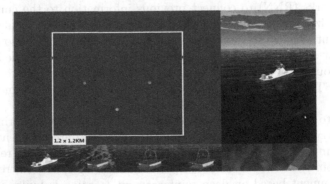

Fig. 5. Initial position. At the initial moment, the USVs is dispersed in its desired position according to the needs of the detection.

Table 1. The parameter settings.

Parameter	Value
Marine environmental noise (dB)	NL0 = 75
Ship self-noise (dB)	NLS = 0
Working frequency (Hz)	f = 4000
Pulse width (ms)	T = 0.4
Array directional gain (dB)	DI = 13
Expected target strength (dB)	TS = 13
Active sound source level (dB)	SL = 205

To quantify the effectiveness of the proposed algorithm, we rasterize the
1.2 km * 1.2 km area where the task is performed, and set the current USVs'
positions with parameters as Table 1 displays, such as marine environmental
noise, ship self-noise, operating frequency, pulse width, base directivity gain,
expected target intensity and active sound source level.

According to the performance evaluation software, the probability of target
detected can be evaluated in grid form, as Fig. 6 shows. We deduce the performance evaluation process in reverse, *i.e.* given the current position of the target
(the grid), the expected area of the USVs can be obtained, and then verify the
proposed method by comparing expected area with actual position of each USV.

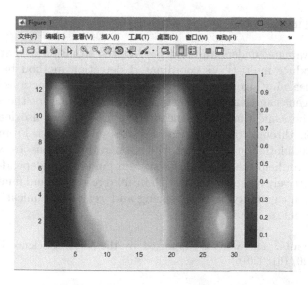

Fig. 6. Schematic diagram of the performance evaluation.

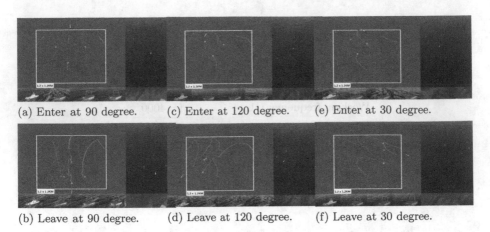

(a) Enter at 90 degree.   (c) Enter at 120 degree.   (e) Enter at 30 degree.

(b) Leave at 90 degree.   (d) Leave at 120 degree.   (f) Leave at 30 degree.

Fig. 7. Experimental result. The target enters and leaves the 1.2 km * 1.2 km area at 30°, 90° and 120°.

A total of 3168 data was intercepted from the simulation experiment, and the actual position of the six USVs and the target was obtained. During the verification process, the values of the parameters are consistent with the parameter settings of the detection subsystem, as shown in Table 1. Among the 3168 pieces of data, there are 2275 pieces of data satisfying the requirements, which reaches the correct rate of 71.81% and verify the effectiveness of the proposed method.

5   Conclusion

To real-time evaluate, understand and predict the situation of marine environment, we introduce multi-USVs coordinated detection method based on deep reinforcement learning algorithm DDPG. Different reward functions are designed so that each agent can learn its own strategy by modeling for the marine environment. At the same time, with the help of LSTM, we also learn the timing information through the sequence of states and actions. From the results shown in the simulation environment, the cooperative actions are verified. Our research work can help the multi-USVs system guide the independent response to changes, effectively complete tasks with limited resources and finally have continuous detection capability in weak sensing and weak communication condition to a certain extent.

Acknowledgments. This work is supported by the Natural Science Foundation of China (U1435220) (61802016).

References

1. Labrinidis, A., Jagadish, H.V.: Challenges and opportunities with big data. Proc. VLDB Endow. **5**(12), 2032–2033 (2012)

2. Jitao, S., Gao, Y., Bingkun, B., Snoek, C., Dai, Q.: Recent advances in social multimedia big data mining and applications. Multimed. Syst. **22**(1), 1–3 (2016)
3. Leskovec, J., Rajaraman, A., Ullman, J.D.: Mining of Massive Datasets, 2nd edn. Cambridge University Press, Cambridge (2014)
4. Sutton, R.S., Barto, A.G.: Introduction to Reinforcement Learning. MIT Press, Cambridge (1998)
5. Littman, M.L.: Markov games as a framework for multi-agent reinforcement learning. In: Proceedings of the Eleventh International Conference on Machine Learning, pp. 157–163 (1994)
6. Schmidhuber, J.: A general method for multi-agent reinforcement learning in unrestricted environments. In: Adaptation, Coevolution and Learning in Multiagent Systems: Papers from the 1996 AAAI Spring Symposium, pp. 84–87 (1996)
7. Busoniu, L., Babuska, R., De Schutter, B.: A comprehensive survey of multiagent reinforcement learning. IEEE Trans. Syst. Man Cybern. Part C Appl. Rev. **38**(2), 156–172 (2008)
8. Matignon, L., Laurent, G.J., Le Fort-Piat, N.: Independent reinforcement learners in cooperative Markov games: a survey regarding coordination problems. Knowl. Eng. Rev. **27**(1), 1–31 (2012)
9. Panait, L., Luke, S.: Cooperative multi-agent learning: the state of the art. Auton. Agents Multi-Agent Syst. **11**(3), 387–434 (2005)
10. Konda, V.R., Tsitsiklis, J.N.: Onactor-critic algorithms. SIAM J. Control Optim. **42**(4), 1143–1166 (2003)
11. Grondman, I., Busoniu, L., Lopes, G.A.D., et al.: A survey of actor-critic reinforcement learning: standard and natural policy gradients. IEEE Trans. Syst. Man Cybern. Part C (Appl. Rev.) **42**(6), 1291–1307 (2012)
12. Williams, R.J.: Simple statistical gradient-following algorithms for connectionist reinforcement learning. Mach. Learn. **8**(3–4), 229–256 (1992)
13. Lillicrap, T.P., et al.: Continuous control with deep reinforcement learning. arXiv preprint arXiv:1509.02971 (2015)
14. Mnih, V., et al.: Asynchronous methods for deep reinforcement learning. In: International Conference on Machine Learning, pp. 1928–1937 (2016)
15. Sutton, R.S., Barto, A.G.: Reinforcement Learning: An Introduction. MIT Press, Cambridge (1998)
16. Zhang, C., Lesser, V.: Coordinating multi-agent reinforcement learning with limited communication. In: Proceedings of the 2013 International Conference on Autonomous Agents and Multi-agent Systems, pp. 1101–1108. International Foundation for Autonomous Agents and Multiagent Systems (2013)
17. Foerster, J., Assael, I.A., Freitas, N., Whiteson, S.: Learning to communicate with deep multi-agent reinforcement learning. In: Advances in Neural Information Processing Systems, pp. 2137–2145 (2016)
18. Silver, D., Lever, G., Heess, N., Degris, T., Wierstra, D., Riedmiller, M.: Deterministic policy gradient algorithms. In: Proceedings of the 31st International Conference on Machine Learning, pp. 387–395 (2014)
19. Mnih, V., et al.: Human-level control through deep reinforcement learning. Nature **518**(7540), 529 (2015)
20. Lowe, R., Wu, Y., Tamar, A., Harb, J., Abbeel, O.P., Mordatch, I.: Multi-agent actor-critic for mixed cooperative-competitive environments. In: Advances in Neural Information Processing Systems, pp. 6379–6390 (2017)
21. Hochreiter, S., Schmidhuber, J.: Long short-term memory. Neural Comput. **9**(8), 1735–1780 (1997)

22. Vaneck, T., Manley, J., Rodriguez, C., Schmidt, M.: Automated bathymetry using an autonomous surface craft navigation. J. Inst. Navig. **43**(4), 407–419 (1996)
23. Bertram, V.: Unmanned surface vehicles - a survey. Skibsteknisk Selskab (2008)
24. Enderle, B., Yanagihara, T., Suemori, M., Imai, H., Sato, A.: Recent developments in a total unmanned integration system. In: AUVSI Unmanned Systems Conference, Anaheim (2004)
25. Yang, W., Chen, C., Hsu, C., Tseng, C., Yang, W.: Multifunctional inshore survey platform with unmanned surface vehicles. Int. J. Autom. Smart Technol. **1**, 19–25 (2011)
26. Caccia, M., et al.: Sampling sea surfaces with SESAMO: an autonomous craft for the study of sea-air interactions. Robot. Autom. Mag. **12**(3), 95–105 (2005)
27. LeCun, Y., Bengio, Y., Hinton, G.: Deep learning. Nature **521**(7553), 436–444 (2015)
28. Lowe, R., Wu, Y., Tamar, A., Harb, J., Abbeel, P., Mordatch, I.: Multi-agent actor-critic for mixed cooperative-competitive environments. In: Advances in Neural Information Processing Systems, pp. 6382–6393 (2017)
29. Boutilier, C.: Learning conventions in multiagent stochastic domains using likelihood estimates. In: Proceedings of the Twelfth International Conference on Uncertainty in Artificial Intelligence, pp. 106–114 (1996)
30. Nielsen, M.A.: Neural Networks and Deep Learning. Determination Press (2015)
31. Bertsekas, D.P.: Dynamic Programming and Optimal Control. Athena Scientific, Belmont (2005)

EC-Bench: Benchmarking Onload and Offload Erasure Coders on Modern Hardware Architectures

Haiyang Shi[✉], Xiaoyi Lu, and Dhabaleswar K. Panda

Department of Computer Science and Engineering, The Ohio State University,
Columbus, USA
{shi.876,lu.932,panda.2}@osu.edu

Abstract. Various Erasure Coding (EC) schemes based on hardware accelerations have been proposed in the community to leverage the advanced compute capabilities on modern data centers, such as Intel ISA-L Onload EC coders and Mellanox InfiniBand Offload EC coders. These EC coders can play a vital role in designing next-generation distributed storage systems. Unfortunately, there does not exist a unified and easy way for distributed storage systems researchers and designers to benchmark, measure, and characterize the performance of these different EC coders. In this context, we propose a unified benchmark suite, called EC-Bench, to help the users to benchmark both onload and offload EC coders on modern hardware architectures. EC-Bench provides both encoding and decoding benchmarks with tunable parameter support. A rich set of metrics, including latency, actual and normalized throughput, CPU utilization, and cache pressure, can be reported through EC-Bench. Evaluations with EC-Bench demonstrate that hardware-optimized offload coders (e.g. Mellanox-EC) have lower demands on CPU and cache compared to onload coders, and highly optimized onload coders (e.g., Intel ISA-L) outperform offload coders for most configurations.

1 Introduction

Replication, a redundancy scheme that replicates data across multiple machines and racks, is widely used to guarantee high reliability and availability against the most failure scenarios in distributed storage systems. Since the data being generated increases rapidly every day, petabytes of storage in today's data centers are becoming common. As a result, distributed systems cannot tolerate such a significant storage overhead brought by using N-way replication, even though disk storage is inexpensive today.

To this end, latest distributed storage systems, such as Google Colossus [6], Facebook HDFS-RAID [1,36], the Quantcast File System [27] and Microsoft

This research is supported in part by National Science Foundation grants CCF#1822987, CNS#1513120, IIS#1636846, and OAC#1664137.

© Springer Nature Switzerland AG 2019
C. Zheng and J. Zhan (Eds.): Bench 2018, LNCS 11459, pp. 215–230, 2019.
https://doi.org/10.1007/978-3-030-32813-9_18

Azure Storage System [15], are transforming to the use of Erasure Coding (EC) scheme, which offers high reliability and availability at a prominently low storage overhead [35,42]. For instance, Reed-Solomon [34] is a popular family of erasure codes used in Google Colossus, Facebook HDFS-RAID, and many others. The Reed-Solomon codes with a 6 + 3 configuration, i.e., three parity chunks for every six data chunks, which delivers the same level of fault tolerance as 4-way replication scheme does, has a storage overhead of 50%, while 4-way replication has a storage overhead of 300%.

The trade-off of deploying erasure codes in distributed storage systems instead of replication is performance. The use of erasure coding results in a significant increase in computation overhead due to the time-consuming EC encoding and decoding operations. With such a trade-off, the erasure-encoded distributed storage systems should benefit from modern high-performance hardware architectures. The advancements in CPU/GPU architectures and network interconnects have enabled the design of high-performance erasure coding libraries [16,24] for alleviating the compute overheads involved in erasure coding-based storage resilience. This motivates us to believe that erasure coding could be a viable primary fault-tolerance mechanism for next-generation distributed storage systems.

High-performance EC coders can be categorized in two general ways: (1) EC Onload, where host-based libraries such as Jerasure [30] and Intel ISA-L [16] are employed, and, (2) EC Offload, wherein Mellanox InfiniBand HCA and GPU-like accelerators based libraries such as Gibraltar [8] and Mellanox-EC [23] are leveraged. With the increased compute and remote I/O required for computing and distributing EC-coded files, EC onload can enable higher storage efficiency that is inherent to erasure-coded storage, at the cost of performance and CPU usage. On the other hand, the high CPU usage can be alleviated with the help of EC Offload designs, that offload computation to the Mellanox HCAs or GPU devices, but suffer the loss of performance due to its limited compute capabilities in comparison to CPU cores.

As we can see, efficient EC coders can play a significant role in designing next-generation distributed storage systems. However, each of these EC coders has different APIs, implementations, and performance characteristics. To guide the users to choose an appropriate one for their target platforms, the community needs a unified and easy-to-use benchmark suite to measure the performance and expose the insights of different coders.

Unfortunately, there does not exist such a benchmark suite for distributed storage systems researchers and designers to benchmark, measure, and characterize the performance of these different EC coders. To address this issue, in this paper, we propose a unified benchmark suite, called **EC-Bench**, to help the erasure coding researchers and distributed storage system designers to benchmark both onload and offload EC coders on modern hardware architectures. EC-Bench provides both encoding and decoding benchmarks with tunable parameter support. The supported parameters include the number of data chunks, the number of parity chunks, the number of bits in a word, and the size of each chunk. To help the users to understand the EC coders in multiple dimensions, EC-Bench reports a rich set of metrics including latency, actual and normalized throughput, CPU utilization, and cache pressure.

With EC-Bench, we conduct experiments on four open-source libraries (i.e., Jerasure [30], ISA-L [16], Gibraltar [8], and Mellanox-EC [23]) to evaluate the performance of onload and offload erasure coders. Our in-depth evaluation exposes impressive performance insights for different coders on modern CPU, GPU, and InfiniBand architectures. For instance, the experiments illustrate that hardware-optimized offload coders (e.g., Mellanox-EC) have less CPU utilization and cache pressure than onload coders, and highly optimized onload coders (e.g., Intel ISA-L) perform much better than offload coders due to the use of advanced instruction sets.

The rest of the paper is organized as follows. Section 2 presents the necessary background on EC. Section 3 presents our proposed design for EC-Bench. Section 4 describes our detailed evaluation. Section 5 discusses related studies. Finally, we conclude in Sect. 6.

2   Background

2.1   Erasure Coding

Conventionally, a storage system tolerates faults by replicating data to different nodes and racks. For example, GFS, HDFS, and Ceph apply 3-way replication as their default storage mechanisms [11,39,43]. Unfortunately, replicating a tremendous amount of data can incur significant storage overhead. Therefore, erasure coding (EC), which can offer the same reliability as or higher than replication with much lower storage overhead, becomes an attractive alternative. The Reed-Solomon (RS) code and its variations are the most popular erasure codes employed in distributed file systems (e.g., HDFS, Ceph, QFS, Google Colossus, Facebook f4, Baidu Atlas and Backblaze [3–6,18,26,27,43]). In general, the input data is split into chunks with a fixed size (i.e., *chunk_size*). An RS coder, denoted as $RS(k, m)$, computes m parity chunks for k data chunks. These $k + m$ chunks are organized as a group called *stripe*. For chunks belonging into the same stripe, $RS(k, m)$ is able to recover the entire stripe from up to m chunk losses, with a storage overhead of m/k. In contrast, the replication scheme has to store $m + 1$ replicas to achieve the same reliability; thus the storage overhead of replication is as high as m. For example, the $RS(6, 3)$ code has a storage overhead of 50% and delivers the same fault-tolerance as 4-way replication that incurs a 3x overhead. One of the disadvantages in applying erasure coding to storage systems, however, is high pressures of erasure operations on system performance.

2.2   Onload and Offload Erasure Coders

To overcome the high computational costs involved with erasure coding, two broad categories of coders have been proposed in the community to take advantage of modern hardware capabilities: (1) onload coders, which are highly optimized for advanced CPU capabilities (e.g., Intel SSE [41] and AVX [17]), and,

(2) offload coders, which offload erasure operations to accelerators (e.g, GPU [8], Host Channel Adapters (HCA) [24]). These hardware-optimized erasure coders can potentially facilitate EC to be employed as a viable choice for fault-tolerance in modern distributed storage systems.

3   EC-Bench Design

In this section, we discuss the design details, parameter space, and main metrics of our benchmarking framework, i.e., EC-Bench.

3.1   Design

EC-Bench consists of two benchmarks, one for encoding and one for decoding.

> **Encoding Benchmark:** For encoding benchmark, a large in-memory data file of size D are split into multiple data blocks of size $k \times chunk\_size$. Each encoding operation of the evaluated erasure coder encodes a piece of data block into $k + m$ data and parity chunks.
>
> **Decoding Benchmark:** In order to generate data and parity chunks (i.e., stripes), such that we can mimic chunk corruption by nullifying some chunks, a preprocessing stage before performing decoding operations is necessary. In the preprocessing stage, it encodes a large in-memory data file of size D into multiple encoded stripes of size $(k+m) \times chunk\_size$, and randomly zeros m chunks out of $k + m$ chunks in each encoded stripe. After the preprocessing stage, each decoding operation of the evaluated erasure coder recovers an encoded stripe. To fairly compare all erasure coders, both data and parity chunks need to be recovered in the benchmark. For some erasure coders, such as Gibraltar [8], which only recover data chunks in decoding, we will re-encode to recover corrupt parity chunks.

3.2   Parameter Space

As aforementioned in Sect. 2, the most important parameters for all erasure coders are the number of data chunks k, the number of parity chunks m, the number of bits in a word w, and the size of each chunk $chunk\_size$. Therefore, in EC-Bench, the values of k, m, w, and $chunk\_size$ may be chosen at the discretion of the user and according to the constraints of erasure coders to evaluate.

3.3   Metrics

In addition to latency and throughout, which are the most typical metrics for benchmarking erasure coders, we also introduce *CPU utilization* and *cache pressure* as main metrics to evaluate onload and offload erasure coders. In this section, we clarify the definition and describe the approach used for each metric in EC-Bench.

Latency. The latency in EC-Bench is defined as the time spent on erasure coding operations (i.e., encoding and decoding).

Throughput. The throughput in EC-Bench is defined as the size of data and parity chunks divided by the time spent on erasure coding operations (i.e., encoding and decoding). Let D denote the size of k data chunks, and t denote the time consumed by erasure coding operations. Such that the size of each chunk is D/k. As illustrated in Sect. 3.1, for both encoding and decoding operations, the erasure coder operates on k chunks and generates another m different chunks. It means that each benchmark will output an in-memory data file of size $D \cdot (k + m)/k$ given an input of size D. Hence, the definition of throughput turns out to be:

$$\text{Thr} = \frac{D}{t} \cdot \frac{k + m}{k} \tag{1}$$

As shown in the equation, the value of throughput is related to k and m. Sometimes, however, it is helpful to compare the throughput across different combinations of k and m. Therefore, we also introduce the normalized throughput as a metric. Since for both encoding and decoding operations, it generates $D \cdot m/k$ bytes worth of coding data. Studies [29,44] demonstrate that it takes $k - 1$ XOR operations to produce a byte. Therefore, if we define the normalized throughput as the number of XOR operations taken place in erasure coding operations divided by the time consumed, the metric is fair for all combinations of k and m. Thus, the normalized throughput is represented as:

$$\text{Thr}_{\text{norm}} = \frac{D}{t} \cdot \frac{(k - 1) \cdot m}{k} = \frac{(k - 1) \cdot m}{k + m} \cdot \text{Thr} \tag{2}$$

CPU Utilization. A well-known advantage of offload architecture is the low-consumption of CPU cycles, which frees up CPU for computation tasks and finally increases overall system efficiency and performance. Therefore, another important metric to differentiate onload and offload erasure coders in EC-Bench is CPU utilization. To precisely get the CPU utilization of each evaluated erasure coder, we employ PAPI [40] APIs to collect the total number of CPU cycles consumed by erasure coding operations. We define CPU utilization as the total number of consumed CPU cycles divide by the time spent on erasure coding operations. Its equation representation is:

$$\text{CPU Utilization} = \frac{\text{CPU cycles}}{t} \tag{3}$$

Cache Pressure. Concerning the architecture characteristics of onload and offload erasure coders, cache pressure is another vital metric introduced in EC-Bench. With the fact that, for a specific erasure coder, the maximum performance point is achieved when the coder makes the best use of the L1 cache [29], cache pressure is at least a complementary to other metrics to explore performance differences between onload and offload coders. For who is developing a new erasure code, cache pressure may as well be a non-trivial metric to analyze performance bottleneck. PAPI APIs are used to collect the number of cache misses in different cache levels. Therefore, cache pressure is defined as the total number of L1 cache misses divided by the time spent on erasure coding operations. Therefore, its formula is:

$$\text{Cache Pressure} = \frac{\text{L1 Cache Misses}}{t} \tag{4}$$

4   Evaluation

In this section, we conduct experiments on four open-source libraries with EC-Bench to evaluate the performance of onload and offload erasure coders. This section also includes additional details on our experimental setup and results.

4.1   Open Source Libraries

These four erasure coder libraries are freely available from various resources on the Internet. The following list represents their descriptions.

Jerasure: Jerasure [30] is a CPU-based library released in 2007 that supports a wide variety of erasure codes. The w of Reed-Solomon code in Jerasure could be 8, 16, or 32.

ISA-L: Intel Intelligent Storage Acceleration Library (ISA-L) [16] is a collection of optimized low-level functions including erasure coding. The erasure coding functions are optimized for Intel instructions, such as Intel SSE [41], vector [17], and encryption instructions. The w of Reed-Solomon code in ISA-L is fixed to 8.

Gibraltar: Gibraltar [8] is a GPU-based library for Reed-Solomon coding. The Reed-Solomon code in Gibraltar is based on $GF(2^8)$, which means it has a fixed $w = 8$.

Mellanox-EC: Mellanox-EC [24] proposed by Mellanox is an HCA-based library for Reed-Solomon coding. The erasure coding operations are handled in host channel adapters (HCA). The w of Reed-Solomon code could be 4 and 8 in the latest ConnectX-5 IB NICs.

4.2   Experimental Setup

Our cluster consists of 20 nodes, and each is equipped with 2.40 GHz Intel(R) Xeon(R) CPU E5-2680 v4 (28 cores, 32 KB L1 cache, 256 KB L2 cache, and 35 MB L3 cache), 128 GB DRAM, two K80 GPUs, and a ConnectX-5 IB-EDR (100 Gbps) NIC. The operating system employed in the cluster is CentOS 7.2. Other necessary drivers and libraries are CUDA 8.0, Mellanox OFED 4.2, PAPI 5.2.0.0 with perf 3.10.0, Jerasure 2.0, ISA-L 2.18.0, Gibraltar[1], and Mellanox-EC[2]. Note that Jerasure in our experiments is compiled without SSE support,

---

[1] Github: https://github.com/jaredjennings/libgibraltar,
commit: c93f9d8c3be70ded173822cdca2e51900a3f5ed1.

[2] Github: https://github.com/Mellanox/EC,
commit: 00bf091aa14322baf4425f8a6d5d134e91fe2a5c.

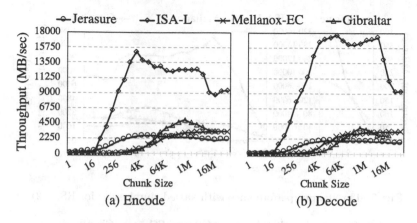

Fig. 1. Throughput performance with varied chunk sizes for RS(3, 2)

such that Jerasure represents onload erasure coder with common instruction sets while ISA-L with advanced instruction sets.

Experiments in this paper are all conducted with Reed-Solomon code as it is the only common erasure code among chosen libraries as illustrated in Sect. 4.1. We also fix the value of w into 8, such that all onload and offload coders are comparable. Let $RS(k, m)$ denote the configuration of Reed-Solomon code computing m parity chunks for k data chunks. We examine onload and offload coders with four popular configurations, $RS(3, 2)$, $RS(6, 3)$, $RS(10, 4)$ and $RS(17, 3)$ used by HDFS, Ceph, QFS, Google, Facebook, Baidu and Backblaze [3–6,18,26,27], etc.

4.3 Experimental Results

It is well-known that decoding operations are similar to encoding operations for RS code. The throughput performance of encoding and decoding for $RS(3, 2)$ depicted in Fig. 1 demonstrates that encoding performance and decoding performance of all selected coders have similar trends. One interesting observation in the figure is that the decoding performance of ISA-L to recover m (m equals 2 in Fig. 1) lost chunks is better than its encoding performance to generate m parity chunks. In the experiment, the m-by-m matrix used for decoding has a smaller size than the generator matrix (i.e., a k-by-m matrix) for encoding, such that the decoding operation requires less compute power; thus, erasure coders, especially high-performance erasure coders such as ISA-L, deliver better decoding performance.

Since both encoding performance and decoding performance of different coders have similar tendencies, we only show encoding results in this section due to space limitation. In our experiments, Gibraltar coder is not able to run with $chunk\_size = \{32\,\text{MB}, 64\,\text{MB}\}$, such that corresponding numbers in the following figures are left blank.

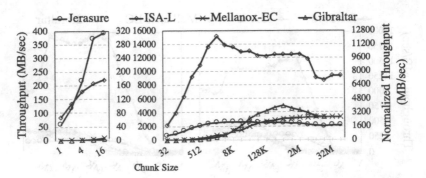

Fig. 2. Throughput performance with varied chunk sizes for RS(3, 2)

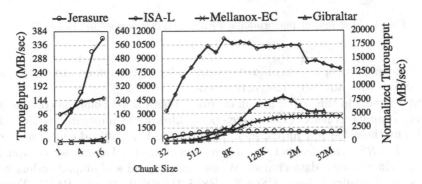

Fig. 3. Throughput performance with varied chunk sizes for RS(6, 3)

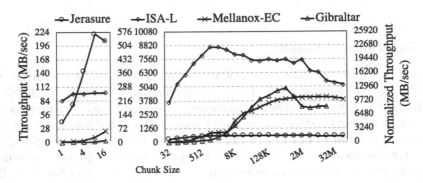

Fig. 4. Throughput performance with varied chunk sizes for RS(10, 4)

Throughput. Figures 2, 3, 4 and 5 depict throughput performance comparisons among onload and offload coders with various chunk sizes ranging from 1 byte to 64 MB. Normalized throughput is showing on the right-hand-side y-axis, and each data point in the figures corresponds to two values, i.e., throughput and normalized throughput. In all experiments, onload coders outperform offload coders for small chunk sizes. For instance, in Fig. 2, both Jerasure and ISA-L

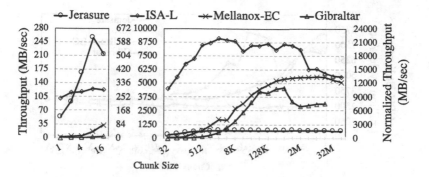

Fig. 5. Throughput performance with varied chunk sizes for RS(17, 3)

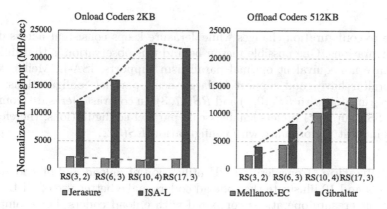

Fig. 6. Normalized throughput performance of onload and offload coders across multiple configurations. The chunk sizes for onload and offload coders are fixed into one of their near-optimal chunk sizes. In this case, 2 KB for onload coders and 512 KB for offload coders.

perform better than Mellanox-EC and Gibraltar with chunk sizes smaller than 32 KB. On the other hand, throughput performance of offload coders improves significantly with increasing chunk sizes, and offload coders are able to defeat some onload coders if chunk size is large enough. Figure 2 demonstrates that Mellanox-EC and Gibraltar coders outperform Jerasure once chunk size is larger than 32 KB. The reason behind the increasing throughput of offload coders with growing chunk sizes is that large chunk sizes alleviate the overhead of transferring data from host to device [10]. In Figs. 3, 4 and 5, we observe trends similar to the trend demonstrated in Fig. 2.

Normalized Throughput. After being normalized, throughput performance across different configurations is comparable [29]. Figure 6 shows how the normalized throughput performance of onload and offload coders changes across multiple configurations (e.g., $RS(3,2)$). ISA-L, Mellanox-EC and Gibraltar coders are

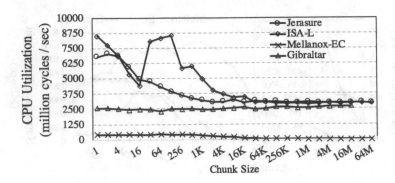

Fig. 7. CPU utilization with varied chunk sizes for RS(3, 2)

sensitive to configuration changes while Jerasure keeps consistent across different configurations. One possible reason behind this observation is that different coders have nonequivalent optimal parallelism supports. ISA-L, Mellanox-EC, and Gibraltar have good support to larger-scale parallel configurations; thus, they perform good with $RS(10, 4)$ and $RS(17, 3)$. In contrast, Jerasure (compiled without SSE support) prefers smaller-scale parallel configurations; therefore, it achieves its best performance with configuration $RS(3, 2)$.

CPU Utilization. Considering CPU utilization of onload and offload coders, Figs. 7, 8, 9 and 10 illustrate that offload coders make better use of CPU cycles to carry out erasure operations compared with onload coders. For example, it shows that, in Fig. 7, Mellanox-EC consumes 0.41 million cycles per second while running with a chunk size of 64 MB. In the meantime, Jerasure and ISA-L take 2950.5 and 2932.23 million cycles per second, respectively. Another observation is that CPU utilization for both onload and offload coders decrease with an increase in chunk size.

Figures 7, 8, 9 and 10 also show an interesting fact that ISA-L deals with chunk sizes smaller than 32 bytes and other chunk sizes in two different approaches (details in the implementation of function *ec_encode_data_avx2* [2]). That's why in Figs. 7, 8, 9, 10, 11, 12, 13 and 14, there are big jumps in the curves of ISA-L in the cases of 32 bytes.

Cache Pressure. The cache pressures of onload and offload coders are depicted in Figs. 11, 12, 13 and 14. Though Gibraltar has more L1 cache misses than ISA-L for some chunk sizes, the overall cache pressure introduced by offload erasure coders is less than that introduced by onload coders. Within all coders, Mellanox-EC influences cache least, while Jerasure has constant pressure on cache for relatively large chunk sizes. The different cache behaviors of ISA-L around *chunk_size* = 32 across four chosen configurations (e.g., $RS(3, 2)$) also indicate the same observation in Sect. 4.3 that ISA-L has two internal approaches to carry out chunk sizes smaller than 32 bytes and other chunk sizes.

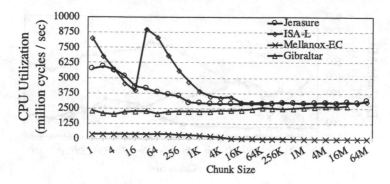

Fig. 8. CPU utilization with varied chunk sizes for RS(6, 3)

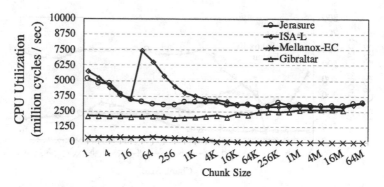

Fig. 9. CPU utilization with varied chunk sizes for RS(10, 4)

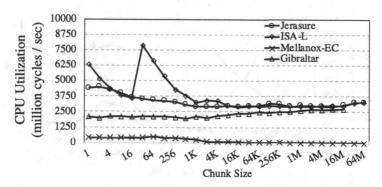

Fig. 10. CPU utilization with varied chunk sizes for RS(17, 3)

5   Related Work

Over the years, as erasure coding becomes an attractive alternative to replication, several works have been focusing on employing erasure coding for performing

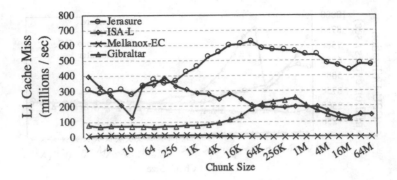

Fig. 11. Cache pressure with varied chunk sizes for RS(3, 2)

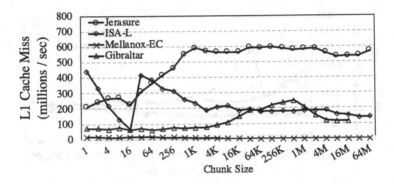

Fig. 12. Cache pressure with varied chunk sizes for RS(6, 3)

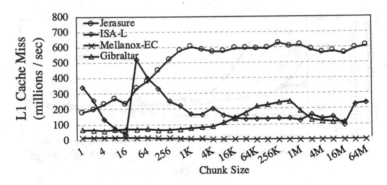

Fig. 13. Cache pressure with varied chunk sizes for RS(10, 4)

data recovery on data centers and benchmarking erasure coders for performance evaluation.

Erasure Coding for Storage Systems: Erasure codes, especially Reed-Solomon code and its variations, have been adopted in famous storage systems [3–6,18,26,27,43], because of its higher reliability with lower storage

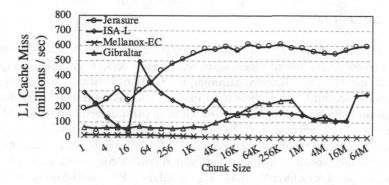

Fig. 14. Cache pressure with varied chunk sizes for RS(17, 3)

overhead. To further reduce the overhead introduced by erasure coding, some research works are proposed, such as Partial-Parallel-Repair [25], Repair Pipelining [20], and [9,32,33]. Several researchers have also designed many other classes of erasure codes to reduce the computational complexity involved in Reed-Solomon codes [7,12–15,19]. In the meantime, erasure coding is also being utilized to design key-value stores, including Cocytus [45], EC-Cache [31], and RDMA-accelerated Memcached with online EC support [37].

Hardware Acceleration and Optimizations for Erasure Coding: Motivated by the advanced features supported by modern CPU architectures, many research works [16,22,28] are enabling the design of high-speed EC by taking advantage of instruction sets like SSE, AVX, etc. Along similar lines, [24] and [8] proposed offload approaches to reduce CPU consumption and leverage the capabilities of GPUs and next-generation network adapters, respectively. On the other hand, our previous work [38] has proposed a new concept **Multi-Rail EC**, which enables upper-layer applications to leverage available high-performance hardware in parallel to accelerate erasure coding.

Benchmarking Erasure Coding Libraries: Recent studies have evaluated onload erasure coders with metrics throughput or latency. For instance, [21] performs several experiments to test the running times of some popular software-based onload erasure coders. [29] conducts a throughput performance evaluation and examination of open-source erasure coding libraries and contributes a way to normalize throughput performance across different configurations (e.g., $RS(3, 2)$, $RS(6, 3)$ and $RS(10, 4)$).

The increased focus on employing EC in storage systems and enabling EC on modern hardware serves as a motivation of this paper. Based on our knowledge of modern hardware architectures, we propose a benchmark which supports latency and throughput metrics as well as architecture-related metrics, such as CPU utilization and cache pressure, to fully evaluate different erasure coders, especially onload and offload coders.

6   Conclusion

In this work, we design a benchmark framework (i.e., EC-Bench) for evaluating erasure coders, especially for onload and offload coders. EC-Bench supports four main metrics (i.e., latency, throughput, CPU utilization, and cache pressure), which we think are sufficient to explore the performance characteristics of onload and offload coders fully. Through in-depth performance evaluations of four erasure coders, we demonstrate that EC-Bench is able to reveal their performance differences in terms of throughput, CPU utilization, and cache pressure. The performance results illustrate that onload coders consumes more CPU and cache resources than offload coders (e.g., Mellanox-EC), and highly optimized onload coders (e.g., Intel ISA-L) typically outperform offload coders.

References

1. Facebook's Erasure Coded Hadoop Distributed File System (HDFS-RAID) (2010). https://github.com/facebookarchive/hadoop-20
2. ec_highlevel_func.c (2018). https://github.com/intel/isa-l/blob/master/erasure_code/ec_highlevel_func.c#L98
3. Apache Hadoop 3.0.0-alpha2 (2017). http://hadoop.apache.org/docs/r3.0.0-alpha2/
4. Backblaze Online Backup (2015). https://www.backblaze.com/blog/reed-solomon/
5. Ceph Erasure Coding (2016). http://docs.ceph.com/docs/master/rados/operations/erasure-code/
6. Colossus: Successor to the Google File System (GFS) (2012). https://www.systutorials.com/3202/colossus-successor-to-google-file-system-gfs/
7. Corbett, P., et al.: Row-diagonal parity for double disk failure correction. In: Proceedings of the 3rd USENIX Conference on File and Storage Technologies, pp. 1–14. USENIX Association, Berkeley (2004)
8. Curry, M., Skjellum, A., Lee Ward, H., Brightwell, R.: Gibraltar: a Reed-Solomon coding library for storage applications on programmable graphics processors. Concurr. Comput.: Pract. Exp. **23**(18), 2477–2495 (2011)
9. Dimakis, A.G., Godfrey, P.B., Wu, Y., Wainwright, M.J., Ramchandran, K.: Network coding for distributed storage systems. IEEE Trans. Inf. Theory **56**(9), 4539–4551 (2010)
10. Fujii, Y., Azumi, T., Nishio, N., Kato, S., Edahiro, M.: Data transfer matters for GPU computing. In: 2013 International Conference on Parallel and Distributed Systems (ICPADS), pp. 275–282. IEEE (2013)
11. Ghemawat, S., Gobioff, H., Leung, S.T.: The Google file system. ACM SIGOPS Oper. Syst. Rev. **37**, 29–43 (2003)
12. Greenan, K.M., Li, X., Wylie, J.J.: Flat XOR-based erasure codes in storage systems: constructions, efficient recovery, and tradeoffs. In: 2010 IEEE 26th Symposium on Mass Storage Systems and Technologies (MSST), pp. 1–14. IEEE (2010)
13. Hafner, J.L.: WEAVER codes: highly fault tolerant erasure codes for storage systems. In: Proceedings of the 4th Conference on USENIX Conference on File and Storage Technologies - FAST 2005, vol. 4, p. 16. USENIX Association, Berkeley (2005)

14. Huang, C., Xu, L.: STAR: an efficient coding scheme for correcting triple storage node failures. IEEE Trans. Comput. **57**(7), 889–901 (2008)
15. Huang, C., et al.: Erasure coding in windows azure storage. In: USENIX Annual Technical Conference, Boston, pp. 15–26 (2012)
16. Intel Intelligent Storage Acceleration Library (Intel ISA-L) (2016). https://software.intel.com/en-us/storage/ISA-L
17. Introduction to Intel® Advanced Vector Extensions. https://software.intel.com/en-us/articles/introduction-to-intel-advanced-vector-extensions
18. Lai, C., et al.: Atlas: Baidu's key-value storage system for cloud data. In: 2015 31st Symposium on Mass Storage Systems and Technologies (MSST), pp. 1–14. IEEE (2015)
19. Li, M., Lee, P.P.: STAIR codes: a general family of erasure codes for tolerating device and sector failures. Trans. Storage **10**(4), 14:1–14:30 (2014)
20. Li, R., Li, X., Lee, P.P., Huang, Q.: Repair pipelining for erasure-coded storage. In: Proceedings of the 2017 USENIX Annual Technical Conference (USENIX ATC 2017), pp. 567–579 (2017)
21. Luby, M.: Benchmark comparisons of erasure codes (2002)
22. Marov, A., Fedorov, A.: Optimization of RAID erasure coding algorithms for Intel Xeon Phi. In: 2016 IEEE International Conference on Networking, Architecture and Storage (NAS), pp. 1–4. IEEE (2016)
23. Mellanox. HDFS Erasure Coding Offload Plugin (2016). https://github.com/Mellanox/EC/tree/master/HDFS
24. Mellanox. Understanding Erasure Coding Offload (2016). https://community.mellanox.com/docs/DOC-2414
25. Mitra, S., Panta, R., Ra, M.R., Bagchi, S.: Partial-parallel-repair (PPR): a distributed technique for repairing erasure coded storage. In: Proceedings of the Eleventh European Conference on Computer Systems, p. 30. ACM (2016)
26. Muralidhar, S., et al.: f4: Facebook's warm BLOB storage system. In: Proceedings of the 11th USENIX Conference on Operating Systems Design and Implementation, pp. 383–398. USENIX Association (2014)
27. Ovsiannikov, M., Rus, S., Reeves, D., Sutter, P., Rao, S., Kelly, J.: The quantcast file system. Proc. VLDB Endow. **11**, 1092–1101 (2013)
28. Plank, J.S., Greenan, K.M., Miller, E.L.: Screaming fast galois field arithmetic using Intel SIMD instructions. In: 11th USENIX Conference on File and Storage Technologies (FAST 2013), San Jose, pp. 298–306. USENIX Association (2013)
29. Plank, J.S., et al.: A performance evaluation and examination of open-source erasure coding libraries for storage. In: Proccedings of the 7th Conference on File and Storage Technologies, FAST 2009, pp. 253–265. USENIX Association, Berkeley (2009)
30. Plank, J.S., Simmerman, S., Schuman, C.D.: Jerasure: a library in C/C++ facilitating erasure coding for storage applications (2008)
31. Rashmi, K.V., Chowdhury, M., Kosaian, J., Stoica, I., Ramchandran, K.: EC-Cache: load-balanced, low-latency cluster caching with online erasure coding. In: 12th USENIX Symposium on Operating Systems Design and Implementation (OSDI 2016). USENIX Association (2016)
32. Rashmi, K.V., Nakkiran, P., Wang, J., Shah, N.B., Ramchandran, K.: Having your cake and eating it too: jointly optimal erasure codes for i/o, storage, and network-bandwidth. In: FAST, pp. 81–94 (2015)
33. Rashmi, K.V., Shah, N.B., Gu, D., Kuang, H., Borthakur, D., Ramchandran, K.: A solution to the network challenges of data recovery in erasure-coded distributed storage systems: a study on the Facebook warehouse cluster. In: HotStorage (2013)

34. Reed, I.S., Solomon, G.: Polynomial codes over certain finite fields. J. Soc. Ind. Appl. Math. **8**(2), 300–304 (1960)
35. Rodrigues, R., Liskov, B.: High availability in DHTs: erasure coding vs. replication. In: Castro, M., van Renesse, R. (eds.) IPTPS 2005. LNCS, vol. 3640, pp. 226–239. Springer, Heidelberg (2005). https://doi.org/10.1007/11558989_21
36. Sathiamoorthy, M., et al.: XORing elephants: novel erasure codes for big data. Proc. VLDB Endow. **6**(5), 325–336 (2013)
37. Shankar, D., Lu, X., Panda, D.K.: High-performance and resilient key-value store with online erasure coding for big data workloads. In: 2017 IEEE 37th International Conference on Distributed Computing Systems (ICDCS), pp. 527–537. IEEE (2017)
38. Shi, H., Lu, X., Shankar, D., Panda, D.K.: High-performance multi-rail erasure coding library over modern data center architectures: early experiences. In: Proceedings of the ACM Symposium on Cloud Computing, pp. 530–531. ACM (2018)
39. Shvachko, K., Kuang, H., Radia, S., Chansler, R.: The hadoop distributed file system. In: 2010 IEEE 26th Symposium on Mass Storage Systems and Technologies (MSST), pp. 1–10. IEEE (2010)
40. Terpstra, D., Jagode, H., You, H., Dongarra, J.: Collecting performance data with PAPI-C. In: Müller, M., Schulz, A., Nagel, W. (eds.) Tools for High Performance Computing 2009, pp. 157–173. Springer, Heidelberg (2010). https://doi.org/10.1007/978-3-642-11261-4_11
41. Using Intel® Streaming SIMD Extensions and Intel® Integrated Performance Primitives to Accelerate Algorithms (2016). https://software.intel.com/en-us/articles/
42. Weatherspoon, H., Kubiatowicz, J.D.: Erasure coding vs. replication: a quantitative comparison. In: Druschel, P., Kaashoek, F., Rowstron, A. (eds.) IPTPS 2002. LNCS, vol. 2429, pp. 328–337. Springer, Heidelberg (2002). https://doi.org/10.1007/3-540-45748-8_31
43. Weil, S.A., Brandt, S.A., Miller, E.L., Long, D.D., Maltzahn, C.: Ceph: a scalable, high-performance distributed file system. In: Proceedings of the 7th Symposium on Operating Systems Design and Implementation, pp. 307–320. USENIX Association (2006)
44. Xu, L., Bruck, J.: X-code: MDS array codes with optimal encoding. IEEE Trans. Inf. Theory **45**(1), 272–276 (1999)
45. Zhang, H., Dong, M., Chen, H.: Efficient and available in-memory KV-store with hybrid erasure coding and replication. In: 14th USENIX Conference on File and Storage Technologies (FAST 2016), Santa Clara, pp. 167–180. USENIX Association (2016)

Algorithm and Implementations

Benchmarking SpMV Methods
on Many-Core Platforms

Biwei Xie[1(✉)], Zhen Jia[2], and Yungang Bao[1,3]

[1] State Key Laboratory of Computer Architecture,
Institute of Computing Technology, Chinese Academy of Sciences, Beijing, China
{xiebiwei,baoyg}@ict.ac.cn
[2] Department of Computer Science, Princeton University, Princeton, USA
zhenj@cs.princeton.edu
[3] University of Chinese Academy of Sciences, Beijing, China

Abstract. SpMV is an essential kernel existing in many HPC and data center applications. Meanwhile, the emerging many-core hardware provides promising computational power, and is widely used for acceleration. Many methods and formats have been proposed aiming at better performance of SpMV on many-core platforms. However, there is still lack of a comprehensive comparison of SpMV methods to show their performance difference on sparse matrices with various sparse patterns. Moreover, there is still no systematic work to bridge the gap between SpMV performance and sparse pattern.

In this paper, we investigate the performance of 27 SpMV methods with 1500+ sparse matrices on two many-core platforms: Intel Xeon Phi (Knights Landing 7250) and Nvidia GPGPU (Tesla M40). Our work shows that no single SpMV methods is optimal for all sparse patterns, but some methods can achieve approximately the best performance on most sparse matrices. We further select 13 features to describe the sparse pattern and analyze their correlations to the performance of each SpMV method. Our observations should help other researchers and practitioners to better understand the SpMV performance and provide implications to guide the selection of suitable SpMV method.

Keywords: Benchmarking · SpMV · Many-core · Evaluation

1 Introduction

SpMV (sparse matrix-vector multiplication) is critical to the performance of many HPC [1,2] and data center applications [3,4]. Especially in many large-sized linear systems and eigenvalue problems, SpMV dominates the computation as well as the overall execution time. Meanwhile, the evolution of many-core processors provides promising computational power for the acceleration of SpMV.

Since the performance variance among different SpMV methods is usually huge, design or select an appropriate SpMV method is important and not easy

© Springer Nature Switzerland AG 2019
C. Zheng and J. Zhan (Eds.): Bench 2018, LNCS 11459, pp. 233–247, 2019.
https://doi.org/10.1007/978-3-030-32813-9_19

for most of the time. There are several factors that affect the performance and make it difficult to design a one fit all solution. (1) **Sparse pattern.** The memory access pattern of SpMV is determined to the the sparse pattern of the input matrix, which is also known as the distribution pattern of non-zero elements. The input-dependent and irregular data layout of sparse matrices results in random memory accesses, which introduces great difficulty in designing a unified SpMV method to handle all the cases. (2) **SpMV methods and Implementations.** Targeting different application scenarios or sparse matrices with different patterns, SpMV methods are designed with diverse considerations, and thus that show much different performance. Moreover, the same SpMV method from different packages with different implementations, might also show huge different performance. (3) **The underlying hardware.** The design decision of many-core architecture also affects the final SpMV performance a lot. SpMV methods designed for one specific many-core architecture might show poor performance on another many-core architecture. For example, one SpMV method designed for GPGPU might gain poor performance on Intel Xeon Phi. In conclusion, a systematic analysis, which fully considers the diversity of sparse patterns, SpMV methods, and hardware platforms, is motivated.

SpMV has been researched for decades on plenty of new architectures and accelerators [5–9]. In addition to designing a specific SpMV method, there are also a lot of existing work trying to bridge the performance gap between the sparse pattern and underlying hardware [10–13]. Those work selects features to represent the sparse pattern and train models to select SpMV methods automatically using supervised [14] or unsupervised [15] machine learning/deep learning algorithms. Researchers in any field are always interested in broader or most latest research effort. So does SpMV field. Since the best method 2 years ago may not be a perfect one for now. Meanwhile, it would be helpful to perform a thorough analysis on the relationship between sparse features and SpMV performance, which may provide us insights on how to select the features to profile sparse matrices. We distinguish our work from existing ones from three perspectives: more cutting edge SpMV methods, larger number of sparse matrices for characterization, and more delicate sparse pattern analysis.

In this paper, we investigate the performance of 27 SpMV methods on more than 1500 sparse matrices, based on two advanced many-core platforms: Intel Xeon Phi (Knights Landing 7250) [16] and Nvidia GPGPU (Tesla M40). We further investigate previous work and finally select 13 features, which are widely used to describe sparse pattern. We take those features as likely candidates to describe sparse patterns and analyze their correlations to the performance of the SpMV methods. We conclude our observations and implications as following:

- No single SpMV method can efficiently deal with all the sparse patterns, but some SpMV methods can achieve the best or approximately the best performance for most sparse matrices.
- The widely used methods, like CSR, CSC and DIA, are not able to compete with the newly proposed solutions, e.g., CVR and CSR5, from the perspec-

tive of performance. Counter-intuitively, even DIA is designed for diagonal matrices, its performance is not the best for them as expected.
– Different SpMV methods show diverse sensitivities to sparse patterns.

This paper is organized as follows. Section 2 gives the benchmarking methodology. Section 3 analyzes the experimental results, and Sect. 4 concludes.

2   Benchmarking Methodology

2.1   Selected SpMV Methods

Many SpMV methods have been proposed with various design considerations. Some famous packages provide diverse and stable SpMV implementations, like

Table 1. The list of chosen SpMV methods.

ID	SpMV methods	Input formats	Package	Platform	OpenSource	Short name
1	COO	COO	MKL-intel [17]	X86	No	
2	CSR	CSR	MKL-intel	X86	No	
3	CSC	CSC	MKL-intel	X86	No	
4	DIA	DIA	MKL-intel	X86	No	
5	IE	CSR	MKL-intel	X86	No	
6	BSR	BSR [21]	MKL-intel	X86	No	
7	ESB Dynamic	ESB [22]	MKL-intel	X86	No	ESB-d
8	ESB Static	ESB [22]	MKL-intel	X86	No	ESB-s
9	CVR	CVR	CGO'18 [23]	X86	Yes	
10	CSR5	CSR5	ICS'15 [24]	X86	Yes	
11	VHCC	VHCC	CGO'15 [25]	X86	Yes	
12	CSRcuSparse	CSR	cuSparse [18]	GPGPU	No	CSRcu
13	BSRcuSparse	BSR	cuSparse	GPGPU	No	BSRcu
14	HYBcuSparse	HYB	cuSparse	GPGPU	No	COOcu
15	COOCUSP	COO	CUSP	GPGPU	Yes	COOCU
16	CSRCUSP	CSR	CUSP	GPGPU	Yes	CSRCU
17	ELLCUSP	ELLPACK [26]	CUSP	GPGPU	Yes	ELLCU
18	HYBCUSP	HYB	CUSP	GPGPU	Yes	HYBCU
19	DIACUSP	DIA	CUSP	GPGPU	Yes	DIACU
20	CSRMagma	CSR	Magma [20]	GPGPU	Yes	CSRMA
21	BSRMagma	BSR	Magma	GPGPU	Yes	BSRMA
22	ELLMagma	ELLPACK	Magma	GPGPU	Yes	ELLMA
23	SELLPMagma	SELLP	Magma	GPGPU	Yes	SELLP
24	ELLPKMagma	ELLPacket	Magma	GPGPU	Yes	ELLPK
25	ELLRTMagma	ELLRT	Magma	GPGPU	Yes	ELLRT
26	Merge	CSR	SC'17 [27]	GPGPU	Yes	
27	CSR5GPU	CSR5	ICS'15 [24]	GPGPU	Yes	CSR5g

MKL [17] from Intel, cuSparse [18] from Nvidia, CUSP [19] and Magma [20] from open-source community. We choose SpMV methods from these packages with overlapping, since even for the same SpMV method, different implementations result in various performance. Finally, 27 SpMV methods are selected (Table 1).

2.2 Selected Features

Based on a comprehensively investigation of existing work, we select 13 features (Table 2) to describe the sparse patterns, which include 7 basic features related to the whole matrix and another 6 row features reflecting the characteristics of neighboring rows. The full list of the selected features are shown in Table 2. Meanwhile, we use both the *average value* (abbreviated as *avg*) and *coefficient of variation* (abbreviated as *cv*) of the row features for better description.

Table 2. Selected features of sparse matrix

1	numRows	m: number of rows
2	numCols	n: number of columns
3	numNonZeros	nnz: number of non-zero elements
4	density	$nnz/(m \times n)$: density of non-zero elements
5	nonEmptyRows	me: number of non-empty rows
6	numDIAs	number of such diagonals
7	densityDIA	$nnz/(numDIAs * n)$: density of non-zero elements on diagonals
8	$nnzRow_i$	number of non-zero elements in row i
9	$lengthRow_i$	col[las] - col[fir]: the distance between the last and the first element in row i
10	$densityRow_i$	$nnzRow_i/length_i$: the density of non-zero elements of row i
11	$numBlockofRow_i$	number of blocks in row i. A block indicates consecutive non-zero elements
12	$lengthBlockofRow_i$	the average length of the blocks in row i
13	$patternSection_i$	Sparse pattern by section, which is the sum of the coefficient of variation value of all features in section i

Take *nnzRow* for example, Eqs. 1 and 2 show the computation method of its *average value* and *coefficient of variation* in respective. We further compute *coefficient of variation* of all features by section, which consists of multiple consecutive rows. The *coefficient of variation* of a specific feature in a specific section shows the similarity of the rows in this section on this feature. We name the sum of the *coefficient of variation* of all features in a section, *patternSection* (sparse pattern by section), which shows the similarity of the sparse pattern of neighbouring rows in this section.

$$avg\_nnzRow = nnz/me \tag{1}$$

$$cv\_nnzRow = \frac{\sqrt{\frac{1}{me}\sum_{i=1}^{me}\left(nnzRow_i - avg\_nnzRow\right)^2}}{avg\_nnzRow} \tag{2}$$

2.3   Hardware Configuration

We conduct the experiments on two popular many-core platforms: Intel Xeon
Phi and Nvidia GPU. They are both widely used for acceleration in many areas,
like scientific computing and deep learning, but with totally different architecture
design decisions. The details of them can bu found in Table 3.

Table 3. The configuration of experimental platforms.

	Xeon Phi	GPU
	Knights Landing	Tesla
Architecture	Knights Landing	Tesla
Model	7250	M40
Details	# of cores: 68	# of SMs: 24
	# of HT/core: 4	# of coes/SM: 128
	SIMD width: 512	warp size: 32
	L1 cache: 32 KB(D) + 32 KB(I)	shared memory/SM: 48 KB
	L2 cache: 1024 KB/two cores	L2 cache: 3 MB
	Memory: 16 GB MCDRAM	Global Memory: 24 GB
	96 GB DDR4	

2.4   Data Sets

To cover the diversity of sparse patterns, we choose the well-known SuiteSparse
Matrix Collection [28], which includes 4700 sparse matrices covering more than
100 application scenarios. These sparse matrices are different from each other
on scale and the distribution pattern. We discard sparse matrices which are
too small, and finally select 1500+ sparse matrices for our evaluation, covering
various scenarios like social network, web graph, road network, and etc.

2.5   Experimental Methods

We choose 27 SpMV methods listed in Sect. 2.1 as our workloads: 11 on Intel
Xeon Phi and 16 on GPGPU. For the workloads that need input parameters, we

use the recommended value or the default value. For workloads on Intel Xeon Phi, we adjust the thread number (from 1 to 4) and report the best one. For workloads on GPGPU, we use default values for the number of blocks and the number of threads. For all workloads, we run 1000 iterations and calculate the average SpMV execution time. As to the compiling flag options, on Intel Xeon Phi, we use '-xMIC-AVX512 -qopenmp -std=c++0x -mkl -O3'; on GPGPU, we use '-m64 -fopenmp -lgomp -w -gencode=arch=compute_52,code=sm_52'. Additionally, we set MCDRAM in 'flat' mode, and use 'numactl --membind=1' to set the workloads run in MCDRAM on Intel Xeon Phi.

3   Experimental Results

In this section, we will firstly analyze the performance of each SpMV method. Then, we compare the number of sparse matrices each method can achieve the best or approximate best performance on. We further perform correlation analysis between the features of sparse matrices and SpMV method performance.

3.1   SpMV Performance

The experiment results of the 27 SpMV methods are sorted by nnz (the number of non-zero elements) for better demonstration. We report both the running-time (in millisecond) and the throughput (in GFlops). The workload performance on Intel Xeon Phi is shown in Fig. 1a to j. GPGPU ones are given in Fig. 1l to 2g.

Performance Analysis on Intel Xeon Phi. Some SpMV methods, like CSR, IE, CSR5 and CVR, show good performance on both small and large sparse matrices with various sparse patterns. As nnz increases, the throughput of these SpMV methods first grow fast and then become slow. The throughput of CSR, IE and CSR5 decrease when dealing with large-scale sparse matrices, while that of CVR is more stable. In addition, COO, CSC, and DIA, which are widely used in real-world scenarios, show much poorer performance than expected.

The relationship between the performance of DIA and nnz seems to be random, since the performance of DIA is mainly determined to the number of diagonals and the density of the non-zero elements on these diagonals, rather than nnz. Besides, BSR, ESB-d and ESB-s show plain performance, but their throughput generally keep growing when the sparse matrix scales up. Additionally, these three workloads are more sensitive to the sparse pattern, thus that the sparse matrices with similar scale but different sparse patterns show much different performance. This is the main reason of the 'glitch' in Fig. 1f, h and g.

Performance Analysis on GPGPU. The same SpMV method from different packages show huge performance variances. The CSR in cuSparse, CUSP and Magma show much different performance. CSR in CUSP is more stable and

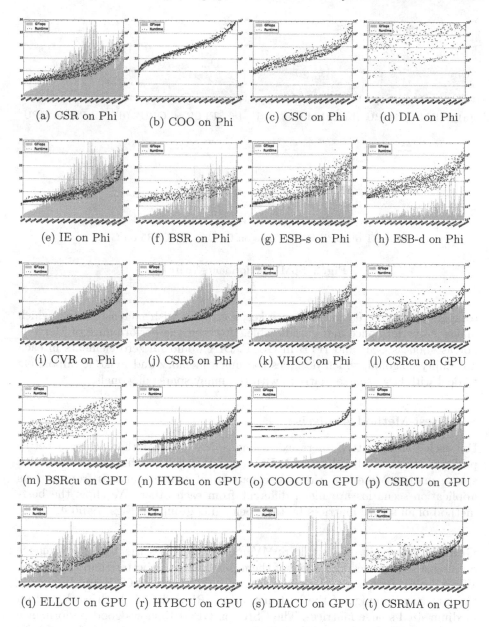

(a) CSR on Phi   (b) COO on Phi   (c) CSC on Phi   (d) DIA on Phi

(e) IE on Phi   (f) BSR on Phi   (g) ESB-s on Phi   (h) ESB-d on Phi

(i) CVR on Phi   (j) CSR5 on Phi   (k) VHCC on Phi   (l) CSRcu on GPU

(m) BSRcu on GPU   (n) HYBcu on GPU   (o) COOCU on GPU   (p) CSRCU on GPU

(q) ELLCU on GPU   (r) HYBCU on GPU   (s) DIACU on GPU   (t) CSRMA on GPU

Fig. 1. SpMV performance (part I)

performs much better than the other two on large sparse matrices. HYB exists in both cuSparse and CUSP, but the latter shows higher throughput in general.

For BSR, HYB, ELL and DIA, the 'glich' indicates their sensitivity to the sparse pattern, which means their performance are quite dependent on the distribution pattern of the non-zero elements. Merge SpMV is stable and insensitive

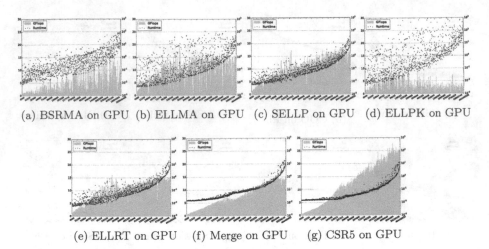

(a) BSRMA on GPU   (b) ELLMA on GPU   (c) SELLP on GPU   (d) ELLPK on GPU

(e) ELLRT on GPU   (f) Merge on GPU   (g) CSR5 on GPU

Fig. 2. SpMV performance (part II)

to sparse patterns. Its performance keeps growing with increasing *nnz*, which makes its performance more predictable. However, the performance of Merge is not as good as CSR and HYB in CUSP. DIA would fill zero elements in each nonempty diagonal, which occupies too much memory and make it impossible to deal with large sparse matrices with too many sparse diagonals.

3.2   Best-Method Analysis

For each sparse matrix, there exists one SpMV method that achieves better performance than all other ones. We name this method best-method of this sparse matrix. Moreover, the sparse pattern of sparse matrices from various application scenarios are much different from each other. We show the best-method of all sparse matrices by their belonging groups in Figs. 3 and 4.

General Analysis. No single SpMV method achieves the best performance on all sparse matrices, but some of them perform much better than the others. When dealing with large sparse matrices on Intel Xeon Phi, CVR and IE occupy the largest percentage of the best-method. CSR5 and CSR both work well on medium-sized sparse matrices. The CSR5 on GPGPU shows good performance on large sparse matrices, while CSR from cuSparse and ELLpack from CUSP suit well on medium and small-sized sparse matrices.

Quantitative Analysis of Best-methods. For better performance comparison, we collect the number of sparse matrices in which each SpMV method can achieve the best performance. Moreover, we also compute the corresponding ratio for better demonstration and show them in Tables 4 and 5.

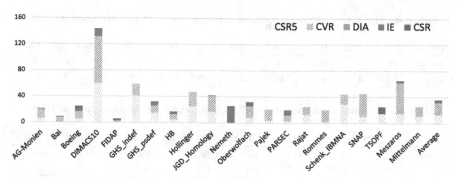

Fig. 3. Distribution of Best-SpMV methods on Phi over groups (only the groups with more than 20 sparse matrices are shown).

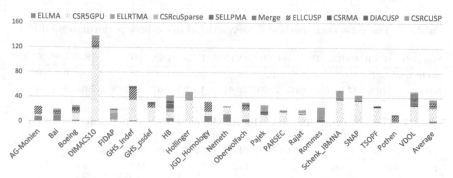

Fig. 4. Distribution of Best-SpMV methods on GPU over groups (only the groups with more than 20 sparse matrices are shown).

On Xeon Phi, CVR and CSR5 perform much better than other SpMV methods, and occupy 50.4% and 32.55% of the sparse matrices in respective. In other words, CVR and CSR5 together show best performance on a large part (83%) of sparse matrices. Meanwhile, COO, CSC and ESB-d achieve the best performance on no sparse matrix. Given an arbitrary sparse matrix, there would be at least one SpMV method performs better than them. VHCC, ESB-s, DIA and BSR achieve best performance only on several sparse matrices on Intel Xeon Phi. There are many diagonal pattern sparse matrices included in our data sets, but DIA achieves the best performance on only one of them. It means that even for a sparse matrix with diagonal pattern, DIA might not be the best choice.

On GPGPU, the distribution of best-method is pretty scattered. CSR5 performs best on most sparse matrices, which occupies 55.9%. In General, SpMV methods from CUSP perform better than that from cuSparse, and the latter achieves best performance on only 35 sparse matrices in total. ELLPack (from both CUSP and Magma) related SpMV methods, like ELLPack, SELLP and ELLRT from Magma show good performance, which means the design of ELL-

Table 4. The ratio that each method achieves the best performance on Phi.

Methods	CVR	CSR5	IE	CSR	VHCC	ESB-s	DIA	BSR	ESB-d	CSC	COO
Optimal	689	445	114	109	4	4	1	1	0	0	0
Ratio	50.4%	32.55%	8.34%	7.97%	0.29%	0.29%	0.07%	0.07%	0	0	0

Table 5. The ratio that each method achieves the best performance on GPU.

Methods	CSR5GPU	CSRCU	ELLCU	ELLMA	SELLPMA	ELLRTMA	Merge	DIACU
Optimal	757	148	114	80	61	53	41	40
Ratio	55.9%	10.9%	8.4%	5.9%	4.5%	3.9%	3%	2.9%
	CSRcu	CSRMA	HYBcu	HYBCU	ELLPKMA	COOCU	BSRcu	BSRMA
Optimal	30	21	5	2	0	0	0	0
Ratio	2.2%	1.5%	0.36%	0.14%	0	0	0	0

Table 6. The ratio each method achieves the close-to-best performance on Phi.

Methods	CVR	CSR5	IE	CSR	VHCC	ESB-s	DIA	BSR	ESB-d	CSC	COO
A-Optimal	957	650	192	192	6	25	1	5	4	0	0
Ratio	70%	47.55%	14.04%	14.04%	0.44%	1.83%	0.07%	0.36%	0.29%	0	0

Table 7. The ratio each method achieves the close-to-best performance on GPU.

Methods	CSR5GPU	CSRCUSP	ELLCU	ELLMA	SELLPMA	ELLRTMA	Merge	DIACU
Optimal	869	188	148	132	156	162	59	45
Ratio	64.2%	13.9%	10.9%	9.7%	11.5%	11.9%	4.3%	3.3%
	CSRcu	CSRMA	HYBcu	HYBCU	ELLPKMA	COOCU	BSRcu	BSRMA
Optimal	79	79	10	70	5	0	0	1
Ratio	5.8%	5.8%	0.7%	5.1%	0.36%	0	0	0.07%

pack is effective on GPGPU. In contrast, HYB from both cuSparse and CUSP show best performance only on limited number of sparse matrices.

Quantitative Analysis of Close-to-Best-Methods. Sometimes, when we choose a SpMV method, it does not need to be the best, if its performance is quite close to the best-method. We re-collect the number of sparse matrices each SpMV method can achieve the close-to-best (within 10% worse than the best performance) performance and show them in Tables 6 and 7. On Intel Xeon Phi, the ratio of CVR increases from 50.4% to 70% and CSR5 from 32.55% to 47.55%. On GPGPU, the ratio of CSR5 increases from 55.9% to 64.2%.

Summary. The widely used SpMV methods, like CSR, CSC and DIA, show much poorer performance on both Intel Xeon Phi and GPGPU than expected. Newly proposed methods, like CVR and CSR5, show quite good performance. Existing work on the research of auto-selection of SpMV methods, which prefers

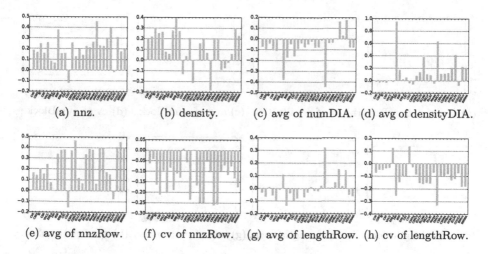

(a) nnz.   (b) density.   (c) avg of numDIA. (d) avg of densityDIA.

(e) avg of nnzRow.   (f) cv of nnzRow.   (g) avg of lengthRow.   (h) cv of lengthRow.

Fig. 5. Analysis of the relationship between the performance and the features (*nnz*, *density*, *numDIA*, *densityDIA*, *nnzRow*, *lengthRow*)

to take CSR, CSC, DIA, ELL, and COO as candidates, should take the newly proposed methods into consider.

3.3 Correlation Analysis of Performance and Sparse Pattern

We compute the values of selected features that are used to describe sparse pattern and analyze the relationship between performance and sparse pattern.

NNZ. *nnz* indicates the number of non-zero elements. Ignoring the distribution pattern of these non-zero elements, we firstly analyze the correlation between the performance and *nnz*. Positive correlation means that as *nnz* increases, the throughput of the SpMV method keeps growing despite of the sparse pattern. In addition, high positive correlation indicates corresponding SpMV method attains predictable performance. In Fig. 5a, most SpMV methods show positive correlation, while COO and ELLPK show negative correlation, which means their throughput will decrease as *nnz* increases.

Density. *Density* is a metric used to describe the sparsity of a sparse matrix. Lower *density* indicates sparser matrix. Figure 5b shows the correlation of performance and *density*. For most SpMV methods, the sparser the matrix is, the lower throughput they can achieve, since sparser matrix often indicates more irregular memory references and thus poor performance.

Diagonal. The correlation of performance and the two diagonal related features: the *number of diagonals* and the *density of diagonals*, are shown in Fig. 5c

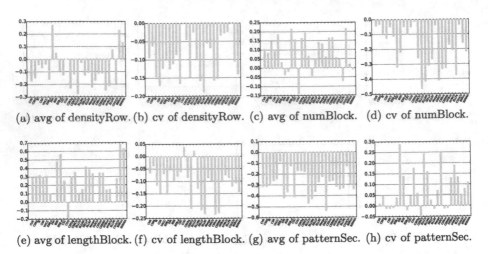

(a) avg of densityRow. (b) cv of densityRow. (c) avg of numBlock. (d) cv of numBlock.

(e) avg of lengthBlock. (f) cv of lengthBlock. (g) avg of patternSec. (h) cv of patternSec.

Fig. 6. Analysis of the relationship between the performance and the features (*densityRow, numBlock, lengthBlock,* and *patternSection*)

and d. The performance of DIA on both Intel Xeon Phi and GPGPU show negative correlation between the *number of diagonals* and throughput, and positive correlation between the *density of diagonals* and throughput. DIA is suitable for sparse matrices whose non-zero elements are compactly distributed along a small number of diagonals.

NNZ by Row. *nnzRow* indicates the distribution of the number of non-zero elements in each row. Figure 5e and f show that DIA on Intel Xeon Phi is insensitive to *nnzRow*, but DIA on GPGPU shows positive correlation. The performance of most SpMV methods show negative correlation to the coefficient of variation of *nnzRow*, except COO and ELLCU.

Length by Row. *LengthRow* is the distance between the first element and the last element in a row. Larger *lengthRow* indicates larger memory reference span, which might result in poorer cache utilization. In Fig. 5g and h, the performance of DIA on both Xeon Phi and GPGPU show negative correlation, since larger *lengthRow* often indicates more sparse diagonals.

Density by Row. In Fig. 6a and b, most SpMV methods show negative correlation between performance and the *density by row*. In other words, if the non-zero elements are scattered in each row, the performance of these SpMV methods would be poor.

Blocks by Row. In Fig. 6c, d, e and f, most SpMV methods show positive correlation to the *numBlock*, while BSR shows that the less the *numBlock* is, the better performance it achieves. As to the average length of the blocks by row, the performance of most SpMV methods show positive correlation.

Sparse Pattern by Section. The feature *patternSection* indicates the similarity of distribution of non-zero elements of the rows in a specific section. Figure 6g and h show that, for most SpMV methods, the more similar the pattern of rows in each section are, the better performance they would achieve.

Summary. Different SpMV methods have different correlation and sensitivity to each feature. It makes more sense to select the features, which are obvious positive or negative to the performance of given SpMV methods, to describe the sparse pattern or to train a SpMV method auto-selection model.

4   Conclusion

In this paper, we comprehensively investigate the performance of 27 SpMV methods on two many-core processors: Intel Xeon Phi and GPGPU. Our experiments show that some widely used SpMV methods/formats, like CSR, CSC and DIA, are not so efficient as expected. Newly proposed methods, like CVR and CSR5 show much better performance. Moreover, we analyze the correlation between SpMV performance and 13 selected features based on more than 1500 sparse matrices. Features with obvious correlation to the performance of some SpMV methods are more recommended to be selected to describe sparse pattern. Our observations and implications will help researchers to better understand the relationship between the SpMV performance and the sparse pattern.

Acknowledgement. This work was supported partially by National Key R&D Program of China (2016YFB1000201), and the National Natural Science Foundation of China (Grant No. 61420106013), and Youth Innovation Promotion Association of Chinese Academy of Sciences (2013073).

References

1. Ravishankar, M., et al.: Distributed memory code generation for mixed irregular/regular computations. In: Proceedings of the 20th ACM SIGPLAN Symposium on Principles and Practice of Parallel Programming, PPoPP 2015, pp. 65–75. ACM, New York (2015). http://doi.acm.org/10.1145/2688500.2688515
2. Venkat, A., Hall, M., Strout, M.: Loop and data transformations for sparse matrix code. SIGPLAN Not. **506**, 521–532 (2015). https://doi.org/10.1145/2737924.2738003
3. Wang, L., et al.: Bigdatabench: a big data benchmark suite from internet services. In: Proceedings of the 20th IEEE International Symposium on High Performance Computer Architecture, HPCA 2014, pp. 488–499, Feburary 2014
4. Jia, Z., Wang, L., Zhan, J., Zhang, L., Luo, C.: Characterizing data analysis workloads in data centers. In: Proceedings of the IEEE International Symposium on Workload Characterization, IISWC 2013, pp. 66–76, September 2013

5. Liu, C., Xie, B., Liu, X., Xue, W., Yang, H., Liu, X.: Towards efficient SpMV on sunway manycore architectures. In: Proceedings of the 2018 International Conference on Supercomputing, ICS 2018, pp. 363–373. ACM, New York (2018). http://doi.acm.org/10.1145/3205289.3205313

6. Buono, D., et al.: Optimizing sparse matrix-vector multiplication for large-scale data analytics. In: Proceedings of the 30th International Conference on Supercomputing, ICS 2016, pp. 37:1–37:12. ACM, New York (2016). http://doi.acm.org/10.1145/2925426.2926278

7. Pinar, A., Heath, M.T.: Improving performance of sparse matrix-vector multiplication. In: Proceedings of the 13th ACM/IEEE Conference on Supercomputing, ICS 1999. ACM, New York (1999). http://doi.acm.org/10.1145/331532.331562

8. Yavits, L., Ginosar, R.: Accelerator for sparse machine learning. IEEE Comput. Archit. Lett. **99**, 1 (2017)

9. Greathouse, J.L., Daga, M.: Efficient sparse matrix-vector multiplication on GPUs using the CSR storage format. In: Proceedings of the ACM/IEEE International Conference for High Performance Computing, Networking, Storage and Analysis, SC 2014, pp. 769–780. IEEE Press, Piscataway (2014). https://doi.org/10.1109/SC.2014.68

10. Abu-Sufah, W., Abdel Karim, A.: Auto-tuning of sparse matrix-vector multiplication on graphics processors. In: Kunkel, J.M., Ludwig, T., Meuer, H.W. (eds.) ISC 2013. LNCS, vol. 7905, pp. 151–164. Springer, Heidelberg (2013). https://doi.org/10.1007/978-3-642-38750-0_12

11. Li, J., Tan, G., Chen, M., Sun, N.: SMAT: an input adaptive auto-tuner for sparse matrix-vector multiplication. In: Proceedings of the 34th ACM SIGPLAN Conference on Programming Language Design and Implementation, PLDI 2013, pp. 117–126. ACM, New York (2013). http://doi.acm.org/10.1145/2462156.2462181

12. Elafrou, A., Goumas, G., Koziris, N.: A lightweight optimization selection method for sparse matrix-vector multiplication. arXiv e-prints, November 2015

13. Yan, S., Li, C., Zhang, Y., Zhou, H.: YASPMV: yet another SpMV framework on GPUs. In: Proceedings of the 19th ACM SIGPLAN Symposium on Principles and Practice of Parallel Programming, PPoPP 2014, pp. 107–118. ACM, New York (2014). http://doi.acm.org/10.1145/2555243.2555255

14. Sedaghati, N., Mu, T., Pouchet, L.-N., Parthasarathy, S., Sadayappan, P.: Automatic selection of sparse matrix representation on GPUs. In: Proceedings of the 29th ACM on International Conference on Supercomputing, ICS 2015, pp. 99–108. ACM, New York (2015). http://doi.acm.org/10.1145/2751205.2751244

15. Zhao, Y., Li, J., Liao, C., Shen, X.: Bridging the gap between deep learning and sparse matrix format selection. In: Proceedings of the 23rd ACM SIGPLAN Symposium on Principles and Practice of Parallel Programming, PPoPP 2018, pp. 94–108. ACM, New York (2018)

16. Sodani, A., et al.: Knights landing: second-generation Intel Xeon Phi product. IEEE Micro **362**, 34–46 (2016). https://doi.org/10.1109/MM.2016.25

17. Wang, E., et al.: Intel math kernel library. In: Wang, E. (ed.) High-Performance Computing on the Intel® Xeon Phi™, pp. 167–188. Springer, Cham (2014). https://doi.org/10.1007/978-3-319-06486-4_7

18. CUDA CUSPARSE Library: NVIDIA, August 2010

19. Dalton, S., Bell, N., Olson, L., Garland, M.: CUSP: generic parallel algorithms for sparse matrix and graph computations, version 0.5.0. (2014). http://cusplibrary.github.io/

20. Bosma, W., Cannon, J., Playoust, C.: The magma algebra system I: the user language. J. Symb. Comput. **243**–**4**, 235–265 (1997). https://doi.org/10.1006/jsco.1996.0125

21. Ashari, A., Sedaghati, N., Eisenlohr, J., Sadayappan, P.: An efficient two-dimensional blocking strategy for sparse matrix-vector multiplication on GPUs. In: Proceedings of the 28th ACM International Conference on Supercomputing, ICS 2014, pp. 273–282. ACM, New York (2014). http://doi.acm.org/10.1145/2597652.2597678

22. Liu, X., Smelyanskiy, M., Chow, E., Dubey, P.: Efficient sparse matrix-vector multiplication on x86-based many-core processors. In: Proceedings of the 27th ACM International Conference on Supercomputing, ICS 2013, pp. 273–282. ACM, New York (2013). http://doi.acm.org/10.1145/2464996.2465013

23. Xie, B., et al.: CVR: efficient vectorization of spmv on x86 processors. In: Proceedings of the 16th IEEE/ACM International Symposium on Code Generation and Optimization, CGO 2018 (2018)

24. Liu, W., Vinter, B.: CSR5: an efficient storage format for cross-platform sparse matrix-vector multiplication. In: Proceedings of the 29th ACM International Conference on Supercomputing, ICS 2015, pp. 339–350. ACM, New York (2015)

25. Tang, W.T., et al.: Optimizing and auto-tuning scale-free sparse matrix-vector multiplication on Intel Xeon Phi. In: Proceedings of the 13th IEEE/ACM International Symposium on Code Generation and Optimization, CGO 2015, pp. 136–145. IEEE Computer Society, Washington (2015)

26. Bell, N., Garland, M.: Implementing sparse matrix-vector multiplication on throughput-oriented processors. In: Proceedings of the ACM/IEEE Conference on High Performance Computing Networking, Storage and Analysis, SC 2009, pp. 18:1–18:11. ACM, New York (2009). http://doi.acm.org/10.1145/1654059.1654078

27. Merrill, D., Garland, M.: Merge-based parallel sparse matrix-vector multiplication. In: Proceedings of the ACM/IEEE International Conference for High Performance Computing, Networking, Storage and Analysis, SC 2016, pp. 58:1–58:12. IEEE, Piscataway (2016). https://doi.org/10.1109/SC.2016.57

28. Davis, T.A.: The University of Florida sparse matrix collection. NA DIGEST (1997)

Benchmarking Parallel K-Means Cloud Type Clustering from Satellite Data

Carlos Barajas[1(✉)], Pei Guo[2], Lipi Mukherjee[3,4], Susan Hoban[4],
Jianwu Wang[2], Daeho Jin[5], Aryya Gangopadhyay[2], and Matthias K. Gobbert[1]

[1] Department of Mathematics and Statistics, University of Maryland,
Baltimore County, USA
{barajasc,gobbert}@umbc.edu
[2] Department of Information Systems, University of Maryland,
Baltimore County, USA
{peiguo1,jianwu,gangopad}@umbc.edu
[3] Department of Physics, University of Maryland, Baltimore County, USA
lipimuk1@umbc.edu
[4] Joint Center for Earth Systems Technology, University of Maryland,
Baltimore County, USA
hoban@umbc.edu
[5] GESTAR, USRA and NASA GSFC, Columbia, USA
daeho.jin@nasa.gov

Abstract. The study of clouds, i.e., where they occur and what are their
characteristics, plays a key role in the understanding of climate change.
Clustering is a common machine learning technique used in atmospheric
science to classify cloud types. Many parallelism techniques e.g., MPI,
OpenMP and Spark, could achieve efficient and scalable clustering of
large-scale satellite observation data. In order to understand their differences, this paper studies and compares three different approaches on parallel clustering of satellite observation data. Benchmarking experiments
with k-means clustering are conducted with three parallelism techniques,
namely OpenMP, OpenMP+MPI, and Spark, on a HPC cluster using
up to 16 nodes.

Keywords: Parallel computing · High performance computing · MPI ·
OpenMP · Spark · K-means Clustering

1 Introduction

The climate of Earth tends to maintain a balance between the energy reaching
the Earth from the Sun and the energy leaving the Earth to space. This is
also known as Earth's "radiation budget". The components of the Earth system
contributing to the radiation budget include Earth's surface, atmosphere, and
clouds [10,18]. The study of clouds, including their frequency of occurrence,
location, and characteristics plays a key role in the understanding of climate

© Springer Nature Switzerland AG 2019
C. Zheng and J. Zhan (Eds.): Bench 2018, LNCS 11459, pp. 248–260, 2019.
https://doi.org/10.1007/978-3-030-32813-9_20

change. Thick clouds in the lower atmosphere primarily reflect the incoming solar radiation and consequently cool the surface of the Earth. However thin clouds in upper atmosphere easily transmit the incoming solar radiation and also trap some of the outgoing infrared radiation emitted by the Earth's surface and radiate it back downward. This process consequently warms the atmosphere and surface of the Earth. Usually, the clouds in the upper atmosphere have a colder cloud top that traps the energy in form of outgoing longwave emission. As a result of the trapped energy, the temperature of the Earth's atmosphere and surface increases until the longwave emission to space is balanced by the incoming solar shortwave radiation.

Two parameters that are directly related to the heating and cooling effects of clouds are cloud optical thickness (COT) and cloud top height (CTH) which is related to cloud top pressure (CTP). COT is a measure of the thickness of cloud which largely determines the reflection of sunlight, i.e., the cooling effects of clouds. The thicker the cloud the stronger the reflection. The CTP also plays a role in the warming of clouds in the thermal infrared region (greenhouse effect). For example a cloud with high CTP and low COT would result in warming affect but a cloud with a high CTP and high COT would result in a net 0 or "neutral" effect. For this reason, the satellite retrievals of the cloud COT and CTP are often portrayed in a joint histogram of COT and CTP.

We can study these variables using NASA satellite data such as Moderate Resolution Imaging Spectroradiometer (MODIS) and Cloud-Aerosol Lidar and Infrared Pathfinder Satellite Observation (CALIPSO). The clouds can be studied through atmospheric modelling, where computer simulations are used in conjunction with field measurements and lab studies to further our understanding of cloud physics. In this work, we use MODIS data for five years (2005–2009) and employ k-means clustering to identify the prominent cloud types.

K-means clustering is a widely applied unsupervised machine learning algorithm. When the input data is large, the speed of k-means clustering should be considered. In our study, we apply three different implementations of parallelized computation of k-means clustering: OpenMP, OpenMP+MPI, and Spark. The contributions of this paper are: (1) implementations of three different parallelization techniques on k-means clustering (2) using performance comparisons of these three different parallelized techniques.

2   Background

2.1   Cloud Joint Histograms

COT and CTP are recorded by a satellite from the snapshot of a cloud which we visualize with the 2-D joint histogram [13]. The International Satellite Cloud Climatology Project (ISCCP) cloud type is used in order to interpret the histogram [17]. With this categorization, it is easy to link the joint histogram data to real world clouds as shown in Fig. 1.

It is natural that multiple cloud types occur in the same $1° \times 1°$ grid cell. Consequently individual joint histogram data (representing one time and one

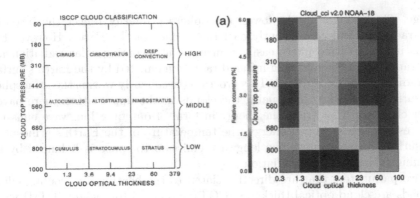

Fig. 1. Left: Cloud type definitions can be extrapolated using joint histograms where the joint-histogram is broken up into regions which are blocked according to cloud-type. Additional information on this technique can be seen in [17]. Right: The joint histogram of cloud top pressure and cloud top thickness suggesting high frequency of stratocumulus clouds.

location) has great variability. This is the reason why the concept of "cloud regime" was created. In short, the cloud regime is the concept representing the domain mixtures of cloud types.

2.2 K-means Clustering

In order to cluster the cloud types based on their properties (COT, CTP) as shown in Fig. 2, we used k-means clustering. The general idea behind K-means clustering is grouping data according to distance where distance is a measure of similarity [9].

K-means is an unsupervised clustering algorithm. It starts with choosing k cluster centers (centroids) in the space representing the data objects. Next each data object is assigned to a cluster center with the closest Euclidean distance. After assigning all data to some centroid a new position for the k centroids are calculated. If the centroids move such that they have a smaller mean distance the new clusters are kept and the old centroids are discarded. Then the previous steps of assigning and calculating are repeated until the centroids' movement is negligible [14,15].

The k-means algorithm is sensitive to the initialization of randomly selected cluster centers [9]. To reduce the randomness in the cluster results, it is better to initialize the centroids as sparse as possible. To get stable clustering results, the algorithm can be made to run multiple times, and the within-cluster-variance and Euclidean distance can be used as clustering criteria.

3 Implementation Details

We have three different approaches to k-means clustering in this section. Two were our own implementations and one was provided by Dr. Jin as a baseline to be improved and compared against. Our source code can be found on GitHub [6].

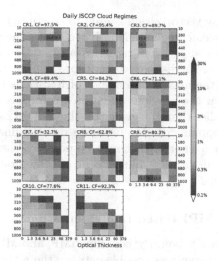

Fig. 2. The cloud regime (CR) centroids of daily ISCCP joint histograms. The cloud fraction (CF) of each regime, the sum of 42 bin values, is also provided. When bin values are larger than 10%, they are explicitly colored [13]. (Color figure online)

3.1   OpenMP Based Implementation

Our initial baseline for improvement was code provided to us by Dr. Jin which uses Python for pre-processing and post-processing of data while leveraging OpenMP enabled FORTRAN for computationally heavy tasks such as the k-means clustering algorithm. The bindings were generated using f2py. We refer to this approach as the OpenMP approach.

The code takes in a binary data file that is a $n \times 42$ multi-dimensional array where the n dimension is the total number of histograms to be used for the k-means algorithm whereas 42 is the number of cloud fraction bins within each histogram. Concisely each row is one joint histogram. The binary data is produced using level 3 MODIS data that is provided in the HDF format. The binary format is more compact on disk and is loaded directly into an array using NumPy. Note that each joint histogram(s) is a data point in the k-means clustering algorithm and will be referred frequently as "record" or "records".

As is typical of OpenMP code the number of threads is set *a priori* with the environment variable OMP_NUM_THREADS. First Python calculates the $k = 10$ initial centroids for k-means clustering using the same idea as the k-means++ initialization algorithm. This attempts to make the initial centroids sparse so that they can each encompass the largest amount of data with minimal, if any, overlap. The first iteration uses the initial centroids as a 0th iteration. All data and the previous iteration's centroids are then passed to the first FORTRAN subroutine, assign_and_get_new_sum, which determines a new centroid and computes the Euclidean distance of each record from the new centroids. The newly generated centroids and respective distances are returned to Python from FORTRAN as two NumPy arrays. To prevent performance loss that comes with using

Python, NumPy's array vectorization is used to compute the mean distances. A vectorized check is implemented with NumPy to determine if the mean distances of the new centroids are superior to the previous iteration's centroids. The centroid set with the best mean distances is kept for the next iteration. This process continues until either the maximum number of iterations is reached, 40, or the mean distance between the previous iteration's centroids and the newly computed centroids is smaller than the given threshold of 0.125 which was provided by Dr. Jin. Once a stopping criterion has been met the final centroids are written to disk in a binary format so that may be post-processed at a later time. A Python script then reads in these binary centroids to produce the several joint histograms seen in Fig. 2.

3.2   OpenMP and MPI Based Implementation

Our first approach uses Cython, Python, OpenMP, and MPI. The total number of records r_t are split as evenly as possible between the p MPI processes such that no process has more than one record compared to any other process. Whereas OpenMP is used in hot computational C loops for increased parallelism. We refer to this approach as OpenMP+MPI.

The load balancing scheme for MPI and OpenMP is discussed on a per node basis as follows. The environment variable OMP_NUM_THREADS is set *a priori* to run time. The Intel OpenMP environment variable KMP_AFFINITY is set to scatter so that threads are distributed as evenly as possible among the cores. Given our HPC testbed the cores per node $c = 16$ in conjunction with some number of processes per node p_n the number of threads per MPI process is computed by $t_p = c/p_n$. This balancing system allows for all node resources to be used, even if $p_n < c$.

Before any k-means calculations begin, each MPI process determines its own process rank and the total number of processes running. The processes use the total number of records and total number of processes to determine their local number of records r_l as $r_l = r_t/p$. In the event that the total number of records cannot be evenly distributed, the remaining records will be distributed such that no processes have more than one record compared to any other process. Then each process reads in its respective records from the same binary data as mentioned in Sect. 3.1. This means that each process knows only of its own records and no data is duplicated across the processes.

First the initial centroids are calculated as mentioned in Sect. 3.1. All data and the previous iteration's centroids are passed to the Cython def function assign_and_get_new_sum, which calls the cdef functions calculate_cl and calculate_outsum. The deterministic behavior of k-means promises that the new cluster produced by calculate_cl is the same on every process. The Euclidean distance computation is where the parallelism plays a role. Figure 3 represents just one of the k many centroids where $p = 2$. Process 0 and Process 1 compute the Euclidean distance from their respective records to the centroid independently of each other. Then the mean distance for all records to the centroid would be computed using a MPI_Allreduce followed by a local division

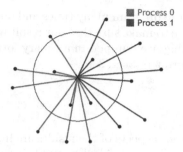

Fig. 3. The general idea for parallelization over a large data set with the repeated calculation. Each black dot is a record and the colored lines tell which process would be handling that Euclidean distance from the current center of the cluster. (Color figure online)

by r_t. OpenMP is implemented with a `pragma omp parallel for` around the record distance calculation loop. Thus the most expensive computation of the k-means algorithm is sped up by splitting r_t into r_l with MPI and multi-threading the record distance calculation with OpenMP.

In the code these distances and clusters are returned from Cython to Python as two NumPy arrays. In actuality the processes collectively compute a global mean distance for each cluster using a `MPI.allreduce` in Python. While the MPI command could have taken place inside the Cython code the idea is to keep the same data transaction style as the FORTRAN code. The MPI call happens in Python rather than Cython. All processes have the same newly calculated centroids, previous iteration's centroids, and respective mean distances to the centroids. So all processes make the same choice on which set of centroids have the better mean distances and discard the other. The stopping criterion and post-processing is the same as in Sect. 3.1.

3.3 Spark Based Implementation

Our second approach is implemented in Python using Apache Spark's scalable machine learning library Spark MLib and the associated API. We utilized Spark 2.3.0 and the built-in k-means algorithm for the cloud regime [1,2]. There are four steps in our applied Spark machine learning workflow: load our data, extract the features, train the model, and evaluate the results.

First we load our data into a Spark DataFrame which is organized as a distributed collection of data by name columns [4]. Upon the creation of the DataFrame it is apparent that our data contained 42 columns which are the bins of the joint histogram. We extracted the 42 features and assembled a features vector in preparation for the clustering. In the clustering process, we set $k = 10$. We changed set the Spark variable `max.iteration` to 40 to make sure that a sufficient number of iterations occurred before the algorithm stopped [3]. We also tried to set larger iteration limits such as 2000, but the run time and clustering result remained similar. So we concluded that 40 iterations are enough in our case. We executed the program many times and output the silhouette with squared Euclidean distance to make sure that our result was relatively stable [14]. The results of the clustering are dumped in a binary format and post-processed using the same Python script in Sect. 3.1.

4   Results

In this section three different aspects of the results are highlighted. Code validity is for testing whether parallelism is implemented correctly. Computation may proceed successfully but the application results could be incorrect. To check the validity of our two implementations we compare our results against the results that are produced by the provided implementation. Performance contains wall clock times with various environment conditions as cataloged in their respective sections for each of the code implementations. Cross-comparison compares all implementations to one another in both qualitative and quantitative measures.

The experiments are conducted on the UMBC High Performance Computing Facility (HPCF) hpcf.umbc.edu. Each node used in our experiments has two eight-core 2.6 GHz Intel E5-2650v2 Ivy Bridge CPUs and 64 GB memory. These nodes are connected by a high-speed quad-data rate (QDR) InfiniBand network.

4.1   Code Validity

When parallelism is involved, we commonly assume that there has to be some numerical drawback. For example, if parallelism is implemented incorrectly, rounding errors can occur, images can degrade in quality, and values that serial code correctly computes are now no longer within an acceptable margin of error. Any code which produces incorrect results in order to improve performance cannot be accepted as correct code. Each of the implementations were run using the same initial parameters in order to mimic the run environment of the OpenMP approach. Additionally all the of the implementations were post-processed using the same Python script so that the images are comparable qualitatively and quantitatively.

First consider Fig. 4. The OpenMP and OpenMP+MPI joint histograms are identical in their order, shape, and colorings. Since the algorithms in the OpenMP approach were recoded line by line in the OpenMP+MPI approach using Cython, it makes sense that the results should be identical. The only fundamental difference between the two coding schema was the major ordering of the data and record splitting via MPI. More importantly, the OpenMP approach and the OpenMP+MPI both used the same Python functions to calculate the initial centroids. The underlying numerical differences between each of the results is inevitable as there is no promise that the FORTRAN compiler and the C compiler will make the same sort of optimizations. Thus the FLOP round off error is most certainly different between each of the three implementations. However the accuracy of COT and CTP need only be accurate within 10^{-3} for the results to be consider good enough in the scope of the problem. The post-processing

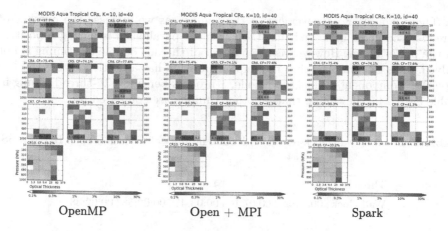

Fig. 4. Post-processed joint histogram results of the k-means final stable clusters for all three implementations. The images are qualitatively identical

script only uses decimals on the order of 10^{-2}. Beyond the quantitative results produced, the qualitative results are seen as the more important use of the joint histogram model as discussed in [13]. This means that the scale, color, shape, and ordering of the histograms play an integral role in determining the accuracy of the implementation compared to the original.

While the implementations are fundamentally different the underlying algorithm is still the k-means clustering algorithm with sparse initialization of the first set of centroids. Even though the Spark code uses open-source libraries rather than personally coded algorithms the qualitative results are identical to the OpenMP approach which was programmed from scratch. The numerical values between each of the post-processed results are functionally identical and as stated qualitatively identical as well.

The major difference is the approach of parallelism. Spark's parallelism uses a completely different methodology than the typical operation of one compute node with OpenMP enabled code. Additionally Spark's data handling is vastly different than the OpenMP+MPI code, yet the results are the same. These differences are irrelevant because the application results computed by all approaches are the within acceptable margins. Therefore both of the alternative implementations can be regarded as accurate parallelized representations of the OpenMP approach, as they show no signs of result degradation.

4.2 Performance

OpenMP. Table 1 presents the recorded times for varying number of OpenMP threads in the OpenMP approach. Clearly as we use more threads the time improves slightly but there appears to be bottleneck. Even though we're using 16 threads (see the final column) the time is not 16 times faster. We can use the best speed possible from these results as a baseline to compare other results to. There is a clear improvement in the timings as we increase the number of threads used. This indicated that the OpenMP parallelism is having a positive on the performance. However as the number of threads double the timing is not halved. This then implies that the implementation has a bottleneck beyond the OpenMP components. Thus the 1-node, 1-process-per-node, 16-thread timing in Table 1 shall be the timing that all other timings are compared too.

Table 1. OpenMP wall clock results with total number of threads used in HH:MM:SS.

Threads	1	2	4	8	16
Wall clock	00:14:59	00:07:10	00:03:47	00:02:58	00:02:38

Table 2. OpenMP+MPI wall clock results with Nodes and Processes Per Node in HH:MM:SS.

Nodes	1	2	4	8
1 ppn	00:01:01	00:00:34	00:00:17	00:00:08
2 ppn	00:01:23	00:00:41	00:00:20	00:00:11
4 ppn	00:01:50	00:00:54	00:00:28	00:00:16
8 ppn	00:02:42	00:01:22	00:00:45	00:00:29
16 ppn	00:04:47	00:02:32	00:01:29	00:01:07

OpenMP+MPI. The MPI results in Table 2 show that as the number of processes per node increase the performance decreases. Consider the 8 node column of the table. As the number of processes per node increase the times gradually worsen at an increasing rate until the timing from eight processes per node to sixteen processes per node doubles. This same behavior is consistent for all node columns. Thus we can say that there is an optimal load balancing issue that must be addressed. The most optimal way to take advantage of all cores on a node in this case is to use the minimal amount of MPI processes and maximum number of threads per process. This cuts down on the communication required between processes and allows for a collection of nodes to be used mainly for threads. These threads are lightweight and require no intercommunication of data to function. For all rows as the number of nodes used increases the performance also increases which is the expected strong scalability outcome.

The data set fits comfortably within the total memory capacity available. Meaning that there is less memory contention and one process per node performs more optimally than expected. On dual socket nodes the minimal number of processes required for optimal performance of memory bound code has been concluded to be two processes per node. This allows one process and its respective threads to be placed on their own processor [5, 16]. Once larger data sets approach the node memory limit of ≈62 GB MPI should start to demonstrate a clear performance improvement as the communication time becomes a small player in the overall timing results.

Spark. Table 3 is the run time table of our Spark implementation. In Table 3 by increasing nodes from 1 to 4 our spark program wallclock time decreases significantly from 9 min to less than 3 min. However when scaling up from 4 nodes to 8 nodes, the timings do not change significantly, despite the continued decrease from just under 3 min to around 2 min. The reason is that during most of the run time Spark is working on loading data into the Spark DataFrame. The actual calculating time of the centroids in Spark with 4 nodes is around 7 s, and with 8 nodes, it is only 4 s. We conclude that performance did not improve much by increasing the number of nodes. This is because the size the data set (3 GB) is not big enough to make a significant difference and there's an overhead when loading the data into the DataFrame.

Table 3. Spark wall clock results with total number of nodes used in HH:MM:SS.

Nodes	1	2	4	8
Wall clock	00:09:03	00:06:16	00:02:51	00:02:09

4.3 Cross Comparison

Implementation Comparisons. The first step in implementing MPI was to convert the FORTRAN code into C code to maintain high performance and ease the MPI parallelization. MPI is better equipped to handle C's native ordering (row major). In contrast CPython API is rather terse and unwieldy. Thus when trying to implement a simple interface a great deal of boilerplate code has to be written. The use of Cython removes a large amount of the API complexities because Cython will automatically generate the CPython API compatible C code from the Cython code and properly optimize for C-like performance. Fortunately the Cython handler is an executable that comes bundled with a modern NumPy distribution at or beyond 1.14+. The Cython handler converts the Cython code into C using the CPython API. The generated C code is compiled to a dynamically linked library which can be imported directly into Python. This process is similar to how `f2py` works for the original FORTRAN implementation. One benefit is that Cython allows any C function to be used inside the Cython code. The major benefit is that Cython also allows for C speed memory accesses via `Memoryviews`. A `Memoryview` provides a closer interface to the heap than NumPy arrays. This allows the block of memory controlled by the NumPy array to be changed as if it were created using `malloc`. With all these tools in place the

FORTRAN code was converted line by line into Cython code and all original NumPy arrays were converted into row-major format so that they are compatible with the C-style arrays that MPI prefers. Importantly Cython allows for easy integration of OpenMP into the `cdef` functions, which means that portions of the code needed to be refactored into `cdef` and `def` portions [7].

Lastly mpi4py is used to integrate MPI into the Python portion. Since Cython handles the computation efficiently, MPI was only tasked with chopping the data into smaller portions and sharing minor amounts of data. An `MPI.allreduce` is used for reducing integers and simple datatypes. Whereas we used `MPI.Allreduce` for reducing NumPy arrays efficiently.

The Spark code is so fundamentally different from the other two implementations, a comparison would just be reiterating the implementation described in Sect. 3.3.

Wall Timings. All but the bottom left three timings in Table 2 are better than the best timing in Table 1. Consider the best timing from the OpenMP approach. This OpenMP timing is 2× as fast as the slowest single node performance time for the MPI enabled code. However this timing takes twice as long as the fastest single node performance time. The 1 node 1 process per node timings in Table 2 use the same amount of resources as the best timing in Table 1. This indicates that the benefits of Cython, rather than MPI, are to thank for the jump in performance. By enabling MPI and using 8 nodes we get a mere 8 s run time. This is 18× faster than the OpenMP performance time and approximately 7.5× faster than the single node OpenMP+MPI code.

Consider the timings in Table 3 compared to the timings in Table 1. Observe the single node performance of Spark in this case the OpenMP approach is 3.4× faster than the Spark approach. It is not until Spark uses 8 full nodes before it is able to compete with the single node performance of OpenMP. Even then it is only 1.2× faster.

The main reason for the under performance of Spark is that the data set is very small and the communication time and initial overhead of Spark far outweigh the actual computation needed to solve the problem. Similarly as we increase the number of MPI processes it is clear that the communication time is a large price to pay despite very minimal amounts of communication. The problem size is small enough that communication still plays a big role in performance timings and OpenMP+MPI has the least amount of overheard when using only one process per node is used which is why this row of timings dwarf all other results.

5   Related Work

The reasons for running benchmarks vary considerably. One may wish to test the capability of new hardware as seen in [5]. The idea of transcoding a problem into multiple languages and use different underbelly computation code is commonplace in the sphere of development. Even on the exact hardware we utilized for our implementations, there have been several transcoding performance studies. For example: the performance of numerical solvers in Julia, R, and Matlab which is found in [16]. In [12], k-means clustering is used as a comparison of other machine learning techniques on Hadoop using their benchmarking suite HiBench. OpenMP applications and k-means clustering are tested in [8]. Another benchmarking work on parallel computing among different parallel programming approaches includes Hadoop, Spark, and Hive database. This proved that different programming methods could cause more than 100 times difference in running speed [11]. However there are no specific combinations that reflect our language choice and application problem.

6 Conclusions

Both parallel implementations managed to correctly compute the same clusters as the original code. Only OpenMP+MPI implementation managed to outperform the original code with the same amount of resources at its disposal. Only OpenMP+MPI managed to outperform the original implementation when using more resources than the original code was capable of using.

However, the demonstration of increased performance of both parallel implementations was severely limited by the lack of data. Spark is designed to handle data on the TB scale, yet we only used 3 GB. These results are not indicative of what would happen given 20+ GB of data. In our Spark application, we basically use only its default level of parallelism. By configuring higher parallel level to load data, or upload data to HDFS might improve the speed of our Spark program. Moreover, Spark application utilizes Python, and the programming in Python itself is slower than programming in FORTRAN and C. So we cannot conclude that Spark is an inferior implementation in this current stage. We only can conclude that it might need more tuning work to make it optimized and competitive.

When MPI scaled is scaled to multiple nodes always the performance always proved. One point is that when MPI is run with multiple nodes using one process per node the total number of threads increase proportionally. However when the number of processes increased beyond one process per node, performance decreased indicating that the data set is also too small for MPI communication. Ordinarily this would be a smaller price to pay for increased parallelism but was not in our case.

In the future we would like to test these parallel implementations with much larger data sets. We propose that both Spark and MPI will have significant increases in performance beyond the original code once scaled up to 20+ GB.

Acknowledgment. This work is supported by NSF grant with number OAC–1730250 and NASA grant 80NSSC17K0366. The hardware used the UMBC High Performance Computing Facility, which is supported by NSF grants (CNS–0821258, CNS–1228778, and OAC–1726023) and the SCREMS program (DMS–0821311), with additional substantial support from UMBC.

References

1. Apache Software Foundation: Apache spark - unified analytics engine for big data. https://spark.apache.org/. Accessed 15 June 2018
2. Apache Software Foundation: MLlib | Apache Spark. https://spark.apache.org/mllib/. Accessed 15 June 2018
3. Apache Software Foundation: Spark MLlib Python API docs. https://spark.apache.org/docs/latest/api/python/pyspark.ml.html#pyspark/.ml.clustering. KMeans. Accessed 15 June 2018
4. Apache Software Foundation: Spark SQL, dataframes and datasets guide. https://spark.apache.org/docs/2.3.0/sql-programming-guide.html. Accessed 15 June 2018
5. Arora, K., Barajas, C., Gobbert, M.K.: Parallel performance studies for an elliptic test problem on the Stampede2 cluster and comparison of networks. Technical report HPCF-2018-10, UMBC High Performance Computing Facility, University of Maryland, Baltimore County (2018)
6. Barajas, C., Guo, P., Mukherjee, L., Daeho, J.: https://github.com/big-data-lab-umbc/cybertraining/tree/master/year-1-projects/team-2. Source Code
7. Behnel, S., Bradshaw, R., Citro, C., Dalcin, L., Seljebotn, D.S., Smith, K.: Cython: the best of both worlds. Comput. Sci. Eng. **13**(2), 31–39 (2011)
8. Che, S., et al.: Rodinia: a benchmark suite for heterogeneous computing. In: 2009 IEEE International Symposium on Workload Characterization (IISWC), pp. 44–54, October 2009
9. Fauld, J.: Unsupervised learning: association rule learning and clustering, March 2018
10. Graham, S.: https://earthobservatory.nasa.gov/Features/Clouds/?src=share. March 1999
11. Guo, P., Wang, J., Chen, Z.: A comparison of big data application programming approaches: a travel companion case study. In: 2017 IEEE International Conference on Big Data (Big Data), pp. 2869–2878 (2017)
12. Huang, S., Huang, J., Dai, J., Xie, T., Huang, B.: The HiBench benchmark suite: characterization of the MapReduce-based data analysis. In: 2010 IEEE 26th International Conference on Data Engineering Workshops (ICDEW 2010), pp. 41–51, March 2010
13. Jin, D., Oreopoulos, L., Lee, D.: Regime-based evaluation of cloudiness in CMIP5 models. Clim. Dyn. **48**(1), 89–112 (2017)
14. Macqueen, J.: Some methods for classification and analysis of multivariate observations. In: 5-th Berkeley Symposium on Mathematical Statistics and Probability, pp. 281–297 (1967)
15. Polytechnic University of Milan: A tutorial on clustering algorithms: K-means clustering. https://home.deib.polimi.it/matteucc/Clustering/tutorial_html/kmeans.html. Accessed 15 June 2018
16. Popuri, S.K., Gobbert, M.K.: A comparative evaluation of Matlab, Octave, R, and Julia on Maya. Technical report HPCF-2017-3, UMBC High Performance Computing Facility, University of Maryland, Baltimore County (2017)
17. Rossow, W.B., Schiffer, R.A.: Advances in understanding clouds from ISCCP. Bull. Am. Meteorol. Soc. **80**(11), 2261–2288 (1999)
18. Wallace, J.M.: Atmospheric Science: An Introductory Survey. Academic Press, New York (1977)

Correction to: MiDBench: Multimodel Industrial Big Data Benchmark

Yijian Cheng, Mengqian Cheng, Hao Ge, Yuhe Guo, Yuanzhe Hao,
Xiaoguang Sun, Xiongpai Qin, Wei Lu, Yueguo Chen,
and Xiaoyong Du

Correction to:
Chapter "MiDBench: Multimodel Industrial Big Data
Benchmark" in: C. Zheng and J. Zhan (Eds.):
Benchmarking, Measuring, and Optimizing, **LNCS 11459,**
https://doi.org/10.1007/978-3-030-32813-9_15

In the version of this paper that was originally published, reference 3 linked to the wrong website. This has been corrected.

The updated version of this chapter can be found at
https://doi.org/10.1007/978-3-030-32813-9_15

© Springer Nature Switzerland AG 2021
C. Zheng and J. Zhan (Eds.): Bench 2018, LNCS 11459, p. C1, 2021.
https://doi.org/10.1007/978-3-030-32813-9_21

Author Index

Printed in the United States
By Bookmasters